"IT'S

Here is the amazing story of the man who turned a handicap into an inspiration, a living legend who will look you in the eye and tell you he's never failed on a case because his chief investigator is Jesus Christ. His exciting, action-packed life is an inspiring example of the power of Christian faith, and a profound tribute to the burning will to succeed!

With 16 pages of photographs

JAY J ARMES
INVESTIGATOR

JAY J. ARMES AS TOLD TO FREDERICK NOLAN

AVON
PUBLISHERS OF BARD, CAMELOT AND DISCUS BOOKS

AVON BOOKS
A division of
The Hearst Corporation
959 Eighth Avenue
New York, New York 10019

Copyright © 1976 by Jay J. Armes
Published by arrangement with Macmillan Publishing Co., Inc.
Library of Congress Catalog Card Number: 76-18915
ISBN: 0-380-01756-3

First Avon Printing, November, 1977

AVON TRADEMARK REG. U.S. PAT. OFF. AND IN
OTHER COUNTRIES, MARCA REGISTRADA,
HECHO EN U.S.A.

Printed in the U.S.A.

Except for the widely-reported rescue of Christian Brando, the names, addresses and locations connected with the stories have been changed to protect those involved. With the exception of Thomas F. Ryan, no name of any actual client appears anywhere in the book, and any similarity to real persons, living or dead, is entirely coincidental.

JAY J ARMES
INVESTIGATOR

Vi Williams

Best personal regards

All that I am On hope to be

I owe to my Lord.

Sincerely in Him

Jay Armes

9-4-88

1.

If you want to hire the world's greatest private investigator, the first thing you've got to do is discard all your preconceptions about the breed. Jay J. Armes isn't anything like Longstreet or Mannix or Cannon or Harry O or any of that kiss-kiss, bang-bang crowd of cardboard cutouts on television. You won't find his offices in any of the gilded watering places frequented by the international jet set; there is no deep-piled, blond-wooded, tinted-windowed high-rise suite in New York or Los Angeles or London or Paris or Rome, no secretaries in St. Laurent casuals and Gucci pumps. Jay J. Armes, the world's most successful private investigator, works out of El Paso, Texas.

El Paso, Texas? Go ahead and look it up, what little there is to look up. You'll find that it started out as a trading post known as Franklin around 1848, then appropriated the name of its nearest Mexican neighbor, El Paso del Norte. Shortening the name to suit American tongues, the town set out to get itself a reputation for toughness and succeeded with plenty in hand. By the time the railroads came in 1881, El Paso was a hardcase town. It was here in 1882, down on the sidewalk by the Capri Theater, that City Marshal Dallas Stoudenmire died with his boots on. Just across the street is the site of the saloon where Johnny Selman blew out John Wesley Hardin's light back in '95. This is the town where Pat Garrett, tall slayer of Billy the Kid, was once collector of customs: the far western corner of Texas and the center of the southern New Mexico border.

Today, it's still a border town, but nearer a vacation jumping-off point than anything else. Just across the Rio Grande lies Ciudad Juarez, and beyond that, all of Mexico. In 1974, more than thirty-six million people crossed the Jaurez–El Paso line, and El Paso Customs reported trade worth $448 million in exports and $510 million in imports.

El Paso lies at an elevation of thirty-seven hundred feet, straddling the lowest all-weather pass through the Rocky Mountains. The population of the city hovers around the 360,000 mark and has grown 16.5 percent since 1960. It's a good place to live, always sunny and rarely cold, the people friendly and hospitable, many of them speaking both English and Spanish. Yet to most Americans, the town has remained the place you drive through on the way to do some duty-free shopping in Juarez, or to go to the horse races or the bullfights.

To hoteliers, it is the birthplace of Conrad Hilton. To servicemen, it is a suburb of Fort Bliss. To businessmen, it is a town that produces two and a half million pounds of cement a day, the center of an area that has yielded a third of all the silver mined in the last four hundred years. El Paso also produces cotton clothing and refines copper—a third of the world's supply is produced in nearby New Mexico. Granite, marble and major sand and gravel mining are conducted in El Paso County. There are banking interests (1974 clearings totaled $6.7 billion), three newspapers (one of them Spanish-language), a net effective buying income per household of $11,253, one automobile and one telephone for every one and a half people, and plenty of room to grow.

For all that, El Paso seems likely to be best known around the world because of Jay J. Armes.

He has worked for royalty and movie stars, millionaire tycoons and giant industrial corporations— clients more than willing to ante up the $100,000 retainer he will ask for really tough cases (or "capers," *as he prefers to call them). His conditions of work are unique: he guarantees results. That is not his only claim to uniqueness, however. Jay J. Armes lives in a sprawling mansion that takes up a whole block on North Loop Road in the suburb of Ysleta where he was born—he chooses not to live in a millionaire's ghetto. The appurtenances of the house include a private lake with a two-hundred-foot-long waterfall, the owner's personal menagerie and an African village to match it. Armes is a crack shot, a karate expert, a qualified scuba diver, a pilot and a good enough driver to have raced pro had he wanted to. He owns several planes, and a twin-rudder helicopter sits on the launching pad he designed himself. He has a fleet of automobiles that includes a $37,000 Rolls-Royce and two armor-plated Cadillacs, all built to Armes' personal specifications, plus a Corvette Stingray with electronic equipment that would make anything "Q" ever devised for James Bond look like a badly-made Morse tapper.*

He is accompanied everywhere he goes by an armed bodyguard who is part Sioux Indian, and who keeps a carbine always within easy reach. There have been a lot of tries at assassinating Jay Armes, but he's hard to kill. He never goes anywhere without his special .38 snubnose in its Myres holster.

His life-style is, quite literally, astonishing. He spends at least one hour of every day of his life working out in the private gymnasium that he designed and built for himself at a cost of $90,000. Another hour is spent on the air-conditioned target range—also designed and created by Armes—in a concrete bunker beneath his home. He walks into a cage containing his two black panthers or another holding a huge Siberian tiger as coolly as he steps into his custom-equipped black Cadillac limo with its surveillance cameras and closed-circuit screen. He manages on a maximum of four hours' sleep and often none at all. He eats sparingly, neither smokes nor drinks (not even coffee), although *he's not intolerant of other people doing either. He travels all over the world on assignment yet finds time to run a correspondence school for private investigators. It has a large number of students and he wrote every word of its curriculum himself. He worships regularly at the Immanuel Baptist Church of El Paso, to whose work he contributes one-tenth of his not inconsiderable income. Despite a workload that would tire an ox, he has managed to make time to campaign vigorously against slothful police work by running for sheriff of El Paso County, to cooperate with a company creating a whole range of toys based on him, and to prepare for a television series about his life and cases in which he would play himself.*

Jay J. Armes isn't a particularly tall man, but he's big and wide-shouldered and walks light on his feet like a good middleweight. He has a ready smile, and a deceptively mild voice and demeanor. Unfailingly polite, he wears his black hair fashionably long, with sideburns that conceal his ears. He doesn't look much like the man shaking hands with Marlon Brando in the photograph that hangs in the waiting room, or the man who modeled for the sign outside his offices. Nevertheless, all three are Armes. Changing appearance is almost a necessity in his line of business and he does so at will.

He wears lightweight suits with shoulder epaulettes and turned-back cuffs. They look faintly military, somewhere between a uniform and a safari jacket, and he has 750 of them, all different materials cut to the same pattern, tailored to conceal the holstered .38. His way of speaking is soft, his vowels Texas-rounded. He comes on so much like a good ole boy that it is easy to miss the steel beneath the softness.

In becoming the world's best-known private investigator, Jay J. Armes has amassed wealth, possessions, fame and the kind of life-style that goes with them. He has a beautiful Chinese wife, fine healthy kids, satisfied clients in every corner of the world and a job he loves to do; but nobody handed them to him on a plate. He started way down at the bottom of the pile, and to get where he is he had to climb faster and harder and fight tougher than most. Because he is, in the most literal sense of the words, a self-made man, and has become what he is in spite of a truly incredible handicap.

He has no hands.

You could look upon my hooks as a handicap, I suppose, although I never do, not anymore. To me, they're an inspiration, but I won't pretend it was always like that. You can't imagine what it's like to be a teenager with no hands: it's sheer unadulterated hell. When they first fitted hooks to my arms, I remember thinking that everyone was going to stare at me as if I was some sort of freak, and it frightened me. I didn't want anyone to see me, and it took me a long while to get used to it. But I did: you have to. It's a long way from easy, though.

I wasn't Jay J. Armes, then. I was born Julian Armas. I had two brothers and two sisters and my father worked in a grocery store. We lived on Dixon Road in Ysleta and we weren't rich and we weren't poor, just everyday normal.

I was an ambitious kid, and I wanted to get ahead. I knew the only way to do that was be like Avis and try harder. By the time I was eleven years old, I had four jobs. I delivered the morning papers on my bicycle, getting up at 4:30 A.M. so I could do that and then rush across to bottle-feed sixty calves for a local farmer before I went to school. After school was out, I'd deliver the afternoon papers and then bottle-feed my "babies" again. After supper I had a job down at the local movie house, where I doubled as an usher and ticket collector. I didn't have any clear idea of what I was going to be, or anything. I just knew what I didn't want to be. I didn't want to end up doing manual labor on a farm, or being a glorified delivery boy until I got too old. I was aiming for the stars.

I learned how to take care of myself very early. One

of my less savory sidelines was a loansharking operation I ran in school. I'd loan quarters to the other kids at the beginning of the week and collect fifty cents at the weekend when they got their pocket money. Sometimes they'd renege, and I'd have to whip them to get paid. I nearly got thrown out of school when the principal found out what was going on. He made me promise to quit loaning money in school and I did. I always keep my promises. I started up again on a street corner opposite the entrance to the school, and settled any differences after school hours.

By the time I was twelve, I had a firm ambition. I wanted to be a doctor. I had a doctor friend in Ysleta, and he answered all my questions patiently, loaned me books, encouraged my interest. If he was performing minor surgery, he would let me watch, and he would describe operations that I wasn't permitted to see. He said I had the makings of a surgeon in me, and I had dreams of myself in white mask and gown, a regular Dr. Kildare. Then all those dreams were shattered, literally blown to bits.

I remember it all so well. It was a sleepy May evening, and I was playing in my backyard with an older boy that I knew, Dickie Caples. He was a good-looking kid, about eighteen then. His parents, who owned real-estate and office buildings in El Paso, were quite well off. Dickie even had his own car, which was a great source of envy among us other kids, although it probably saved my life. That evening, Dickie had gotten hold of a box of railroad torpedoes, and brought them to our house. We got an icepick and pried the box open. Inside were some containers. I took one of them out and tore off the seal. It exploded in my hands.

The effect was exactly the same as if I had detonated a stick of dynamite and the next thing I remember is being face down near a tree about twenty feet away. I was trying to get hold of the trunk of the tree to get to my feet. I couldn't get a grip on the tree and it puzzled me. It simply didn't occur to me that I no longer had any hands.

I managed to get to my knees and then stand upright, and I saw now that I was covered in blood, and my mangled hands were squirting more of it, like two water hoses. I looked around and saw Dickie running out of the yard. I thought he was running to get help, and I ran after him. In fact, he was running in sheer terror.

"Dickie!" I shouted in anguish. I couldn't catch up with him and I was frightened. "Get the car, get the car!"

He turned around and looked at me. I must have looked like Satan coming up out of hell.

"What?" he said.

"Get the car, take me to the doctor's in Ysleta!" I said. "Hurry, hurry!"

Dickie ran to the car and yanked the door open for me. He couldn't look at my arms. I got into the car and sort of folded them across my body. The pain was coming in sweeping waves now, and it was awful, awful. I remember that my blood was squirting so strongly that the windshield became slick and opaque with it, and Dickie couldn't see to drive. He had to wipe the glass clean with his hands. By the time we got to the doctor's, Dickie was soaked in my blood as well.

We ran into Dr. David Cameron's office. There was a pregnant woman sitting on a chair by the wall, waiting to see him. She looked up startled as we burst in, and then she saw my hands. Her eyes rolled up in her head and she fainted. I ran around her sprawled body and started kicking on the door of the doctor's office. I was already light-headed from loss of blood, but I kicked in desperation and after a moment the doctor jerked the door open, his face angry, all set to tell someone off. When he saw me his eyes widened, and he yanked me inside. Within seconds he had tourniquets on and slid a needle into my upper arm. His white jacket was spattered with blood. He never spoke a word, and I remember his face was set and serious as he worked on me. He was a fine doctor, a fine man. The painkiller he had given me worked fast, and I remember feeling disengaged and uninvolved as telephones shrilled and people ran in and out of the office. I answered questions someone asked me, and then I remember the ambulance's siren screaming on the way to the hospital.

At the hospital Dr. Cameron told my father that there was no way they could save my ruined hands. He went into detail about the injuries, but it didn't mean anything to me. I guess I was in shock; I didn't even cry when he said they would have to amputate both hands above the wrist. My father agreed, his face full of pity and pain and concern. I remember he had tears in his eyes when I asked him to forgive me.

So they did what they had to do, and then I began to realize what had happened to me. I wanted to die. I lay there in the hospital, and as far as I was concerned, the world had come to an end. I didn't want to talk with anyone, not even my parents or my brothers and sisters. I didn't want to do anything. I just lay on my side and stared at the wall and thought black, black thoughts.

"Why me?" I kept thinking. "Why me?"

Tears of self-pity would fill my eyes, and I would look at the huge balls of cotton-stuffed bandage on my arms and hate the *things* beneath them. I didn't want ever to have to look at them. I loathed my own ruined body.

Then one day I realized how totally selfish I was being. All the love of my family and friends, all the help and concern of the doctors, it was being wasted on me. I suddenly realized that I wasn't really saying "Why me?" at all. What I was saying was "Why not somebody else?" It was as if someone somewhere had heard my question and told me the answer: *why not you?* I'm not going to call it a miracle, it wasn't anything like that; but to me, at that particular moment, the effect was miraculous. I started to get better. I quit feeling sorry for myself. I asked the doctors to check me out for artificial hands and I thanked the Lord that I was still alive. I've never felt sorry for myself since that day, never felt that I got a rawer deal than the next man. I came to terms with myself, I guess. I decided that maybe losing my hands was in the Lord's plan for my life, that somehow this was the way it was meant to be. And I vowed that I wasn't going to be just as good as I'd been before the accident. I was going to be even better.

HANDLESS NEWSPAPER CARRIER, 12 YEAR OLD
JULIAN ARMAS WHO LOST HIS HANDS IN AN ACCIDENT
DEMONSTRATES HOW EASILY HE CAN HANDLE HIS
JOB AS A TIMES NEWSPAPER CARRIER WITH THE USE
OF HOOKS. JULIAN NEEDS NO ASSISTANCE IN EITHER
THE FOLDING OR THE DELIVERY OF THE NEWSPAPERS.

Julian Armas, 12-year-old *Times* carrier in Ysleta, who lost both hands in an accident nearly two years ago, has not let his physical handicap interfere with either his normal activities or his ambitions for the future. The youth's hands were blown off in May, 1949, while he was experimenting with a railroad torpedo in the yard of his Lower Valley home.

His hands were so badly mangled after the torpedo exploded that they had to be amputated at the wrists, but Julian has learned to use his hand hooks so expertly that he can do anything a normal person can do with his own hands—climb trees, comb his hair, shoot a gun. He folds his own newspapers before he delivers them on his route.

"When I first got my hooks, I thought I couldn't stand to have people stare at me all the time," he said, "but soon I got used to it and now I don't mind the staring."

Julian also has a pair of artificial hands which

he uses for "dress." Despite his handicap, the boy
has taken part in school athletics. He played end
guard on his grammar school football team and
was a member of the 220-yard relay team last
year. Now that he has enrolled in Ysleta High
School, Julian believes that he should forget about
athletics and get down to some serious study. His
ambition is to become a lawyer, but he is also
going to keep up his study of chemistry and other
sciences of which he is very fond. . . . His hobbies
are collecting coins and military souvenirs and
reading detective books. Julian's closest pal is
"Butch," a two-year-old German shepherd who
served as his master's hands before Julian got his
hooks, opening doors and doing similar small
tasks for him.

"I'm really proud of Butch," Julian boasted.
"He's the smartest dog I know. I trained him as
they do the Army dogs, and he can crawl under
fences and disarm anyone."

Julian's ability to carry out his tasks cannot be
overrated. Jack Smith, District Circulation Manager of the *Times,* praised the boy's capabilities
by pointing out that since Julian took over his
route, circulation in that area had increased.

"He gives us exceptional service," Smith said.

Julian, son of Mr. and Mrs. Pete Armas, has
two brothers, Pete Jr. and Constantino, veterans
of the Navy, and two sisters, Beatriz and Eva.

That article from the El Paso *Times* says as well as
anything how hard I worked to lead a normal life.
What it doesn't say is exactly how hard *hard* was. I
had a unique operation: a tunnel was made in my
biceps and a pin placed right through them so that the
muscles themselves would provide the "power" to operate the hooks. In learning to use them, I had to de-
velop those muscles two to three times more than the
average person, and if you think that was easy, you're
dreaming.

I had to relearn everything: from scratch. All of a sudden something as commonplace as tying a shoelace became a major engineering feat. Opening doors, buttoning a shirt, writing my name, I had to learn them all the way a child in kindergarten learns the alphabet. I won't try to describe the pain that's an inseparable part of all this, but there is some. Of course, I had to be stubborn and refuse to go to the rehabilitation center; I simply wouldn't think of myself as handicapped, needing help. I was going to do it all my way. My way turned out to be the hard way, but that's the way I did it. When I got through, I could do a lot more without hands than I had ever done when I had them.

The first priority was to learn to ride my bicycle. Once I'd mastered that, I had special grips put on the handlebars of my motor scooter and pretty soon I was ready to go out on my paper route again. I had to relearn how to tie the papers, and the much trickier feat of throwing them from the moving scooter. I got a lot of skinned knees and bruises at first. If anything went wrong with my scooter, I had to be Mr. Fixit, and there the hooks became a positive advantage. My mother had always given me a hard time if I came into the house with grease or oil on my hands. Well, that was no problem anymore.

I did all the normal things kids do. I had dates. I played football and a smack-and-run game of tennis. I went out for track, as it says in the *Times* article, and played end at football. I was the bugler in Troop 95 of the Boy Scouts. I learned how to wash myself, fasten my pants, pick up a cup, eat with a fork, drive a car, turn on a tap.

The hardest thing I had to learn was one everyone else finds relatively simple: opening a screwtop bottle. I spent countless hours, working well into the night, trying to master it. The ability to turn the hand palm up or palm down is called pronation or supination. I have neither, and I got so discouraged when I tried to open screwtops that I'd end up smashing the bottle in a fit of frustration. After a while, I'd shrug and get another one and try again. Eventually I mastered it, although you wouldn't believe how long it took. Then I started in to learn how to put the top back on again.

As I said, you could look upon the fact that I have hooks instead of hands as a handicap, but I don't. You are only handicapped if you think you are. I've spent a lifetime observing people, and I know now that they set their own limitations, create their own inhibitions. Yet a man can be anything he wants to be, do anything he wants to do, as long as he has a star to steer by. I make no secret of the fact that in my case it is Jesus Christ. I'm not proselytizing: I just believe.

When I got started in this business—and it's hard to believe that the years have gone by so fast—there were eighteen detective agencies in the El Paso area alone. I went to see Sheriff Bob Bailey to ask for a letter of recommendation.

"You want to be a private investigator?" he said. "Forget it, kid!"

"Why?" I said.

"Look," he replied, "I haven't seen the shamus yet that didn't end up staring at me from out of one of my cells. We got eighteen agencies out there already, and in a town the size of El Paso that's at least seventeen too many. We need more private eyes like we need more wetbacks. Take my advice and try some other racket."

I told him I'd given it a lot of thought, but that I was determined to go ahead and start up my own agency—with or without his support, but preferably with it. I told him I thought maybe I could do something to give the private investigator a better image.

"I'll believe it when I see it," he said. "But I'll give you a chance."

A chance was all I was asking for, I said. We went to see Chief of Police Reisinger, and although he said it was against his better judgment, he went along with the sheriff, and Private Investigator's License C-00107-3 was issued to Jay J. Armes of El Paso.

I walked out of there determined to succeed and justify their faith in me. I knew what most people thought of the private investigator. They called him a snoop, a shamus, a gumshoe, a peeper, a dick, and they used the words derogatorily, were ashamed if they had to buy his services. If they had a bad experience—and plenty of people did and do—they wrote it off as bad luck, a bum trip. Call it experience, they would shrug, what can you expect? They didn't even go to the police because they had no clear idea of their legal entitlements. So they got suckered by people who couldn't have investigated the theft of a dime from a kid's piggybank.

I wanted to change all that. I wanted people to be able to select an investigator the same way they would a doctor or an attorney—and expect exactly the same kind of ethical behavior. Over the years I have been instrumental in trying to get stiffer regulations to govern the conditions under which private investigators are licensed and operate. I started my school so that newcomers could get a good grounding in the methodology and techniques of the business. There's still a long way to go, but it's a cleaner business these days than it was when I got started. Incidentally, only one of those eighteen agencies I mentioned earlier is still operating in El Paso. The honorable exception is the justly famous William J. Burns Organization, and they're not strictly in my field.

So maybe I'm doing something right.

2.

Jay Armes isn't exaggerating when he says he can do more without hands than can a lot of people who have them. In fact, he can do things that are impossible for anyone with normal hands. On TV and in the movies, you see people whacking away at each other with bare knuckles all the time. In real life, they'd be out of action for a month, with broken hands. Armes doesn't have that problem. Barriers mean nothing to him, either. He can strike and shatter materials that would break even the conditioned hands of a karate master. The ordinary man cannot smash plate glass with his clenched fist, but Armes can. He can pry apart the links of a steel chain, pluck documents from a roaring incinerator, bash his arm through the heavy panelling of a locked door, casually pick up a red-hot blow-torch—and stay in business. For any other man, it would be emergency treatment at the nearest hospital.

His hooks are not just substitute hands. They are, first of all, tools. And after that, weapons. It's only when you see Jay Armes practicing karate or unarmed combat that you realize those ordinarily innocuous hooks are, in fact, lethal. He is hitting that practice bag with fifteen pounds of stainless steel, propelled by the full force of arms and shoulders fully three times as strong as those of the average man. It takes only a little imagination to picture what those gleaming hooks would do to that padded canvas if it were living tissue and bone.

Jay Armes can do so many things with his hooks

that are beyond the capability of a normal person that it is difficult to know where to start listing them. But take knives. Any intern will tell you that people attacked with knives usually have two distinct kinds of injury. There will be the—expected—body wounds, bad enough by any standard; but if the victim has put up a fight, there will also be the ugly mess of their hands and arms, which will have been sliced to shreds in vain attempts to fend off the wicked blade. If anyone comes at Jay Armes with a knife—and plenty have—he can take the cutting edge in his relentless grip, a grip so powerful that it will shatter the blade, without the slightest risk of injury. "This tends to confuse the assailant," Armes grins. You can see where it would.

Take some other examples: the sap, the length of lead pipe, the short strip of viciously-wielded chain. Try to defend yourself against an assailant swinging any of them, and odds are you will end up with shattered forearm bones and crushed hands at best, or a shattered skull at worst. You might as well try to defend yourself with a plastic bag. Armes can take those killing blows on steel that returns as much as it takes —and then reply in kind.

He can lift sharp-edged heavy metal objects which would take off the fingers of another man. He can hang suspended on rope or wall not only indefinitely, but comfortably—no fingers to slip, no wrist muscles to tire and surrender to the strain. He can climb up or down ragged steel cables that would rip normal hands to pieces even when protected by the strongest industrial gloves. He can even swarm up the greased cable of an elevator, holding on where ordinary hands would instantly slip and send the climber plummeting to oblivion. Once, he even stopped a dangerous machine by simply jamming his hook into it. Try that with your hand.

Stretch a cable angling between two points, and Armes can slide down it at speeds that would burn the skin off the hands of even the most hardened gymnast. Hand-over-hand, he is infinitely superior to the rest of us, suspended by his hooks like a coat on a hanger. Think of all the things that burn, bruise, break, tear, slice, shred, or mangle the human hand. Armes is impervious to practically all of them.

In addition to this almost superhuman aspect of the man, there are the implements he has designed to enhance his abilities. Most of them, Armes says, are "still on the secret list," but he will go so far as to say that one of them has to do with cutting sheet metal and another is for bypassing locks of any kind. He can turn the hooks into a powerful electromagnet. A diamond tip attachment transforms one caliper into a highly efficient glasscutter. Another turns the hooks into heavy-gauge wirecutters. They can bend, twist, flatten or crush materials that would tear normal hands to bloody shreds. They can hold a pistol or submachine gun as rock-steady as if the weapon were fixed in a vise, with no concessions to recoil. Yet for all that, Armes has a touch so delicate that he can pick up a cube of Jell-O without crushing it.

Having hooks instead of hands poses one obvious disadvantage—the man who wears them is hardly inconspicuous, something an investigator often has to be. To offset this, Armes went to the most famous of all the Hollywood make-up men and gave him a specification: make a pair of cosmetic "hands" so realistic that even someone sitting next to me won't be able to tell they are artificial. It cost a small fortune, but it vas done. So realistic are they that people who know Jay Armes well sometimes mistake him for his brother when he wears the "hands." He wears them for "dress" occasions and for disguise and undercover work, but for every day he prefers the hooks. He knows what he can do with them.

He will neither confirm nor deny it, but it's a fairly safe bet that among the other "secret weapons" built into the incredible Armes hooks is a device that can turn him into a walking transmitting and receiving

*station, linked permanently to a recording device.
What else, nobody knows but Jay Armes himself, and
he's not talking. Which doubtless explains the mis-
chievous grin that lights up his face when he tells in-
terviewers that he still has quite a few tricks up his
sleeve.*

It began like any other caper, with a phone call.

This one was going to be a little different from
most. Before it was over, I would almost die in a helicopter crash over a remote Mexican village, see my
name in banner headlines all around the world and
help end a decade-long legal deadlock. Of course, I
didn't know any of that when the telephone rang.
Even if I had, I'd still have taken the call.

The international operator told me the call was
from Paris, and the caller Marlon Brando. I had met
"Bud," as they used to call him, when I first went to
California and played a tiny part in one of his early
movies. He came straight to the point, as always.

"My son has been kidnapped, Jay," he said. "I want
you to find him."

I told him I'd just heard the news myself on TV.
There had been no details, just that he'd disappeared.
There's one question that comes right at the top of the
list in kidnapping cases, and I asked it now. No,
Brando said, there'd been no ransom demand.

"All right," I said. "Tell me everything you can."

I already knew a little about the boy's background.
You'd have had to have been living in a Tibetan cave
not to know something about the eleven-year battle
Brando and his ex-wife Anna Kashfi had been fighting
in the courts for permanent custody of the thirteen-
year-old Devi Christian. Now he filled in the details
for me, the ploys and counterploys of the lawyers, the
hundreds of thousands of dollars it had cost and his
concern for the effect it was having on the boy. He
told me that Anna Kashfi was keeping bad company,
that people tried to exploit her because of her connection with him. He also confided that his greatest fear

was that he might unwittingly have stepped on some tender toes with his portrayal of the aging *capo mafioso* Don Vito Corleone in the just-released movie version of *The Godfather,* and that Christian's kidnapping was some sort of reprisal.

That seemed unlikely to me, and I told him why. Gangland kidnappings are seldom for reprisals of the kind he feared. When the underworld decides someone is going to disappear, it's usually for good. If they want to punish someone for a transgression, they usually take it out on him directly. It's the small-time crooks and the amateurs who go in for the other kind of kidnapping, and even they rarely go after the children of celebrities anymore. There is too much press attention, which alerts too many people and makes it difficult to keep the victim hidden. Much easier to take the child of some wealthy businessman whose name means little outside his own home town. They are much easier marks, too.

The only facts Brando could give me were that Christian had been going to a private school in Ojai, California, and that his attorneys in Los Angeles had checked and found that Christian had not been in school since late February, when his mother had taken him out because of a bad case of tonsillitis. I asked him for the name of the attorneys, and told him to have them put together a dossier containing everything that might be relevant to the case. I had that familiar gut feeling that comes to me as I get into a case, the hunch that Anna Kashfi was more deeply involved than perhaps we knew. Don't ask me to explain how it happens: I don't know. But over the years I have learned to respect my hunches. I told Brando my feelings.

"Anything's possible," he said, "but proving it is another matter. I have to stay here in Paris another day or two. I can't get away from this movie until then. As soon as I can, I'll fly to Los Angeles and confer with you. Meanwhile, I want you to get started."

"I already have," I said.

It was perfectly true, because during our conversation I had been asking him some of the questions to which I need answers on any kidnapping case. Every aspect of the daily routine of the kidnapped victim and his family has to be examined in detail. The approach must be systematic, comprehensive and accurate, because the number of options is so huge. The investigator knows only one fact: that someone has disappeared. Whether this someone has been taken north, south, east or west, whether he went voluntarily, whether anyone saw him—the investigator simply doesn't know. So he must have a system, a routine, a modus operandi to establish as many facts as he can.

This one looked tough. We had no information about the boy's appearance at the time of his kidnapping, no information about the house he was living in or who else was there, no clear indication of when he had actually been abducted. I decided to get out to Los Angeles—fast.

Once there, I set up round-the-clock surveillance on Anna Kashfi, and began an intensive neighborhood survey in the district where she lived. This is not a particularly glamorous job. You knock on a lot of doors, ask a lot of questions, pound a lot of pavement, use up a lot of shoe leather. Much of it is thankless and unrewarding, but if done properly, a neighborhood survey can paint you a picture of a subject that no amount of documentary evidence can provide. Basically, the aim of a neighborhood survey is to interview every neighbor and acquaintance of the subject family—those in the houses on each side of theirs, and two or three further along on each side, plus those opposite and diagonal to the house. You check on how long each family has been at that address, whether they have seen any strangers visiting the house, any cars nearby that didn't belong on the street, any changes in route men, delivery men, mailmen, garbage men. People aren't necessarily nosey, but they notice things without even knowing that they have seen them. It's the investigator's job to ferret out those facts, to convince people to tell him things that, actually, he has no right to know.

While this was going on, other agents were checking passersby, looking for people who used the street regularly at certain times of day, asking them if they had noticed anything. Gradually, we began to put together a picture of the days and nights of the ex-Mrs. Brando, and it was none too savory. Her house had been a hangout for a pretty rough crowd, and there had been several fights ending with police intervention after neighbors complained.

We learned that Kashfi and her friend Shirley Hauptmann were involved in a venture called World Travel Academy, which had its headquarters in Mexicali, just south of the border in Mexico. This was quite a break, because it was from there that Kashfi had filed the report that Christian had been kidnapped.

Next we found a lady who had filed a complaint about the people at the Kashfi house. Her name was Marian Conlan, and she was a widow, very prim and proper. She had disapproved most strongly of the goings-on up the street, and as part of her disapproval had written down the registration numbers of the vehicles driven by Kashfi's visitors. She was happy to provide me with a copy of her listings, which were written in a tiny, sloping script with a date alongside. She explained that the dates were those when the vehicles had visited the Kashfi home. The last one noted was March 5, 1972. I asked her if she could remember what kind of car it was.

"No car at all," she said. "It was one of those Volkswagen bus things, a caravan. It had a name on the side. Something about world travel."

"World Travel Academy?"

"That's right," she said, and we were in business.

I sent one of my agents to each of the three twenty-four-hour ports of entry: Tijuana, Tecate and Mexicali. Their instructions were short and sweet—check the records to see if any of the vehicles on Mrs. Conlan's list, and in particular, the red Volkswagen bus, had crossed into Mexico. If any had, there would be a record of it. Mexican authorities retain the title of all vehicles planning to go further into Mexico than twenty-eight kilometers from the border. Anyone attempting to do so without the proper permit is stopped at the patrol points inland and sent back to the border to get one. There are sound reasons for this. Firstly, it prevents professional auto thieves from stealing cars in the United States and unloading them on unsuspecting Mexican buyers. Secondly, it dissuades visiting tourists from selling or hocking their cars in order to raise extra funds with which to play the horses or the roulette wheels or whatever vices they're indulging in south of the border. Believe me, there are plenty to choose from.

While I was waiting for word from the border I made arrangements to charter a Hughes 500 helicopter. I wanted a big bird, something with plenty of power and range, and this civilian version of the Army's OH-6A fitted the bill perfectly. Designed to carry five passengers in comfort, the Hughes 500 will cruise at 140 mph and has a range of well over four hundred miles at five thousand feet. The military version set twenty-three world records in one month of 1966, making it, for my money, one of the best choppers in production. I figured I was going to need the best of everything—including luck—on this caper.

That evening, my agent called me from Mexicali.

"Mr. Armes," he said, "we lucked out. That red Volks went through here Monday."

Four days ago. They could be a long, long distance away by now, but we had a couple of things going for us. One, they'd have had to give some kind of destination for their permit, as well as indicate the length of time they intended to stay in Mexico. Two, they'd have to leave Mexico through their port of entry in order to retrieve the title to their vehicle. So if they tried to slip back into the United States when the pursuit hotted up, we would have someone waiting for them. A couple more questions elicited the information that the owner of the vehicle, one James Barry Wooster, had given his destination as Baja California, and the probable length of his stay as three to four weeks. I told my agent to stay put and gave him a few other things to do until I arrived. Then I telephoned San Diego International and got them to put the Hughes 500 on standby. Ten minutes later I was on my way to Los Angeles Airport, and in another twenty I was drinking a Coke in the first-class compartment of an American Airlines jet bound for Dago, a large-scale map of Baja California spread in front of me.

Baja California is a 600-mile-long finger of pretty inhospitable land, never wider than 130 miles and often much narrower. On the west is the Pacific, and on the east the Gulf of California. The Sierras run down its center like a backbone, and on each coast lies a highway—Highway No. 1 on the western side and Highway No. 5 on the eastern, the latter beginning at Mexicali. It's a good highway (by Mexican standards, anyway) as far as San Felipe (about 130 miles south), as is Highway No. 1 on the western coast to Rosario de Arriba. After that, you're on your own. The road is unpaved for the next 750 miles. Highways 1 and 5 join at Laguna Chapala, crossing into the Southern Territory north of the Vizcaino Desert. At San Ignacio, the road swings east through the mountains and descends to Santa Rosalia, a biggish town on the Gulf. There is a ferry service from there to Guaymas on the mainland, and also an airport—two features that did nothing to brighten my day. Santa Rosalia is about 550 miles from the border as the crow flies. In four days, the fugitives could have made it that far, if not further. There were another six hundred miles of road from there going all the way south to the tip of the peninsula at San Lucas, way down below the Tropic of Cancer.

The statistics the map presented were formidable. There were about two thousand miles of coastline. There was forest, desert and mountain terrain. There were offshore islands and hundreds of tiny little fishing villages hardly meriting a formal name. And all this ground to cover presupposed that the fugitives had told the truth and were, indeed, heading into Baja California. Still, we had to start somewhere, and Baja was as good a place as any. I concentrated again upon the notes compiled by our neighborhood survey in Los Angeles. A rough crowd, our informants had agreed, hippies, long on hair and short on manners, morals, and money. It wasn't likely they would be heading for any of the swankier places or anyplace they would need to check in formally, like a hotel. Not with the kidnapped son of an internationally famous movie star. There were plenty of places all down the Baja coast that weren't much more than wide spots in the road: a trailer camp here, a roadside pull-up there, tin-roof shacks and adobe beer joints squatting squalidly wherever their owners had decided to erect them. I put my money on the fugitives carrying camping equipment—tents, sleeping bags, canned food—for complete mobility.

At Mexicali I rendezvoused with my agent, James Carroll. He had already made the arrangements I had stipulated, and five Mexican Federal Police were standing by to assist me. I told them all I knew: that we were searching for a kidnapped boy of thirteen, who had been taken across the line in a red VW bus by a group of Americans. They promised me—after I paid them in advance—100 percent cooperation in checking out all the villages down the coast. They asked me how far I was planning to go, and I told them that in the first instance we would search as far south as Laguna Chapala. They observed gravely that Laguna Chapala was a very long way, and I as gravely agreed, adding that if we found it necessary to go a great deal further, perhaps even as far as the southern tip of Baja California, then that, unquestionably, was what we were going to do. I then suggested we get started, and told them to get aboard the helicopter.

No chance.

The first one told me in some detail how he couldn't even get into an elevator without becoming airsick. The second said he had nine children, and he had no intention of making orphans out of them by getting into one of those puddle-jumpers. The third, fourth and fifth all had equally inventive minds, and were equally adamant. I tried bribery and I tried flattery and I tried threats. I might have been talking Urdu for all the good it did. They'd seen my hooks, and they didn't plan to go up in any chopper piloted by a man with no hands.

We compromised. I would fly out in the helicopter and begin the air search. They would follow in a four-wheel-drive vehicle, keeping contact with me by radio. If I found anything, I could whistle them over to my position, whereupon they would provide me with all the backup I needed. It wasn't exactly what I'd had in mind, but I knew it was the best I could hope for, so I had to grin and bear it. I stocked up on bottled water and got airborne. The five Federales watched me climb away from the tarmac with the expressions of men who have just heard someone say he plans to jump off the highest tower of the Golden Gate Bridge. I don't think they really expected to see me again.

I began my first sweep, and then my second and my third, working without stopping, conscious of each passing second, as if a giant clock were ticking in the back of my mind. I was always aware of the fact that my quarry was also on the move. They might well head back for some hamlet I'd already searched. They might do a 180-degree turn and head back for the border. They might already be across the Gulf and well on their way into the mainland of Mexico. Their options were limitless, and all I could do was stay aloft as long as possible. I landed only to refuel, or to ask questions in some tiny waterline fishing village or other. I got a lot of dirty looks from the fishermen—they don't take too kindly to someone dropping out of

the skies in a chattering machine that spooks every
underwater creature for ten miles. But I wasn't in the
mood to worry. As soon as I knew a place was
"clean," I was up in the air again. I had decided long
before I headed south not to touch food. The citizens
of rural Mexico have developed a resistance to the
various forms of bacteria indigenous to their country
that North Americans never will, as anyone who's
done a couple of rounds with the complaint known as
Montezuma's Revenge will attest. I subsisted on sugarless gum and bottled water, and I slept as little as I
possibly could. I don't need much sleep at best, and
when I am up against a time problem, as in this instance, I go without any if necessary. As soon as it was
dark, I'd put the whirlybird down somewhere and
make contact with my Federales. We would compare
notes on the places that had been checked out, and
well before dawn I'd be in the air again.

I searched almost without stopping for three days,
and by the middle of the third day I was beginning to
hallucinate. I saw the vehicle I was looking for in
every clump of bushes, every gully, every stand of
timber and bunch of rocks I flew over. The bare dun
ground slipping beneath the fleeting shadow of the
helicopter had a strange, hypnotic effect. I would put
the plane down somewhere near the edge of the ocean
and stumble out into the flat glare of the sun, falling
face down in the surf. I kept awake any way I could.

Meanwhile my brave Federales were heading in my
general direction, stopping now and then for a few
questions here or a cool beer there, maintaining contact with the *maricón* in the helicopter who didn't
even have time to eat. By now my shirt and pants
were indescribably filthy, and I smelled like a goat.
There was a stubble on my chin that would have taken
the edge off a chisel. Still, I pressed on.

The coastline south of San Felipe never looks the
same from one moment to the next. There are rocky
inlets, tiny sheltered bays fringed with sand, ugly ex-

panses of bare broken volcanic rock. Once in a while
there will be a tiny fishing village, huts huddled
against the shelving cliffs facing the sea, rickety boats
beached just above the high-water line. Next there will
be a long finger of rock jutting out into the brilliant
sea, its crest dark with wind-twisted shrubs, followed
by a low flat stretch of sand dunes deserted except for
the scolding, screaming seabirds.

Although there was so much variation, paradox-
ically the coastline began to look familiar to me, and I
started to think I'd already covered it. I just wasn't
thinking straight anymore. I would see that red Volkswagen every place I looked, like a dying man seeing
waterholes in the desert. Landing the chopper, I would
check out my sighting and find to my disgust that it
had been a mirage. By now, my eyes felt as if someone had held them open and poured sand in them. It
would have been the easiest thing in the world to quit
right there; but something drove me on.

On the next day I started again before dawn. There
was a mist over the sea drifting in landward, so I had
to hold the chopper down low, close to the water and
just above her stalling speed, not too far out from the
rocky coastline. Suddenly, as if someone had planted
it there while I blinked my eyes, I saw a huge finger of
rock jutting out of the sea directly in front of me. It
looked as big as the Washington Monument, filling the
entire windshield, jagged and enormous. Even as I
braced myself for the tearing crash of the collision I
instinctively hit every button on the control panel and
that chopper went up like an Atlas missile, all of her
317-hp screaming like a demented banshee. Climbing
at the rate of twenty feet per second, I cleared the top
of the promontory with literally inches to spare, my
entire body bathed in a cold sweat. For the first time I
was thankful the five Federales were not aboard. With
a full load, I'd never have gotten the bird up that high
that fast and we'd have all been dead.

I leveled her off at one thousand feet and hovered,
checking my location. I was about two hundred miles

from the point I'd started at, and perhaps fifty from my point of no return—that imaginary spot on the map when you must return to base or arrange to land somewhere ahead. I made a mental note to check with my men when I had another ten or fifteen miles on the clock, and at that exact moment I saw the tents.

Right below, in the shadow of the pillar of stone I had almost hit, lay a small bay. There were caves in the face of the rocky, sloping cliff that faced the sea, and below these I could see bright red and orange tents pitched on the shelving beach. There was other gear scattered haphazardly around, butane stoves and pans lying beside them. I banked to landward, and as I did, the sun glinted on the chromium of a red Volkswagen bus partially covered with brush and backed under some stunted trees.

I took the plane in a five-mile half-circle away from the camp and then made another pass over the bay. This was no mirage: I had found the fugitives.

I put the helicopter down about a mile from the bay and made my way back on foot. From the top of the cliffs overlooking the beach I could see no sign of activity below: everyone was asleep. I checked, using the big Zeiss binoculars. They brought the license plate of the VW bus so close it could have been parked right in front of my nose. It was the one I was looking for.

I didn't feel excited, or elated. Just satisfied that everything was going good. Now I had to establish whether Christian Brando was down there. I trudged back to the chopper and called up my mercenaries, giving them my position. They were the better part of 150 miles away, but assured me that their arrival was imminent.

I sat in the shadow of the plane and watched the sun climb up the side of the sky. There was nothing I could do but wait, and wait I certainly did. Nearly four hours later they came jouncing up the dirt track making more noise than the combined pipes and drums of the Highland Light Infantry, with a cloud of dust rising behind them that was probably visible in

San Diego. I ran toward them before they could start tooting the horn to attract my attention.

I told them I was sure the people I was looking for were in the camp below, but that I had no way of knowing whether they would put up any resistance. I had seen that they had enough food and other supplies down there for a prolonged stay, so there was no question of waiting them out. I told my men to go on down and see if the Brando boy was there. They demurred, saying that as it was my case, I ought to be in charge of the arrests.

"I have no jurisdiction down here," I said. "You are Federal officers and this is your bailiwick. Now go on down there and arrest those people."

"No, *señor*," the sergeant, whose name was Hernandez said. "You are in command here. Lead, and we will render you support."

I was in no position to argue. I shrugged and went down the shelving cliff fast, my .38 drawn. There was nobody moving on the beach, and I ran up to the first tent and ripped the flap open.

"All right!" I yelled. "Everybody out! Put your hands on your heads and come out here!"

There were a man and a woman inside, both wearing only underwear. They stumbled out into the daylight, eyes bleary with whatever they'd been smoking or drinking the night before. The woman had no brassiere on. They went ahead of me toward the cliff face, eyes wide with fear, and leaned on their hands, legs apart, as I ordered them to do. They had no weapons, so I left them there and hit the second tent, bringing out another two men, and another two from the third. I told them all to keep very, very still, or my men would let them have it. Behind one of the tents was a sleeping bag, occupied by what I thought was another long-haired man. I yanked the bag open and immediately discovered my error. It was a young woman and she was as naked as a jaybird.

"Out!" I snapped. "With your hands on your head!"

"What?" she squawked. "Like *this*?"

"Don't worry, lady," I said. "You're not my type."

I lined her up with the others. They were all shivering slightly, whether from fear or cold I didn't have time to ascertain. I was already opening up another tent. A man naked to the waist was swinging his legs to the ground, a scuba speargun in his right hand. He looked up fast as I came into the tent and started to turn the harpoon toward me.

"Drop it quick!" I said. "Or I'll drop you!"

He let go of the speargun and it fell soundlessly to the ground. I discovered later it was ready to fire. I hustled him out of there and lined him up with the other five men and the two women. They all looked sheepish and about as dangerous as a set of chessmen, but I wasn't taking any chances. I turned around to whistle up my trusty Federales and went stone-cold.

There was no sign of them.

Here was I holding eight full-grown adults at the point of a five-shot pistol, confident that if anyone made a threatening move my mercenaries would step in and blow them away. Instead of which they weren't even close enough to see what was going on. They were up among the bushes on the top of the cliff, about fifty or sixty yards away. If they had opened fire from there, they'd have been just as likely to hit me as anything.

I put the best possible face on it I could.

"Get on down here, men!" I yelled. I wondered what my prisoners would have done if they'd known they had only one man to contend with. I decided not to dwell on it: you can go prematurely gray that way.

As my Federales came warily down the hill, ready for anything now that they were sure nothing was likely to happen, I checked out the encampment again, sure that Christian Brando must be somewhere. There was one more tent, close to the water's edge, and when I went in there, I found a teenage boy wearing only a pair of stained denim pants, who tried to burrow down among the bedclothes to hide from

from me. He was scared stiff, and I could understand why when I caught a look at myself in a mirror hanging on the tent pole. I looked like a Barbary pirate, and what with the hooks and the gun, it was no wonder the kid was scared.

It was Christian Brando and he needed a doctor. He had a high fever and a wracking cough. The floor of the tent was speckled with blood-flecked mucus. He was breathing very badly, and his face was so pale it looked almost blue. I'm no physician, but I know pneumonia when I see it. I told the Federales to put the abductors under arrest and bring them back to the border.

They said they could not do that, because no complaint had been filed against these people in Mexico. I said they had proof before them in the shape of Christian Brando that the Americans were kidnappers, and they agreed. Unfortunately, it would be necessary for Christian to remain in Mexico indefinitely as a material witness if such charges were to be brought. They would do what they were empowered to do: deport the kidnappers from the country as undesirable aliens who, if they ever tried to enter the country again, would be automatically imprisoned.

I had to make an agonizing choice, and I decided that under the circumstances the most important thing was to get Christian to a doctor. I translated what the *jefe*—the senior Federale—had told me to the Americans. They looked relieved, as well they might. If I'd had my druthers, I'd have tossed them into some stinking Mexican *calabozo* and mislaid the key. As it was, it would have to be left to the American authorities to track them down when they came back into the United States.

I put Christian aboard the plane and we flew direct to San Diego, where I had a doctor give him penicillin and some other shots. Then I put in a call to Brando's attorneys, Allen Susman and Norman Garey. They told me that Brando was with them, and he came on the line right away.

"Jay," he said. "I've been waiting to hear from you. When can we get together to discuss things? I've got more information that might be helpful to you."

"Relax," I said. "I'm on my way to Los Angeles now. And I've got Christian with me."

"You've—*what*?"

I told him again, and he still couldn't quite believe it. He asked me to put the boy on the line. Christian was crying with happiness, and saying yes, he was all right, he was coming home, yes, he was fine. The doctor had already okayed his trip, so we got on to the next flight and Christian Brando came safely home.

There were tears and smiles and hugs and handshakes, and flashbulbs popping. Father and son were so obviously overjoyed at being reunited that my tiredness fell off me like an old coat. After a little while Marlon Brando turned to me.

"Jay," he said. "I don't know where to begin thanking you."

"Then don't begin," I said. "Seeing the two of you together is all the thanks I need."

"But Jay," he protested. "Isn't there something I can do for you?" I grinned. He was wearing a beautiful cashmere sport shirt and custom-made slacks. He was immaculately shod, impeccably groomed, handsome, talented, self-assured, the highest-paid actor in Hollywood. I, on the other hand, was wearing the same filthy Levi pants and shirt I'd been wearing since I started on my search. I looked as if I'd been cleaning out the crankcase of a truck, and anyone with any sense was keeping well upwind of me.

"There is one thing," I said.

"Name it," he replied instantly.

"Could you loan me a clean shirt?"

3.

The rescue of Christian Brando took place in March 1972. It made world headlines, and I found myself being pursued by reporters asking for intimate details about the boy and his father. This is one of the greatest problems of my profession, for the relationship between an investigator and his client—certainly as far as I am concerned—is completely inviolate, totally private. That is one of the reasons why in almost every case related in this book the names and locations have been changed. An investigator's relationship with his clients is based upon mutual trust, and I cannot and would not ever betray it. It's one thing to tell you that I have worked for King Faisal or the Burtons or Richard Widmark or Howard Hughes. It's quite another to give you specific information about their problems and how I handled them. The Brando case was a little different: the star and his wife had been battling in the courts for eleven years and there was precious little about their lives that had not been dragged through every newspaper in the world. If the client elects to make his case and my part in it public, that's something else entirely. Until he does, it remains private.

Later I had to appear at several court hearings in connection with Christian Brando's custody. The ex-wife told a confused and unconvincing story about her World Travel Academy friends offering to take both her and the boy on a vacation to Mexicali. Thinking it might improve his condition—he had bronchitis—

she accepted, only to discover that the dates conflicted with her changing her residence. Promising to meet her at Mexicali with Christian, the friends went on ahead with the boy, leaving on Sunday, March 5. When Kashfi arrived at the border, they were not there. She had meanwhile been served with papers requiring her to have Christian in court in Santa Monica on the following Thursday. When the friends from Mexicali didn't appear, she reported Christian's disappearance to the Mexican police. She then telephoned her lawyer, Barry Rose, in Los Angeles. He told her to come back home and leave it to the police, who were meanwhile searching for the boy. On the way back to Los Angeles, Kashfi and her friend Shirley Hauptmann were arrested on a drunk and disorderly charge and spent the night in jail at Salton City. One way or another, the news got into the Mexico City papers, and became a worldwide sensation.

When I went onto the witness stand I told Superior Judge Laurence J. Rittenband about my search for Christian, and the condition in which I had found him. I told him that one of the kidnappers had confessed to me that Anna Kashfi Brando had offered him $10,000 if he would take the boy out of the country.

The whole thing was sheer hell for all parties involved, and I felt really sorry for Marlon Brando, who looked drawn and tired. He now had to go back to Paris and resume work on the movie he was making as though nothing had happened. The case was recessed until the movie was finished. At a later hearing, he was given permanent custody of his son, thus ending nearly twelve years of court action and making him a very happy man.

I think there must have been a representative of every newspaper in the world at those hearings, as well as UPI and AP, the wire services. The case—and my part in it—made world news, but back home in El Paso, they had some trouble accepting that Jay J. Armes, who was being called "the world's best private detective," was the same Jay Armes everyone in town knew. You know what they say about prophets being without honor in their own town. I found it was that way for me.

"Jay Armes, the world's greatest private eye?" they'd say. "How can that be? He grew up right here in El Paso. How did he get to be the world's greatest private investigator?"

I'll tell you this much: it wasn't easy.

There is a song that says that the best things in life are free, but I've found that most of the worthwhile things are earned by the application of either sweat, time, money or blood. Most of the capers I've handled have involved the first three. Once in a while it was all four. Maybe there's an easier way, but if there is I have never found it.

One of the first capers I ever handled involved the disappearance of a four-year-old boy, Stephen Wheeler. His mother was a teacher at the University of Texas in El Paso, his father an engineer who simply disappeared from the family home with the boy while the mother was at school. Stephen's grandparents contacted the police, but the detectives came up empty, all their inquiries dead-ended. At that point the grandparents brought their daughter along to see me. Paul Henderson was a good-looking white-haired man of about sixty, with an erect, almost soldierly bearing. His wife was plump and motherly and smiled a lot. They could have stepped right out of a Norman Rockwell painting. Dorothy Wheeler was in her mid-twenties, a brunette with large, expressive eyes that looked constantly as though tears were about to fall from them.

Henderson took charge of things. He said he understood that I guaranteed results, and I confirmed it. As far as I know, my guarantee is unique in the investigative field. It is given without qualification: I stay on every case until it is finished, no matter what. If a client pays me an agreed retainer, then he gets 100 percent of everything I've got until the case is solved. That's my commitment every time and there are no exceptions.

Henderson then asked me how much I would charge to locate their missing grandson. I stopped him right there and explained that there is a difference between locating someone and bringing someone back from wherever that person is. The first is a simple matter of seek-and-find. The second is infinitely complicated and, if mishandled, can lead to the investigator himself being charged with abduction or even kidnapping. In my business, we are often required—you could almost say are expected—to bend the rules. You have to be very careful not to bend them so far that they break.

They told me they had no information to speak of. Charles Wheeler had simply packed his things, taken the boy and split. They had no idea where he could have gone or even any clear idea of why, all of a sudden, he had taken off. I began the long, careful series of questions that have to be asked in kidnapping or abduction cases. People don't know how much they know. It takes skilled interrogation to elicit that information, a technique based on years of observation and practice. My initial evaluation of the case was that the Hendersons dominated their daughter, who, although she wasn't telling me, had been having trouble with her husband. That might explain his motive in taking the boy away with him. Now we had to find out how, and where.

In a kidnapping or abduction case, there is a good deal of information that, while not especially valuable in itself, can be of immense aid to the investigator. So my first questions to Dorothy Wheeler were about the baby: his physical description, what clothes he might have been wearing and any others that the father had taken from the house. Since there seemed to be no question of anyone else being involved, and no likelihood of ransom being asked, I skipped on to ask them for the names and addresses of all their relatives and friends, whether in the United States or abroad, even people they had not seen for years but to whom, feasibly, Charles Wheeler might turn in time of need. I asked whether he had received any strange letters or telephone calls during the recent months, especially foreign mail. I asked about his place of work and his friends, hobbies, social life. It was a one-dimensional portrait of Charles Wheeler—you would be surprised how one-dimensionally some family members see each other—but it was the foundation of the dossier I would compile on the man.

When we were through, I told them how much I wanted for a retainer. The old man blinked once or twice, and then coughed.

"What about the extras?" he said.

"There are no extras," I said. "That's my fee and that's it."

He looked surprised—perhaps relieved would be a better word—and they left. I immediately got to work following up on the information they had given me. I set up a neighborhood survey in the vicinity of the Wheeler home, sending agents to interview everyone who lived close to or knew the family. Meanwhile I checked out the bank the Wheelers used to make sure no large sums had been deposited or withdrawn, and put other men on the task of checking out all the names and addresses Dorothy Wheeler and her parents had given me.

While all this was going on, I followed up by talking to everyone who had known Charles Wheeler, especially the people at the engineering plant where he worked. Everybody there seemed pretty tight-lipped, and I realized it was because nobody wanted to get in the middle of a custody fight. It's always hard to know who is in the right when children are involved, and obviously his co-workers felt more sympathy for Wheeler, whom they knew and whose story they had doubtless heard over coffee or lunch at one time or another, than for the wife, whom they didn't know.

Finally, we got a break. A secretary who worked at the engineering plant told me that there had been an inquiry regarding Wheeler from South America. She thought it had been a request for a reference, and felt sure that the boss knew where Wheeler was. She said she was also sure that I wouldn't get the information out of him even if I used red-hot pliers. I didn't try.

If Charles Wheeler was in South America, he would have needed a passport to get there. The only place you can get a passport is through the State Department, and anything processed through a government department is a matter of record and can be traced— if you know how! Within twenty-four hours I knew he was going to Bogotá, Columbia, and twenty-four hours later I had the name of Wheeler's next-of-kin there, Thomas McLelland, and his address.

I checked with the Hendersons, but the name meant nothing to them or their daughter. They had never heard that Charlie had any relatives in South America —not that that meant anything because Charlie had always been close-mouthed, tight-fisted and selfish. Why Dorothy had married him they would never understand. I excused myself before the old man got warmed up: I've heard that song before.

Bogotá, here I come, I thought, and called Avianca. They told me I'd have to connect at Miami. I threw a few things into a bag, whistled up my car and hit the road. Twenty-four hours later I was landing at El Dorado Airport in Santa Fé de Bogotá.

It's a fascinating city, the birthplace of the legend of El Dorado (hence the name of the airport) which brought the Conquistadores in search of the Seven Cities of Gold. The legend grew out of the ritual in which the Cacique of Guatavita covered his body with gold dust and floated to the middle of a lake on a raft, accompanied by the *jeques,* or priests. He would then dive into the lake, while the priests threw sacred objects into the lake as offerings to the gods of the waters.

The place has changed quite a lot since then. It's now one of the most modern cities in South America, with skyscrapers, office blocks, enormous apartment houses. The International Center, or El Centro, as the locals call it, is a vast complex of shops and stores and restaurants, all joined by a basic platform. You can buy anything from uncut emeralds to straw hats. The bittersweet smell of roasting coffee is everywhere.

I checked into the Hotel Tequendama where my local agent, Felipe Mes, was waiting for me. He's a big burly guy with jet black hair, huge spatulate hands and a grin as wide as a slice of watermelon. It was too late for us to get started—that would have to wait until morning—but there was plenty of preparation work to do. I wasn't unhappy about the delay, to tell the truth. What with the time differential, the ache in my bones from the mandatory typhoid and yellow fever shots, and the chill in the night air six thousand feet above sea level, I decided to settle for a late dinner and a tactical conference with Felipe. Bogotáns don't eat much before eleven, so we made our plans over a superb seafood meal at La Fragata, not ten minutes from the hotel.

I let Felipe specify the boundaries and limitations within which we would have to work. It is one of my special advantages as an investigator that I have agents such as him all over the world, as well as friends, acquaintances and numerous contacts. It is these people who know the shortcuts, the police procedures, the local customs, the airline schedules. Such knowledge can mean the difference between success and failure. Once in a while it can save your life.

Next morning, Felipe and I were in position outside an apartment house on one of the avenues running east from the Avenida Suba, a middle-class, middle-income area. Bogotán offices open at eight, so we were in place by six: I didn't want to miss our subject. We sat in the Volkswagen I'd rented the preceding evening from Hertz at the Tequendama, our faces hidden behind the local paper, *El Tiempo*. The Hendersons had given me a photograph of Wheeler, and I recognized him immediately as he came out of the building, in spite of the newly-grown Zapata moustache. He was a big well-built man with swarthy skin, wearing a fawn windbreaker and dark slacks. He got into a battered Chevy and drove off past us.

We waited some more. After a while, Felipe touched my arm and pointed with his chin at another man who'd just left the apartment house. He was slat-thin, about forty-five years of age, with thinning gray hair and a long horse face. He was wearing a dark pea jacket and blue pants.

"McLelland," Felipe said. "He works downtown in an architect's office on Avenida Caracas."

We watched McLelland get into his car and drive off, and waited another half-hour for safety before we went over to the apartment. Felipe's information was that the two men had hired a woman to stay with the boy while they were at work, and his information was right. She was a short, squat, dark-skinned Colombian woman who looked almost Indian. Felipe spoke to her in rapid-fire Spanish, telling her that we knew the boy had been abducted from the United States, and that we knew that she knew this and was therefore an accessory to his kidnap. I showed her my credentials and the power of attorney signed by the mother, and told her we must take the boy with us right away. Her eyes dropped and her face turned sullen, impassive. She said that she could not allow us to take the boy without telephoning his father. Felipe looked at me and I shrugged. There was no way we could drag him out of there by main force without creating an international incident.

"*Señora,*" I told the woman. "This is a legal document, and I am here to enforce it now. I understand your loyalty and you must indeed telephone the father of the boy. You will tell him that we have taken Stephen to the Foreign Office, where a disposition will be made. He can meet us there and have his say."

She didn't much like that either, but my credentials

and the legal-looking power of attorney reassured her, as did Felipe's local dialect. Finally, she agreed to the boy's accompanying us, and we hurried out of there with the sound of the telephone dial whirring in our ears as she called Wheeler. We piled into the car and took off—not, of course, to the Oficina de Extranjeria, which is downtown on Carrera 10, but hell for leather to the airport. We covered the dozen kilometers in about five minutes flat, and ran up to the check-in counter. Little Stephen thought it was all a fine game, and was bouncing around with excitement. Nobody was paging us, nobody was looking at us, and most important of all, there were no police coming after us. That was the good news. The bad news was that the plane we'd made the run for was delayed and wouldn't be leaving for at least another hour and a half.

I wasn't about to wait. When that woman contacted Wheeler and he contacted the Foreign Office, they would contact the police and there was going to be one hell of a bang. I didn't want to be around to hear it. We did a hasty rethink. Wheeler would expect me to head direct for the States, anyway. It was possible that he might even try to have the plane intercepted at one of the layovers. It was even possible that he might come after me with blood in his eye. With Stephen in my arms, I identified myself to the airline people as a special investigator. The power of attorney worked like a magic wand. The passport requirements for the boy were waived, and we sailed through customs and immigration on to the next outward-bound plane. It was headed for Lima, Peru. Frankly, I would have willingly boarded a kamikaze as long as it was heading out of Bogotá at that moment. Lima might be a thousand miles in the wrong direction, but it was extremely unlikely that Charlie Wheeler would ever think I'd head *away* from the United States.

Stephen and I had no trouble getting a Los Angeles–bound plane out of Jorge Chavez International that same afternoon, and next day we were back in El Paso. Some detour, I thought.

To my astonishment, there was a welcoming committee of photographers and reporters at the airport to meet us. Mrs. Wheeler had been giving them a blow-by-blow description of the exploits of Jay Armes, and after I called her from Los Angeles she brought them all out to meet us. She wanted me to get recognition for bringing her boy home, solving a case the police had long since given up on and wouldn't have been able to handle anyway. She told them about my unique guarantee, and I got my first taste of being in the headlines.

To tell the truth, I didn't mind at all. I figured I ought to get at least something out of the caper, because the retainer I'd asked from the family was something like $5000 short of the amount I'd spent on air fares alone. However, I'd told them "no extras" and that was that. I guess they didn't mind if I ground my teeth a little, though.

4.

Contrary to all and any preconceptions, the offices of
The Investigators at 1717 Montana Avenue in El Paso
are almost startlingly seedy. Entry to the inner sanctum
is via a corridor that leads into a conference room, adjacent to which is Jay Armes' office. One wall of the
conference room is dominated by a huge painting of a
tiger springing upon some unseen prey. Hidden somewhere among the stripes is a secret peephole through
which the front entrance of the building can be observed, should anyone, for whatever reason, disable
the closed-circuit TV cameras that keep it and the rest
of the building under constant surveillance.

All visitors to the premises are automatically photographed and nobody gets in without having to pass
Armes' bodyguard.

In the conference room there is a blackboard covered with chalk diagrams, and next to it some FBI
Wanted posters, a hat stand with a variety of hats and
coats for disguises and a chamois shoulder holster
holding a snubnose .38 Smith & Wesson. In the center
of the table is a globe of the world, the kind that lights
up to become a table lamp. The chairs are wicker and
the walls are lined with bamboo cane. The fluorescent
light is orange-yellow, a weird and gloomy contrast to
the hard flat Texas sunshine outside. It heightens the
jungle atmosphere created by the cane walls, bamboo-
pole door frames, leopardskin-patterned upholstery
and bizarre African masks on the walls. Armes says it
encourages confidentiality.

On the desk, like toys on the floor of a rich kid's playroom, is a disarray of electronic gadgets: touch-telephone, push-button telephone, dictating machine, cassette recorder, portable walkie-talkie, electrically-operated notepad, calculator-recorder, radiophone. There is a framed snapshot of Armes' seven-year-old son Jay, another of Linda Armes with the other two children, Tracy and Michael.

Facing the visitor is a metal sign that reads JAY J. ARMES CHIEF INVESTIGATOR in Roman capitals. In front of it lie a security officer's badge, a tiny souvenir ashtray (a sign in the waiting room says "Thank you for not smoking") and a Hawaii Five-O badge presented to Armes by Jack Lord, the star of the series, after Armes appeared in a segment of the show playing the role of a villian named "Hookman."

Behind the desk on the visitor's left is a bamboo-frame bookshelf surmounted by a digital clock, more snapshots, and a six-inch-high model of a charging African elephant with enormous white tusks. Behind the investigator's chair the window is boarded up and covered by a Venetian blind. No daylight enters the room.

To the right of the window stands another bookcase containing the seventy-one volumes of Corpus Juris *and the three supplementary volumes of annotations. On top of the bookcase stand two grinning jug-eared African busts and a toy Rolls with a radio in it that someone gave Armes with a note saying it was for the man who had everything.*

The wall adjacent to this bookshelf is covered with framed certificates. They testify to Armes' membership in the International Police Congress (Interpol), the Central Bureau of Investigations in Hollywood, a state of Texas license for The Investigators, another from the Texas Association of Licensed Investigators, a City Occupation License and several from the Training Academy of the El Paso Sheriff's Department. Armes put in more than three times the required hours to get his deputy's commission and his license to carry a gun. Beneath the certificates is a framed plaque carrying a photo of Armes and the motto "An investigator's time and advice are his stock in trade." Beneath it hangs an M3A1 parachutist's machine pistol with a telescopic sight.

High up on the wall in the corner, behind where visitors sit and are least likely to notice it, the closed-circuit TV monitor flickers. On it Armes can see anyone approaching the front of the office. By flicking a switch, other cameras can traverse the sides and rear of the building. He had the system installed after someone sprayed the building with a machine gun one night when he was working late.

Out in back there is parking space for the huge Cadillac Eldorado and another as big. In front of the building there is a screen of see-through concrete, and jagged rocks have been set irregularly into the sidewalk and the frontage of the building. These have a function similar to the closed-circuit television's. They have been put there to avert assassination attempts. The screen of concrete will effectively withstand anything short of a missile. The rocks will prevent anyone from driving any sort of vehicle onto the sidewalk or up alongside the office building. "A tank might make it," Armes says and grins; but that's all.

The Investigators does not advertise. The flamboyant style of its principal is probably all the advertising it needs, but for the record, the organization handles—according to Jay J. Armes' business card— inventory shortages, industrial undercover work, counterindustrial espionage, shadowing, photography, employee background, extortion, forgery and fraud, missing persons, heirs and witnesses, embezzlement and theft, domestic relations, personal injury, hotel and store detection work, bodyguard and special police assignments, plant and building protection, debugging phones and offices, and closed-circuit television installation.

When I graduated from high school I went out to California, quite certain I was going to become a movie star. Even as a kid, I was quite positive in my approach to everything. Determined I was going to do it, sure I was able to do it—and I did it. I broke into the movies, although I never got to be a star. I had a few small parts in features, a lot more bits—nothing that anyone would remember, I suspect. The movies—and my parts in them—were mostly forgettable. Anyone who knows anything about the movies knows that the mid-fifties will never be classed among the vintage years of Hollywood. That was when the entire industry was running scared of the new monster, television.

I saw the writing on the wall very early on in my Hollywood years, and used every spare hour that I wasn't on call at the studios to study. I was mad about languages, and found I had the natural flair of the mimic. I studied as many as I could: German, Italian, French, even Chinese, to add to my own knowledge of English and Spanish, and I continued with the law studies I had begun in high school. I learned to type by the hunt-and-peck system, and got up to sixty words a minute. In my spare time—and I *made* spare time —I also attended the Pasadena Playhouse and studied with the Benbart Players. The drive that is in me now was in me even then. I guess it's because I hate procrastination. All through my life I have seen people putting off doing the things they want to do and it exasperates me, as does having people make me promises they don't or can't keep, appointments they turn up late for or not at all. The most soul-destroying moments of my life are the ones when I am idle. I can't unwind: I never learned how. From boyhood I had conditioned my mind and body that way. Now I can't do anything else. I have to be on the move, doing something, heading somewhere. To me the best is always yet to come, and I enjoy every single thing I do because of it. Because when you do things, you can see the results. Accomplishment is fulfilling in itself.

Altogether I appeared in thirty-six movies and twenty-eight TV shows during the six years I was in California. I did walk-ons, spear-carrying, locations, even stunt work, anything. I had a nice little apartment up on Elevado Avenue, just off Doheny in Beverly Hills. I bought the first of my many Cadillacs. I had lots of girlfriends and lots of fun, and learned the most important thing of all—how to be self-sufficient.

Even then, though, I knew that there would be an end to it, that one day I was going to move on. I was a long way from starving to death, but being a small-time movie actor wasn't the only thing I wanted to do with my life. When I finally got my degree in criminology, I came to the big decision: I was going to become an investigator. And—being me—I had to do it the hard way. I headed back for El Paso, all set to prove Thomas Wolfe wrong: you can go home again.

The welcome I got from Sheriff Bob Bailey and Chief Reisinger of the El Paso Police Department was some way short of rapturous, but I got started anyway. I knew I wasn't going to work anything like any existing detective agency. I had a fairly clear picture of where I was going, and I knew that to get there I had to be not just different, but unique. I had a head start on most people: I had to be the first private detective working with hooks instead of hands. I also knew I would and could work about four times as hard and four times as fast as most of the people I knew who were in the same business. I believed then and I believe now that a person can be whatever he wants to be. It doesn't matter which side of the tracks he comes from. It doesn't matter whether he's white, brown, yellow or black. If he has talent and he has determination, he can make it. All I had to do was prove it.

The hardest thing at first is to let people know that you are there and that you're willing to work harder for them than anyone else. When I got started, I pounded the streets, going from door to door like a carbon-paper salesman, doing it the only way I knew how—the hard way. I set up an office with a secretary and wrote letters to every attorney within a hundred miles. I hired ten agents, all ex-policemen, and sat back waiting for the work to start pouring in.

Nothing happened.

There I was with an overhead that would have crippled Lockheed, ten agents eating me out of house and home, and I wasn't being asked to find a missing dog. Then I hit upon a system that worked. I would go downtown each night and morning, and pick up the newspapers hot off the press. Then, everything that had to do with a crime was clipped—and I do mean everything. Robbery, missing persons, traffic offenses, murder, the whole enchilada. These cuttings became the foundation of a potential case file. El Paso is, after all, a border town, and a never-ending flow of people come into it with nothing but the clothes on their backs, looking for fame and fortune. Some of them find it. The others have to get money any way they can. There is a famous story about the outlaw Jesse James, who was once asked by a newspaperman why he robbed banks. With unassailable logic, Jesse replied, "Because that's where the money is." To small-time crooks from south of the border, El Paso is where the money is.

I would send a letter to anyone who had been the victim of a crime, whatever it was, saying that Jay J. Armes was there to help them. My "movie" name, chosen for me a long time ago by a director at Universal who thought Julian Armas sounded like a Latin lover, was easy to remember. I found then—and I still find—that if I talked to people personally, they retained me. There were more than a few, you can be sure, who did a double-take when they saw that I had hooks instead of hands. They would sit down in my office plainly wondering whether I was competent to handle their problem. My ace in the hole was always the same: I told them I guaranteed results. If I took on a case, I would stay on it, all the way down the line. From that day to this, I've stuck to that rule. That's why I've never had an unsolved case.

I had another advantage: the police attitude toward nonviolent crime. For someone who has been burglarized, the world has come to an end. Many people view it as a form of personal rape, and are appalled and deeply disturbed by it. To the police, it is a routine matter. They see it all the time, and they investigate everything—a burglary or an embezzlement or an abduction—in exactly the same way. It's called routine, and it is. While they're looking for your burglar or someone else's mugger, they're also looking for stolen cars, runaway kids, dope peddlers, bank robbers, escaped mental patients, lunatic assassins, traffic violators, perverts and members of the Symbionese Liberation Army. They are settling family squabbles and busting drunks and enforcing liquor laws and negotiating for pay raises and filling in reports, always filling in reports. Somewhere in there is you.

But not when you come to Jay J. Armes. You get 100 percent of my time and expertise. I'm interested in solving your problem fast, the faster the better for both of us. If your problem isn't solved, then it's still on my mind, I still have to be concerned with it. That's my motivation: I want to get it out of the way, finished, settled. There's none of that *mañana* in my system, none of that "let George do it" attitude. My philosophy is "get it done now," and it has been since I was a kid. Believe me, it works.

Soon I began advertising on radio. I used the old *Dragnet* theme. I suppose there are a lot of people around now who don't even remember the show, which began on radio and then made the transfer to TV so successfully. It was the daddy of all the cops and robbers shows with its laconic hero Sergeant Joe Friday of the Los Angeles Police Department, and its threatening four-chord musical introduction—da de dah-dah! da de dah-dah! da de dah-dah-DAAAAAH! I used this music and followed it with the sound of a woman's scream, and then her voice saying, "Who are you? Who *are* you?" There would be the sound of footsteps, the crash of breaking glass, another scream.

Then the announcer would say, "If this is your problem—if your privacy has been invaded, your safety
threatened, your loved ones frightened—call The Investigators! Night or day—call The Investigators! Let
your problem be their problem!"

It worked like Edison's light bulb. We started getting up to two hundred telephone calls a month, and
more work than we could handle. I took on additional
agents, and set about writing another set of radio com-
mercials, this time with business backgrounds—a boss
finding a shortage but unable to trace the miscreants,
a store suffering from heavy theft but not catching
shoplifters, and so on. Same exhortation at the end of
each one: call The Investigators. "We're on the job
day or night, waking or sleeping. Call 532-5739. Call
The Investigators *now!*"

In a matter of months, we were handling every kind
of investigation there was. I now began organizing a
Hot-Check Detail (HCD) to bring to book people
passing dud or phony checks. The price paid by small
businessmen and supermarkets for this racket runs into
several billion dollars per annum, and when I announced my plans, the El Paso Police Department was
more than happy to lend 100 percent support. They
had file cabinets full of bad check complaints and
knew that few of them would even justify sending out
an officer. A bad check for less than $50 only brings
a misdemeanor rap down on the head of the offender,
and these days there are plenty of people who'll risk a
rap on the knuckles from the judge for $50 worth of
groceries. Literally thousands of such checks were
passed in the El Paso County area each year, and the
stores just had to eat their losses until The Investigators HCD began operation.

I planned the whole thing on an hour-spent-per-
dollar-recovered basis, researching meticulously, and
checking time and again before I set the wheels in motion. Within a year, what had begun as an experiment
became a virtual monopoly, and we were turning over
a lot of money on that one small detail alone.

The next area of specialization I cornered was the business survey. There are very few businesses of any size that aren't interested in the activities of their competitors. Sometimes they want to know how the other guy is doing profitwise, if he is hurting from stock deficiencies, if his 50-percent-off sales are the genuine article, if he is ripe for a takeover. For such people, we perfected the business survey. It's a difficult job and it takes time, but if the investigator knows what he is doing he can get his client any information he wants.

We only work to a specific brief, and the first thing I want to know is what the client wants the information for: industrial espionage is out if the client plans to use it in bad faith. Let us suppose, however, that he simply wants to know—for takeover purposes, or because he is planning to make an offer for the business against an already quoted asking price—how much the firm is worth "on the hoof."

First of all, we have agents pick up the trash before it is collected by the garbage men. Business trash is not like household rubbish. There's not much debris or junk—it's all dry: business papers, labels, envelopes, sales tags and stickers, invoices, delivery notes and so on. It isn't too hard over a short period to put together a picture of the company's customers and suppliers, its general modus operandi. If it's a store or retail establishment, shrinkage can be ascertained by checking coded sales tags that have been removed and thrown out against the new ones in store. If they are having a sale, you can easily check whether it is genuine by the same kind of comparison.

Meanwhile, you obtain the names and addresses of all employees—particularly middle and higher management. Agents are then sent to infiltrate the recreational places patronized by the staff: bars, bowling alleys, tennis clubs, golf clubs, restaurants, cocktail lounges where they meet after work, and so on. Accidentally on purpose the agent gets to know one or more of the employees and by asking the right sort of questions he can evaluate the way the business is being run, staff attitudes toward management, the dodges employees are using to get around the system, and much more. The business survey can assess accurately the profits or losses of a firm, how much pilferage and shoplifting it is suffering, what its staff thinks of management and vice versa, even which employees are on the take in one way or another. Discounts being offered and received, bills being paid or not, the size of the bad debt problem—name it, and it can be obtained.

From there it was but a short step to undercover work, putting agents into businesses as "employees" to uncover thefts, embezzlements and other criminal activities. I became a specialist in finding missing persons—wives, husbands, friends, lovers, children. Every time I concluded a case successfully, my client would become a living, breathing testimonial to The Investigators. In a business where 80 percent of all inquiries come from referrals, that is no small point.

It was the missing persons cases that interested me most. I was always fascinated by the motivation of runaways, and they were always the hardest to psych out. My theory is that to understand your subject, you must try to think like him, ask yourself what he would do. Why is it that one Tuesday, for no apparent reason, John Doe just walks out of his home and never comes back? What is it that makes a wife who's never played around suddenly plunge into a passionate affair with some man she's met at a PTA meeting? What makes a teenager suddenly decide he or she's had it up to here with his or her parents and take off? How do we wound each other so subtly, so infinitesimally, that we never know what we have done until it is too late? Who gives the final push, says the deciding word? Who, finally, pulls the trigger?

I've had such cases all over the world, and they never cease to surprise me. Old men, middle-aged men, women, kids. It's the cases involving kids that break your heart. I got lots of retainers from parents whose children had run away from home, asking me please for God's sake find Johnny, or Jane. They were usually bewildered, these parents, unable to understand why their child would leave home. They would tell me how the youngster had everything, nice clothes, a lovely home, a car, a hi-fi, his own TV, everything. Very few of them have the courage to face up to the truth of the matter, which is that their child ran away from home for the simple reason that they weren't giving him the one thing he really wanted: love.

Kids are pretty smart, and even if running away from home isn't the brightest thing they can do, they do it for what seems to them a damned good reason. Just as an arsonist will leave clues at the scene of his crime, so the runaway is leaving clues for his parents to find. He is telling them something is wrong and needs putting right, and if they still don't see it, he'll run away all over again. Sometimes you can tell this to the parents. Much more often all you do is go out and locate the runaway and bring him back, and watch the reunion and the hugs and kisses and tears. They thank you, thank you from their hearts, and say it will be all right now. So you're out of it, and you leave it at that. There's no point in telling them to be more careful, to give their child the love he needs. There's no point in telling them about all the kids who never come back, the boys who get involved in crime or drugs, the girls who go on the streets or end up dead, raped in an alley. It's a jungle out there and there are animals in it that would put the most savage beast God ever created to shame, but you don't tell them that either. It isn't their world, it's yours. It's the world you go into every day of your life, never knowing whether you'll come out alive. It's not easy to leave my wife and children every morning with that thought hanging over all of us, but that's what they pay me for and that's what I do.

5.

Every day, without fail, Jay Armes spends an hour practicing shooting. Wearing a suit tailored exactly the way his day suits are, he shoots from the standing, kneeling, running, falling and prone positions, using the special .38 snubnose, or a murderous-looking Browning shotgun. He tries as much as possible to simulate real-life conditions, so there are no earmuffs or eyeshades or dinky little cartridge belts such as you see if you make the conducted tour of the FBI shooting range.

Armes is a crack shot with every kind of weapon. He demonstrates the technique for target shooting, and then shows the difference between shooting that way, and shooting on the run, or from the hip. In target shooting, the body is profiled, side-on to the target. The feet are carefully adjusted to get the line of fire correct. The pistol is held pointing at the ground, raised above the target as the breath is drawn in, and descends on the exhalation for the shot. Armes does it that way: his shot rips out a chunk from the right breast of the man-sized target, just as he said it would.

Now he tries it the other way. The gun is in the Myres holster on the left-hand side, butt pointing to the right. He sets the target in motion and brings the gun up quite, but not very, fast, firing one-two-three-four-five about as fast as you say it. The group of holes in the target can be covered easily by the palm of the hand.

The underground range is custom built to Armes'

own design. It is computerized; the targets are moving on-track cutouts, or concealed pop-ups, three of the former and six of the latter. The on-track targets can be programmed to travel forward or backward, stop and go, face, turn and angle. They can be used independently of the pop-up targets or simultaneously. The pop-up targets are synchronized so that as one is hit, another will appear, or two or three will appear at opposite sides of the range, or jump up in line, or one after another, anywhere between ten feet and seventy, for one second or seven.

The target range itself measures one hundred feet long by forty-five feet wide. At the business end there are three shooting channels, each fitted with a control for the targets, and a table with a fitted armrest for shooting "on rest." At the far right-hand side is the master computer control, which also controls the lighting. Darkness, shadows, twilight, neon-lit or sodium-lamplit street, hazy or bright sunshine, all can be produced to order. Steel swing shutters are fitted to each channel. They can be swung to any required angle to simulate half-open doors or angled walls. There is no shooting condition that cannot be reproduced in this chill air-conditioned room.

The range is actually a concrete bunker, lined at each side with three-inch cork to deaden the concussion. At the far end, behind the targets, armor plate eight inches thick deflects all bullets harmlessly into a trough set in the floor, from which a conveyor belt carries them away. There is absolutely no chance whatever of a ricochet.

As a double precaution against accident, a special safety ceiling was installed. It is made of several layers, cork over wood over heavy steel plate over concrete, which would kill any bullet without risk to anyone below should there be an accidental discharge while loading. A special extractor system siphons off the smoke and burnt powder, which is extremely toxic if inhaled. Everything about the target range is designed to the highest standards, the total fail-safe.

Jay J. Armes is not only a deputy sheriff, he is also a constable, and is aware of the irony of a double amputee holding down the job once filled by such redoubtable two-gun men as John Selman, who won his spurs in the Lincoln County range wars. Selman was the bravo who put an end to the forty-notch career of John Wesley Hardin in El Paso's Acme Saloon during the evening of August 19, 1895. Jay Armes doesn't think much of all that "quick on the draw" stuff. "What counts is what you do with the gun when you get it out," he says. "Accuracy. If I tell you I'm going for a seventy-five [one of the numbered locations on one of the targets], then I'll hit it. Left hand, right hand, sitting down or standing on my head. Hitting what you're aiming at is what counts. When I'm shooting, it's like everything else I do—I call my shots. Every time."

During his hour on the target range, Jay Armes will use more than half a dozen different guns from his collection. Despite the hooks, he reloads methodically and without fumbling. When he is firing, there is no tremor, no waver, and—as Armes points out—the recoil of the weapons doesn't bother his steel hands half as much as it bothers the hands of ordinary men. Another advantage is that his hands never get sweaty. There is no danger that when the chips are down, he will try for his gun and it will slip from his hook.

He has remarkable sensitivity in those wicked-looking hooks. He can squeeze the trigger until the double-action gun is on the point of firing, and yet not fire unless he wishes to. A single-action pistol is harder to manage but there aren't too many people using frontier Colts these days, anyway.

He stands with his back to the targets, the pistol in its holster, and sets the controls. As a bell rings, one of the man-sized targets pops up. Armes turns 180 degrees and fires. The target drops back, neatly holed. He turns and faces away again, and again the bell rings. This time the target is on another part of the range. Armes has one second to turn, fire and hit it.

He does it time after time after time, examining the results critically and tutting when his shooting is less than satisfactory.

The important thing about guns is to remember that they are tools, like a spade or a chisel. Put them in the hands of a man who knows how to use them, and they will be used properly. Give them to someone who is irresponsible, and there'll be hell to pay. The man I admire is the one who carries a gun but uses his head instead. You'll get out of more tight corners using your head than you ever will using a gun.

I got a phone call while I was in New York, soon after the announcement that I was working on a case. I got back to the Plaza Hotel quite late, and there was a message asking me to call a Thomas Howard. The name meant nothing to me, but I called the number and the man who answered said he was Thomas Howard, and was I interested in some inside information on the identity of the La Guardia bomber? I told him I was, and he said he knew who had done the job. He said he would tell me who it was for $500. I told him I would have to evaluate the quality of his information, and he said he was staying at this hotel on West Forty-fourth Street, in room 1008. Why didn't I come down and meet him there? We agreed to rendezvous in half an hour, and I just had time to shave, shower and change my shirt before grabbing a taxi and going down there.

The room was on the tenth floor, in an octagonal hallway. I knocked on the door and a man's voice called to me to come in, it was open. I walked in and found myself staring down the barrel of a Ruger Super Blackhawk. They look something like the old frontier Colts, but they are a lot more gun. The makers justifiably claim that with magnum ammunition, the Blackhawk is the most powerful handgun in the world. A friend of mine once remarked laconically that they're useful guns for stopping trains: you just fire at the oncoming locomotive and the bullet will stop it dead.

I stood very still and looked at the man holding the gun. I didn't know him. He had a three-day stubble and a hunted look in his eyes. He wasn't a big man, perhaps five-seven or eight, about 150 pounds. Behind him in the slightly shabby hotel room I saw a couple of liquor bottles in the wastebasket. His eyes were bloodshot and he smelled of whiskey. Every ashtray in the place was full of butts. The place stank.

"Close the door," he said, and I obeyed. You don't argue with a big gun like that, or even with a little one. The little ones can kill you just as dead.

"You're Jay J. Armes?" he said. I nodded, yes, I was. His mouth flattened in an expression that I had to assume was satisfaction.

"I've been living for this moment," the man said. "Just this and nothing else—the day I caught you and killed you, you son of a bitch!"

Let me tell you, when you're in a bind like I was, your mind goes at about a thousand miles a minute. You come up with and discard ideas faster than the blink of an eye, like someone riffling a deck of cards in the back of the mind. I was measuring distances, to see where I could move if I had to. The room was roughly square. There was a television set to my right, and a sofa to my left. Directly to the left of the sofa was a table lamp on a table, and an armchair at a right angle to it. In front of the armchair and behind the man with the gun was a low coffee table. Another sofa stood against the wall on the far right, and there was a doorway through which I assumed lay either the bedroom or the bathroom or both.

"Listen," I said, watching his trigger finger. "You wouldn't want to kill me without me knowing why, would you?"

"You don't know who I am?"

"No," I confessed. "No idea." I really didn't know who he was, but even if I had, I'd have kept on talking. All the time I was watching his trigger finger. If the knuckle whitened, that meant he was going to pull, and I would have to act, no matter what the consequences.

"I lost my family because of you, Armes!" he said. "My wife, my children, everything. That's what you did. That's why I'm gonna kill you."

"I don't even know you," I said. "How could I have done what you say?" I still had my eye on that trigger finger. So far so good, I thought. The longer I could keep him talking, the better my chances were going to be.

"You testified against me," he said. "In my divorce, a year ago."

I ran him through the file in my mind, A, B, C, and suddenly it came to me. His name was Robert Connelly and his wife had retained me, which was why I hadn't recognized him. I had provided the wife with the evidence for her divorce, and she had also been awarded custody of the two young children.

"Mr. Connelly," I said. "Isn't it?"

"You know damned well it is, Armes," he snarled.

"Then you're right," I said, taking the plunge. "I did testify against you. But all I did was tell the truth."

"The truth!" he said bitterly.

"It was the truth, Mr. Connelly," I said. "I was under oath and I told the truth."

"I lost my family on account of you," he said doggedly.

"You want to kill me because I told the truth?" I said. "Now that just doesn't make sense. If I'd told lies about you, I could understand it. But I didn't lie— did I?"

"No," he said grudgingly. "You didn't lie."

"Did I make anything up? Conceal anything?"

Again the shake of the head. There was a faint light of doubt in the bloodshot eyes now, the element of uncertainty as to what to do next. I knew the initiative had passed to me.

"Then you don't want to kill me, do you?" I said. "Give me the gun." I held out my hand, confidently.

"I think I better just kill you anyway," he said, looking at my hand, and then the gun, and then back at me. "You're gonna send me to jail sure if I don't."

"For what?"

"Hell Armes, this is ADW and you know it."

I spread my hands and grinned. I told him this kind of thing happened to me all the time and I never filed charges. He looked at me like a kid who really can't believe he's going to get the red fire truck he asked his Daddy for.

"You mean it?" he said hoarsely.

"Sure," I said, and I meant it. I knew I wasn't safe until I had that gun out of his hand, and I knew there was no way I was going to get it without convincing him that he wasn't going to wind up in jail charged with assault with a deadly weapon. The simple way to convince him was to tell the truth. I wasn't going to prefer charges. I might just beat his head in, but I wasn't going to prefer charges.

"Well," he said, and lowered the gun. As he did I hit him, just about as hard as anyone ever hit anyone. He went down in a heap, cold enough to skate on. I picked up the Ruger and emptied the shells out, putting them into my pocket. Then I went into the closet, where there was a refrigerator. I took the ice bucket out, went into the bathroom and filled it with water, came back, and poured it over Connelly's head. It took three dousings before he came up, kicking and spluttering and cursing. When he saw the Ruger in my hand he suddenly went dead silent and still.

"Uh," he said. "What . . . what you gonna do, Armes?"

I told him I wasn't going to do anything. I told him I was going to walk out of there and let him get on with his life in the hope that he might straighten himself out.

"But it's going to cost you," I said.

"What?" he asked fearfully.

"This," I said, gesturing with the Ruger. "It's too much gun for a little fellow like you."

I left him there in the hotel and I never saw him again. I walked to the corner of Sixth Avenue and took a cab uptown. On the way I reflected on the event that had just taken place, and whether there was anything I could do to make sure it never happened to me again. The fact that I had been armed had meant nothing, because only a lunatic tries for a holstered gun when the other man has the drop. And especially when he has the drop with a gun that would blow a hole through a safe door.

It was right then, as the cab turned onto Central Park South, that I got the idea for the "secret weapon" in my right prosthesis. If, I thought, I had some kind of gun built into my hook, something that could be fired by muscular control, I would never be caught flatfooted by someone like Connelly again. I rushed up to my suite in the Plaza and started making some sketches. What I visualized was a small-caliber pistol, single- or double-shot, built into the right hook and controlled by the same kind of mechanism that operates the prosthesis.

I called a friend of mine, a gunsmith. He told me that there was a single-shot .22 magnum built along the lines I was discussing, although obviously the controls would have to be specially created to fit the surgical specification. Next, I put the problem to a world-famous New York surgeon. He thought about it for ten seconds and then told me that what I wanted was impossible. I've been told that before, and it doesn't dissuade me. I told him why it would work. He told me why it wouldn't. We argued. I insisted. He relented enough to agree to think about it. Ten days later he performed the delicate operation in which the intricate mechanism was grafted into my arm. By flexing a certain muscle, and no other way, I could fire the gun hidden in my right hook. It could not be fired accidentally or involuntarily. One day, it would save my life.

Recently, I was on a TV talk show and the host asked me about my secret weapon, which I proceeded to demonstrate for the audience.

"Well, your secret weapon isn't so secret any more, Jay," the host said. "You just told fifty million viewers what it is."

I just smiled. I didn't tell him about the other arm, and what special equipment is built into it, or what it's for. Nobody knows but myself and the man who installed it, but you can be sure of one thing: it cost a lot of money. I consider it money well spent if it means I can go anywhere, confident that I'm not going to come up empty when everything is riding on me. I feel like the man in that old Tennessee Ernie Ford song, "Sixteen Tons": one fist of iron, the other one steel; if the right don't get you, then the left one will.

6.

One of the first rules you learn in my business is that there aren't any rules. You are dealing with infinitely variable factors—the human heart and mind—and it's as well not to try standardizing the approach to either. My rule is not to have a formula, and not to take one single thing for granted.

Like the day this man just walked into the office and said he'd like to talk to me. It happens all the time, and we have a system to handle such inquiries. My executive secretary and girl Friday, Joyce Peterson, has been with me a long time and knows almost as much about my capers as I do. I think she really enjoys the cloak-and-dagger aspects of the organization, but she is also well aware that anyone coming through the door could be out to kill me—there have been more than a dozen attempts so far. So we screen "wild ones" pretty carefully. Anyone who comes in off the street unannounced and uninvited is called a "wild one." You take special care with those.

Obviously, I can't spell out the routine for you, but I can tell you some of the things that happen. The visitor will be offered something to drink. If the drink is refused, Joyce will ask his help in doing some small chore involving getting the lid off a jar or the plastic box in which a typewriter ribbon is kept. Unwittingly, the visitor has given us his fingerprints. He doesn't know that he has been put in a chair facing a hidden camera that will photograph him full face and profile. Meanwhile Joe Breedlove will be giving him the once-over. I sometimes believe Joe has X-ray eyes. He can spot a hidden gun at twenty yards, and if the visitor is wearing one, then I'm alerted, and various special items in my office are put in readiness. There are at least six separate hidden weapons placed strategically around the place. Some of them can be operated from where I sit: I don't even have to rise from the chair. While he is waiting, our "wild one" is on TV. The closed-circuit camera hidden in the waiting room gives me as close a look at the man as I want. After I've given him the once-over, then, and only then, is he escorted into my office.

The visitor on this occasion had given his name as Tom Ryan and told Joyce that he was from out of town. He was "clean"—not armed. He didn't even look dangerous. Neatly, rather than elegantly dressed in western-style clothes, he was a good-looking man in his sixties with silver-gray hair. I tabbed Ryan as a middle-sized rancher, doing better than break even. I told Joyce to wheel him in, and he sat down on the leopard-skin couch, looking at me and shaking his head impatiently.

"It's your father I want to talk to," he said.

I told him that my father had been dead for some years, and asked if it was a family matter. Ryan said it wasn't, and asked if maybe I had an older brother. I began to wonder what this was all about. I told him I had two older brothers. Constantino is an engineer, and Pete works for the state of California. Ryan looked at me as if I'd begun to grow horns and a tail.

"You're the investigator?" he said. "You're Jay J. Armes?"

There didn't seem to be any point in denying it.

"Well, hell, Mr. Armes," Ryan said, "I'm sorry. The way those boys down at the Morgan Guaranty and Trust talked about you, I figgered you had to be fifty-five, sixty years old."

"I've lived a long life in a short time, Mr. Ryan," I said. "Now, what can I do for you?"

It turned out he'd asked some people at Morgan Guaranty and Trust about me, and they had recommended me very highly, and in doing so had given him a couple of highly-colored accounts of some of my capers. Sometimes these tend to gain a little in the telling.

Once the ice was broken, Ryan began to talk. He told me he had a close friend—who wished to remain anonymous—who was divorced and contributing to the support of his two teenage children. His friend, "let's call him Chandler," hadn't been in touch with either them or his ex-wife for a long time. His bank made the necessary payments to the ex-wife, who was now living in La Jolla, California. Ryan told me that the two girls would call Chandler from time to time, but that he hadn't heard from them lately and he was worried.

"Chandler and I just feel so damned uneasy about the whole setup out there," he told me. "We want you to look it over and report back to me."

I told him what I would need: names, addresses, photographs of the girls if possible, and promised to get to work on it right away. It sounded like a fairly simple matter. Little did I know.

"I'll need a retainer," I told him, and mentioned a figure.

"Aw, just send me a bill," he said offhandedly.

I told him I didn't work that way. When the client paid my retainer—and only then—I began work. He looked surprised, or maybe puzzled would describe it better.

"What's the difference?" he said. "You'll get paid— I'm good for the money."

I repeated my conditions: retainer first, action next. It's not that I am afraid of being bilked, although that has happened more than once. It is simply the way I work, and I make no exceptions. Everyone gets exactly the same treatment, and I do mean everyone, from crowned heads down. Ryan looked at me as if he had no more use for me than a temperance lecturer. With an exasperated gesture he burrowed into the pocket of his cord jacket and came up with a check.

It was folded about ten different ways, and looked as if he'd been carrying it around since about 1901. He flattened it on the desk with the heel of his hand, and then scrawled his signature across it before tossing it over to me.

"There y'are," he said waspishly. "Fill it in. Whatever it takes."

I shook my head and explained it all again. I had given him a figure as my retainer, and that was all I was asking for. No more, no less. Once again Ryan looked at me in that frowning, puzzled way, head cocked to one side.

"Well, I'll add a couple of thousand," he muttered. "Just in case."

I was beginning to get a little exasperated myself, and stopped him for the third time. He didn't argue anymore, just scribbled the amount of my retainer across the check, muttering something under his breath that might have been "Goddamned *landino*." Oldtime cowmen used to call steers that knew all the tricks *landinos*. It's an old Spanish word meaning "savvy" or "crafty." A *landino* was one cow you didn't take any liberties with, and I decided to take it as a compliment, albeit a two-edged one. I also resolved to check out our Mr. Ryan as soon as he left. There was something unusual about him, something I couldn't quite get a handle on.

That's why we run our security check on unannounced visitors. By the time they leave us, we have their fingerprints, photographs, physical description, estimated (or stated) age and stated (if not necessarily true) address, plus their automobile registration. Given that amount of information, I can run down anyone's background in two hours flat. Birth certificates, marriage and divorce records, land records, motor vehicle titles, the records of the police department and the Department of Motor Vehicles, credit bureaus, bank records—all these and more are on file, waiting to be used by the investigator. On top of that my membership in the International Police Congress means that I

can request information from any member police force
in the world. Then there's NCIC—the National Crime
Information Center where all criminal records are cen-
tralized and computerized for instant retrieval. If you
give it a moment's thought, you'll realize how much of
your own life is documented: public utilities know
about your home, mailmen know whom you corre-
spond with, banks how much you are worth, credit
card agencies how much you owe, finance companies
what you're borrowing—and so on. The best investigators can obtain access to all this information, and a lot
more that you don't know about. Bear it in mind, if
you're planning a life of crime.

I flew out to San Diego, rented a car and wove my
way through the interpasses and underpasses on to Interstate 5 heading north for La Jolla. The water across
Mission Bay looked flat and sullen, and a fitful wind
was picking up little whirls of sand and trying to throw
them in my eyes. I tuned in to Station KSON to pick
up some music. Glen Campbell was singing about the
troubles of the Wichita lineman, and I sang along. The
car's the only place I can do it: my wife Linda says I
have a voice like a raven.

The former Mrs. Chandler, Mrs. Wilson as she now
was, lived on a sharply-sloping street just north of
Soledad Park. I set up my neighborhood survey, and
found out in pretty short order that Mrs. Wilson's life
—and family—were in total disarray. In spite of the
fact that Chandler was sending her a lot of money—
one of the people I interviewed said it was $2500 a
month for each of the girls—the Wilsons were going
to hell in a handbasket. The boyfriend was out of
work, hadn't had a steady job as long as most people
could recall. There were loud rows there all the time,
and Mrs. Wilson seemed to spend most of her time
either getting drunk or sobering up so she could get
drunk again. The two girls had run away from home.
I was told that one of them had set off for Canada,
hitchhiking. The second girl had simply gone: nobody

had any idea where. I called Ryan and painted him a picture he didn't like one damned bit.

"Mr. Armes," he said. "You just stay on it. Find those girls, and quick. We want to know where they are and how they are—hear me?"

I heard him, all right. I was surprised the telephone could take it—he sounded mad enough to hunt bears with a switch. I told him I'd get to work right away, and headed back for San Diego. This simple little job had suddenly developed into a rather larger caper, and I was going to have to bring in some assistance. Finding runaway teenagers is not easy. To begin with, they don't file the kind of records adults do. They can also adapt with surprising ease to conditions that their parents will indignantly tell you would disgust them. They'll sleep rough, shack up with undesirables of both sexes, steal food to live—and they can go a long way in a short time, especially if they are attractive kids. Plenty of lonely motorists will stop for a good-looking teenager, even go hundreds of miles out of their way to drop them off someplace. It happens all the time, and it doesn't make a job like mine one little bit easier.

I set up a "control center" at the Little America Westgate downtown. They've gussied the place up some since the days when it was the Westgate Plaza, although I don't know that oversize beds and new decor, however elegant, are necessarily an improvement. However, it was central, and near the airport. I started making calls.

My organization doesn't just have agents all over the United States. We have agents all over the world. Where we don't have an agent, we usually have a live contact. In England, in France, in Sydney or Singapore, I can call a certain number and get action.

Let me explain: there is a difference between "contacts" and agents, obviously. The Investigators has over twenty-four hundred agents on call, but they are not on a full-time retainer basis. I work them in the "Kelly Girl" system. The Kelly Agency will provide a girl to come in and type for you. While she's typing, she's getting paid. When she stops and goes home, you stop paying. I use the same system with my agents. It's the only kind of system an operation like mine could possibly sustain. Any other way and I'd end up in the poorhouse: it doesn't take an awful lot of imagination to work out how much it would cost to have 2462 agents sitting around waiting for me to send them some work. I had a small taste of that when I first set up in business. Never again.

Contacts are something else. Every day, wherever I am, I endeavor to get to know more people, more situations. I make it a point to try to talk to as many people, learn about as many different kinds of jobs and businesses, as I can, every day of the year. This way you get an incredible insight into other people's lives, their jobs, how they feel about things. I learn from everybody, and I'm not ashamed of doing so. The name of the game is contacts—having someone you can call for advice, for help, for suggestions, for information. I've been fortunate enough to work in just about every country in the world. I have helped law-enforcement agencies in those countries solve crimes or prevent them. They are my contacts, just as I am theirs in the United States—it's a mutually beneficial liaison. If I don't have an operative in a certain city, here or abroad, then I turn to my law-enforcement contact. He will provide me with the information I need, or give me the name of a contact. And we're off and running.

It took nearly a month to trace Julie, the younger girl, a month of intensive work by agents and contacts all over the country. Sure enough, it turned out she'd hitchhiked her way into Canada, and was sharing an apartment with two other girls on Cedar Hill in Victoria, British Columbia. Tick off Julie. The best information we could get on the other girl, Cathy, was that she had left the country and was in The Hague, Holland. Once again, I called Ryan and reported my findings.

"Chandler's ex-wife's parents are Dutch," he said. "They live in The Hague and Chandler told me they're a no 'count bunch of zeroes. I want you to go over there and bring his girl home!" He paused, then said, "You need any money?"

I grinned, remembering our first interview, and told him no, I could manage. What I would need was Chandler's Power of Attorney to bring the girl back to the United States. He said Chandler (by then I knew his real name) would get one to me via a law firm in Los Angeles, and he was as good as his word. I met the messenger, a young man in a mohair suit that couldn't have weighed more than sixteen ounces, in that strange and somehow appropriate symbol of Los Angeles International Airport, the 135-feet-high Futuristic Theme building. Its parabolic arches suspend a restaurant nobody ever seems to patronize and an observation deck from which you can see hardly anything except the other terminals. An hour later I was airborne, en route for one of my favorite cities in the world: Amsterdam.

The sweet perfume of the flowers in the market on Singel stayed in my nostrils long after I was beyond the outskirts of the city. I would have loved to spend some time wandering around, shopping for a little present for Linda in the Flea Market on the Waterlooplein, eating a snack from one of the herring stalls, listening to pop songs played on the ornate barrel organs; but there was no time for any of that. I tooled the hired Ford down the long flat straight road to The Hague, getting used to the small vehicle and the strange *Autosnelweg* signs along the motorway—The Hague is called 's-Gravenhage in Dutch. There was one light moment during my fifty-kilometer journey when I saw a sign pointing to a town called Monster, which lies on the southern side of The Hague. I wondered how the people who lived there felt about the inevitable jokes.

The Hague is not a beauty spot. It is primarily a seaport, an oil seaport at that. It has about the same kind of raunchy style as Galveston, if you can imagine Galveston with Gothic architecture downtown. The place where the missing girl was living was in a rundown district near the harbor. I contacted the Dutch authorities—the Dutch police carry the title "Royal," something even the legendary British bobby can't claim—and showed them my credentials and Chandler's power of attorney. They moved with commendable promptitude, and a detective named Jack Somerwil went down there with me to pick up Cathy.

Cathy didn't want to be picked up, and made no bones about it. She was a pretty kid, sixteen or so, with long blond hair streaked silver the way they do it these days. In the end, she gave us no choice, and I headed back to Schiphol with her handcuffed to my left arm, a police sergeant driving the rented Ford.

About half an hour before flight time she tapped my arm and gave me a smile that would have melted Scrooge's heart.

"Mr. Armes," she said, blushing prettily. "I'm awfully sorry, but I have to go powder my nose."

Reasonable enough, I figured. I walked her over to the door of the ladies' rest room and unlocked the cuffs. I told her I was going to wait right outside the door.

"Thank you, Mr. Armes," she said. She really did have a lovely smile, I thought, and leaned against the wall to wait. About five minutes later a little old lady came out of the powder room shaking her head and smiling. I could see she was American: her passport and Pan Am ticket were sticking out of the top of her handbag and I pointed it out to her. She thanked me, and remarked that kids had sure changed since she was a girl. I asked her what she meant.

"That girl in there," she said. "Can't even use the door. She's climbing out through the window, would you believe?"

I believed. I went in there like Gangbusters, mad clear through at having been so neatly taken. Ignoring the screeches of protest and outrage that greeted my appearance, I grabbed Cathy just as she was about to disappear through a window that you would have thought too small to push a mangy cat through. I dragged her back any old which way, and as we sprawled on the floor, I slapped the cuffs back on her. Then I marched her back to our seats near the loading gate for our flight. People were staring at us as if we had come in preceded by a brass band, and Cathy sat rigid, her face a dull, angry red.

"Don't touch me!" she hissed. "Don't even speak to me! I hate you! I *loathe* you!"

I didn't plan to lie awake nights fretting over that. Cathy Chandler had just proved that I couldn't trust her an inch, and I told her so. I also told her that I intended to keep her handcuffed until we were back in the United States. She ignored me. Her mouth was clamped shut, and her jaw muscles all bunched up. Her eyes were hot and angry. She was all tensed up. I've seen jackasses with that look about them when I was a kid. You'd just better make sure you don't get anywhere in back of them. I made a mental note to take the same precautions with Cathy. Given half a chance, she would kick my head in just to see if it was hollow.

She gave me hell for every one of the five and a half thousand miles back to Los Angeles. She insisted on going to the rest room on every plane and in every airport lounge through which we passed. After about the fourth or fifth time, it got so I was almost blasé about it, and told the startled ladies upon whom I was intruding that I'd just close my eyes and forget everything I'd seen. However, if you think being jammed into a washroom with a recalcitrant teenager who hates your guts is fun, forget it. There were more than a few times on that trip when I seriously asked myself what the heck I was doing wet-nursing runaway brats across hemispheres and getting my ankles kicked to shreds for the privilege. Especially when the caper had started out as a little old checkup job that wasn't supposed to take more than a day or two.

I brought Cathy home, and made my final report to Tom Ryan at the Los Angeles offices of his attorneys. Secure in the knowledge that both girls were alive and well—if he noticed that Cathy was madder than a wet hen he affected not to—he asked me to submit my bill as soon as we got back to El Paso.

I gave it to him, itemized—from ten-cent tips to transcontinental air fares. He looked it over and gave a wry smile, shaking his head. He told me afterward that it was the first time in as long as he could remember that he'd seen a bill that wasn't padded. From that day on, Tom Ryan and I became close friends. I was the first man he'd done business with in ages who hadn't tried to rip him off and he began to retain me to look after a lot of other pies in which he had a finger. He had business interests all over America, and many overseas as well. Whenever he wanted something checked out, he would call me in.

"Check it out," he would say. "Spend whatever it takes."

And from that day to this he has never queried one single expense I have incurred in his behalf. We don't even discuss up-front money anymore, and I feel sure that Tom wouldn't mind if I explained why. After he left my office, on that very first day we met, I picked up the battered check he had left as my retainer and called my banker. I told him that I'd just had a client in who gave me an off-kilter reading, and that I'd like him to verify the check.

"Sure, Jay," Ken said. "Who's the signatory?"

I told him the name: Thomas F. Ryan. There was a funny sound at the other end of the phone, as if Ken was choking on a fishbone. After a moment he asked me to tell him what the man looked like. I described Ryan: graying hair, in his sixties, wearing western-style clothes. Ken burst out laughing.

"You really don't know who he is?"

"No," I said. "I really don't know who he is."

"Jay," Ken said, "Thomas Fortune Ryan the Third is one of the richest men in the United States, if not in the world. He used to own Braniff Airlines. You didn't offend him, did you?"

"Who, me?" I said.

7.

I don't think I offended Tom Ryan at all. As a matter of fact, I know I didn't, because today he and I are not only friends but business associates. We jointly own Radium Springs Projects, a hot springs property of over 150 acres twenty-two miles from Las Cruces in New Mexico. The land contains underground thermal springs holding water with a constant temperature of 190°C. Plans have been mooted for a thermal power plant on the site, although at the moment they are only at the drawing-board stage.

Tom and I share a relationship based on mutual trust, and I know how lucky I am to have a partner upon whom I can rely implicitly. Some other people aren't quite so lucky: take Harold Lake, for instance.

It was a Monday morning, May 18, 1970. I was in my office when I saw a visitor come in. He was a big man in a plaid lumberman's jacket and cord slacks. I watched him on the closed-circuit TV and saw that he was arguing with Joyce. I flipped the switch of the intercom. He was insisting upon seeing me and no one else, and Joyce was having a little trouble getting him to sit down so she could go through the checkout routine. I buzzed her and told her not to bother: I knew Lake, who was president of one of the largest food distribution organizations in the Southwest, Sierra Foods. I'd done some work for him on another occasion, and knew that he serviced discount stores, military commissaries, wholesale outlets and supermarket chains, and carried at all times an inventory in excess of $2 million. Harold Lake wasn't what you'd call a wealthy man, but he was a long way past just doing well.

I asked him what his problem was and he told me he had an inventory shortage of $30,000. He wanted me to find it, and he also wanted me to find the thief so that he could, as he put it himself, making a pantomime motion of strangling someone, choke the S.O.B. with his bare hands.

"They can't do this to me," he said. "I've treated them like my own family. I've helped them with money when they were in trouble. I've paid their school bills, doctor bills, I've paid their rent. And they still go and do this to me."

"Who is 'they,' Mr. Lake?"

"I don't know, dammit!" he snapped. "If I knew I wouldn't be talking to you!"

I started asking some questions. Although he had an inventory shortage, he was adamant in his stance that none of his own employees were responsible, that he had things arranged in such a manner that it was impossible for anyone to rip him off. Nevertheless, he was $30,000 in the hole, and it was making him mad enough to eat beef with the hide on. We discussed his inventory control, which sounded better than adequate. I asked him if he had sufficient shrinkage to account for the loss. What little he had could never have accounted for a $30,000 loss. So it had to be a thief. Or thieves. I said as much, and he shook his head vehemently.

"There's no way, Mr. Armes," he said. "I'm there every day, from the time we open in the morning to the time I lock up at night."

He told me that he had about seventy employees, all of whom had been with him for years. I could see that it wasn't the loss of the money that was eating at him: it was the betrayal of his trust. His eyes were teary as he told me about his business, and he emphasized his points with hands scarred from years of hard labor.

Nobody had ever given Harold Lake a free ticket to ride: he'd obviously worked for every cent he had. Now someone he trusted was stealing him blind.

"I want you to find out who's doing this to me," he said. "I can't sit still for it anymore."

I told him I would take his case, but that I would need a retainer. He asked me how much, and I told him: $10,000 up front, another $10,000 when I came up with the solution.

"Twenty thousand dollars to locate thirty?" he said angrily. "If you're going into the holdup business, Armes, the least you could do is wear a mask."

"I guarantee results," I reminded him. "And believe me, that's how much it will take."

"Let me get this straight," he said. "I ante up twenty thousand, and you guarantee to get my thirty grand back?"

I told him that I couldn't give him that kind of guarantee. What I would guarantee was to find out where the money had gone and to find out who was responsible for taking it. Lake got up slowly off the couch and leaned both hands on the desk, sticking his chin forward at me.

"That's not a hell of a lot of guarantee for twenty thousand dollars," he said. "I can't see where you'd be worth it."

"Sit down, Mr. Lake," I said, "and I'll tell you a story."

He sat down with a look on his face that said it had better be a damned good one. I told him about the woman who called in a plumber to fix a dripping tap. The plumber fitted a washer and was gone in ten minutes, and sent in a bill for $10. The woman sent it back with a note saying she could get a washer in any hardware store for a nickel, so maybe the plumber would care to rewrite his bill with that in mind. He rewrote the bill, and sent it back. This time it said "For supplying one washer, ten cents. For knowing how to fit it, $9.90." The lady paid up.

"Uh," Lake said as I finished. He'd gotten the point,

and he sat there squinting at me out of those shrewd, faded blue eyes.

"When do I have to pay you this ten thousand?" he asked.

"Right now," I said.

He gave a grin and pulled out his checkbook. Ten minutes later we were in business. The first thing I asked him to do was to let me have access to all his personnel files. He agreed, but pulled a typewritten list out of his pocket and handed it to me. I asked him what it was, and he told me it was a list of all the people on his staff that he didn't want me to investigate.

"Charlie Tarr there, he's been with me for twenty years, no way he could be involved," he said. "Ken Whitehorn there, he's been with the firm fifteen years, and so has Tom Flynn. I love that boy like a son, he's been a real hard worker. I paid for the delivery of all his children. Tom wouldn't flimflam me. Jane Osborn there, she's been—"

I stopped him in midsentence and told him that I was not only going to investigate every single one of his employees, I was also going to investigate *him*.

"Now wait just a damned minute—" he began angrily.

I stopped him again and told him: my way, or not at all. He gave me that look from beneath the eyebrows again, and then nodded, as though making a decision.

"You just better be as good as they say you are," he growled, and left me to it.

I shut off all calls, and began to evaluate the case. There were two options from which to choose. It was either an inside job, which Lake vehemently said was not the case, or it was not. I considered his business, the distribution of fresh and canned foods, eggs, cheeses, perishables, and then I thought about what I would do if I were a thief. I've never heard of any gang hijacking a truckload of cheese or eggs or canned tomatoes. The pros go for quick turnover, which means cigarettes, liquor, imported cameras, easily disposable clothing like ladies' tights, jewelry—but not food. Have you ever had someone sidle up to you on a street corner and offer you a good deal on a pound of pastrami? No. Mr. Lake, I thought, it's an inside job, and whoever is ripping you off is exchanging the goods for hard cash.

From that premise I then had to put myself into the position of the employee contemplating the thefts. Where would the weak points in the chain be, where the easiest areas to score? How would *I* do it? Decision: it had to be between the warehouse and the customer. Question: to whom were the goods being sold? Decision: smaller stores, perhaps, who would buy at fifty cents on the dollar with no questions asked as to provenance. By the end of the afternoon I had a pile of scribbled notes, a lot of unanswered questions and a headache. I took them all into the Corvette Stingray and hit the road for Dallas, where Sierra Foods has its headquarters.

"Big D," as the city is known, isn't anything like the Easterner's mental picture of a Texas city. It has none of the rough-and-ready frontier atmosphere you can still see in El Paso, or even in nearby Fort Worth (which Dallas snobs call "Cowtown"). It is the fourth-ranking city in the United States for home offices of publicly-owned corporations, and also for the number of million-dollar businesses. More than four out of the five hundred largest industrial corporations in the *Fortune Directory* have offices or representatives in Dallas, which is also one of the three largest fashion markets in the United States. It had the largest airport in the world—bigger than the island of Manhattan and built at a cost of $800 million—until Montreal out-Texased it, and a macabre worldwide fame as the city in which President John F. Kennedy was assassinated in November 1963. Apart from all that, it's a nice place.

I checked into the Fairmount and then went over to Sierra Foods to pick up the personnel records. The warehouse was on the west side of town, at the end of a cul-de-sac situated between Irving Boulevard and the

Trinity River. Then back across the Continental Viaduct to the meeting with my agents. Our first priority: check out all the employees.

We start without any preconceptions at all. My evaluation is that the missing money is the result of an inside job. We can go through every employee's records, and come up empty. We can follow blind alleys without number and have to retrace our steps, and every one of them hurts, in money, sweat and time. But there is no other way to do it. Only by process of elimination can you get a handle on a suspect, and we do that following what is essentially a Sherlock Holmes dictum: when every possibility, no matter how remote, has been explored and discarded, the facts remaining, however bizarre they may appear, must point to the truth.

So, we begin. We check out every job application, every item of information given. By the time we have finished, we know a great deal about each employee: where he lives, what his habits are, what his family life is like. We know what kind of car he drives, what kind of TV set he owns, what kind of bills are coming in, what kind of credit he has—and whether any or all of these things match his earnings. The employee you are looking for is the one who is spending more than he earns, and you can only isolate him by eliminating all the others. It may, of course, be a group of employees, but the rules remain constant. Once the employees who are "clean" are eliminated from our inquiries, we zero in on the ones who seem to be living better than their paychecks warrant.

Then we check out their bank records and any other savings they may have, how much they have on deposit. Against all these figures we set their total earnings at present, and for the preceding year. We make careful note of the size and number of checks they are writing, and most especially to whom. Don't ask me to go into too much detail about how we obtain this information; just let me observe that tellers are well named.

Once we had a handle on our suspects at Sierra Foods (there were a lot more than even I had expected), we began surveillance, calling in more manpower from the field to maintain it. Some of our suspects were truckdrivers for Sierra Foods, so we bugged their vehicles. Posing as an inspector of the Dallas Department of Motor Vehicles carrying out a routine check, I placed audio-transmitting devices in the cab of each suspect vehicle, and another in the rear end of the truck. The first would transmit any conversation that went on in the driver's cab; the second would provide us with information on what kind of deals the driver might be making, and with whom. The bug in the driver's cab is always a problem: it has to be far enough way from the engine so it won't be drowned by the noise, yet near enough to the driver to pick up his speech. At the same time, it has to be "invisible." All this is far from easy to do, and you can appreciate that it doesn't come cheap. Such equipment is very intricate and very expensive, and 99 percent of investigators simply can't afford it because it spends so much of its life on a shelf. To me, it's an essential. I want to finish every case as fast as I can; it's good for me and it's good for my client. The longer it goes on, the more it costs both of us.

Once the bugs are in position, an agent is assigned to each truck and in his car a small FM-signal receiver is installed. It will be adjusted to a low-band frequency matching that of the transmitter, and one that is well away from any other FM station to avoid interference. Linked to the agent's FM-signal receiver is a micromini wire recorder so that we have a permanent record of the actual conversations that are being heard.

Harold Lake provided us with a complete roster of all deliveries the trucks were scheduled to make, and the amount of merchandise each was slated to deliver. My agents would log and record everything his drivers said and did until we got a break.

On June 1, fifteen days after Harold Lake retained me, we broke the case wide open. We had worked out the thieves' routine step by step. We had tape recordings of them discussing how they would have to make a "heavy delivery" because they had a payment due on the house or a balloon note on a truck or a dentist bill. They were in collusion with some of Sierra Foods' best customers—bakeries, supermarkets, discount houses, even the military.

My agents observed one driver and his helper deliver to a bakery where they were supposed to unload ten cases of eggs, fifteen cases of butter and two fifty-five-gallon drums of cooking oil. It was still dark when the truck rolled up at the ramp, but they watched through a special sniperscope, whose infrared lens turns night into day and magnifies the object being watched. The actual delivery was twenty cases of eggs, thirty cases of butter and four drums of oil. Another refrigerated semitruck delivered sixty cases of eggs, forty-five cases of butter, two hundred cases of milk, one hundred cases of five-pound cans of oil, eighty cases of sugar, a hundred cases of salt, forty cases of macaroni, three hundred cases of baby food, two hundred cases of coffee, and three hundred blocks of processed cheese. It took them the best part of a morning to unload the stuff, and when we checked the dockets we found that the actual order was considerably less than half the amount delivered. And so it went on.

It was almost foolproof. Seven drivers were shifting enormous quantities of merchandise while confederates inside the warehouse covered up the losses with forged dockets. They were concentrating upon the easy-to-lose perishables—eggs, butter, flour, coffee. Who could categorically state that this gross of eggs was stolen, this other not? How could you go into a huge bakery and point to one hundred bags of flour and say they were the ones missing?

After the drivers and their partners in crime quit work, we kept them under surveillance. They led us to a vacant garage they were using as a warehouse to hold stock. It was like an Aladdin's cave in there, full to the roof with merchandise of every conceivable kind. The code numbers and docket tags on the boxes were photographed, and the locks resealed.

We located more merchandise at the homes of some of the suspects, who numbered twelve in all, recovering something like $15,000 worth of goods. I obtained a search warrant and went into the garage warehouse with Harold Lake beside me. His eyes were as big as dinner plates when he saw the stuff. There was more than $90,000 worth of goods in there.

Warrants were then obtained for the arrest of the manager of the commissary at the military base, the owner of a huge bakery chain and several others who had been deeply involved in receiving and concealing goods stolen from Sierra Foods, which had been going on not for just a few months but over a five-year period. Harold Lake hadn't been ripped off for $30,000—the figure was closer to a quarter of a million dollars.

We recovered almost half of that figure in merchandise, and I had the satisfaction of seeing nine of the culprits sentenced to five-to-ten year stretches in the penitentiary. Five others drew sentences of between three and five years. Every one of them who had been an employee of Sierra Foods had been on the list of people Harold Lake had insisted we not investigate.

I doubt he got the same satisfaction in watching them go down that I did. He just couldn't believe it, not any of it. These were his employees, his friends— his surrogate children. He hadn't wanted to file charges against them, but he knew in the end he must. The fact that he got back every penny that he'd lost from the insurance and the bonding companies didn't seem to mean a thing to him.

We said goodby at the doorway of the office block. He looked old and tired, all the fire gone out of him.

"They were my friends, Mr. Armes," he said. "My friends. I just can't believe it."

I think what he meant was, I can't believe my friends would break my heart. But that was exactly what they had done.

8.

The Sierra Foods caper is a perfect example of why
Jay Armes needs and owns such a bewildering array of
sophisticated hardware. His kind of investigating re-
quires the very best there is, and the very best there is
costs thousands and thousands of dollars. So much, in
fact, that local and federal law-enforcement agencies
sometimes find themselves in the embarrassing position
of having to ask him to lend them equipment that
their own budgets do not permit them to purchase.
Fascinated by whatever is new, Jay Armes is presently
exploring the possibilities of developing a portable laser
gun, which, if perfected, would be able to cut through
brick walls or steel doors like a knife through butter.

In his library at the house on North Loop, its
shelves sagging beneath the weight of encyclopedias
and how-to books, reference works, dictionaries, alma-
nacs, atlases and neatly labeled videotape cassettes,
there is a stunning collection of gadgetry that puts to
shame even the selection downtown.

Optical microscopes up to around 2500X, electron
microscopes with ten times that magnifying power,
chemical analysis kits, fingerprinting kits as good as if
not better than anything owned by the FBI, eight or
ten different kinds of tape recorders ranging from a huge
reel-to-reel Ferrograph to a tiny voice-actuated device
that will fit into a vest pocket without making a bulge.
All the famous names, and some not so well-known
outside espionage circles, like Nagra and Uher. A
briefcase with a built-in two-way radio transmitter-

receiver, pushbutton antenna and concealed camera and recorder that looks like any other Madison Avenue lunchbox. A micromini recorder, the smallest made anywhere in the world, that will tape silently and efficiently for two hours at a time. "Bugs" of all shapes, sizes and descriptions. The largest will transmit a signal for up to ten miles, the smaller ones five. They range in size from kitchen matchbox to sugar cube. Cameras big, medium, small, tiny—Minolta and Minox and Canon and Leica and Nikon, and the smallest photographic device made, the mini Bolax. Its lens is so fine that the tiny negatives will allow enlargement to mural size without loss of detail. There are lenses that look like small howitzers, filters, infrared attachments for night photography, cameras with voice- or movement-actuated shutters, heat-sensitive devices, silent motorized rewinds, infrared lenses.

There are contact microphones with stethoscope attachments for listening through walls. They have jackplug attachments so that a recorder can be plugged into them. If the man in the next room changes his mind, you can hear him, Jay Armes says. There is a radio transmitter that looks like a wristwatch. There are six or eight different pairs of binoculars, including the special German CEMP infrared glasses that will not only render night into day but are also equipped with a built-in camera that photographs what the watcher is seeing with equal clarity simply by pressing a button. A range finder no bigger than Grandfather's pocket watch that will measure inches or miles with equal accuracy, an astronomical telescope that brings the moon up so close you feel you are on it. The giant debugger, a $10,000 miniaturized miracle, which will smell out any electronic device in a room no matter where hidden, is designated Signal Device Locator 10/ R4. It costs clients $1000 a throw, but clients pay gladly to forgo the pleasure of having their place ripped apart by less sophisticated searchers. In one corner stands a TV monitor set linked to a closed-

circuit television camera system and a videotape recorder. In another corner is a scuba diver's oxygen tank and wet suit, flippers and mask: Jay Armes is a qualified underwater searcher too. And there are guns, guns, guns, everyhere you look.

A rifle rack holds a Winchester .44-40 repeater, a bolt-action sporting rifle and the special tranquilizer rifle that fires paralyzing darts and was once used to put a $2 million embezzler to sleep in Rio so he could be smuggled out of the country and brought back to face the music. It is fitted with a Superscope, the infrared telescopic sight developed during the Vietnam War. Using it, the sniper can shoot with devastating accuracy even in pitch darkness. There is a huge tiger skin on the floor—you are never far away from the tiger motif when you are with Jay Armes. There is a selection of telescopic sights, mostly European in origin: the Walther 4-diopter, an Ajack 4X, a small SIM Zj42, an American Redfield variable power (3-9X).

The wall to the right of the desk is festooned with handguns. Two .25 automatics, two .22 automatics, a Starr automatic target pistol, a .22 snubnose revolver, a .38 Smith & Wesson, a .38 Colt Special with a five-inch barrel, a .32 purse gun, a Walther P38 and a Beretta 7.65-mm automatic, a GLC/OSS M1942 .45 single-shot pistol that's certainly a collector's item. These are all used to frame the glass-fronted display case that houses Jay Armes' special collection: a Luger PO8, a Colt M1911 .38 on a .45 frame, a snubnose .38 Colt revolver with an ivory grip, a Ruger Blackhawk .44 magnum, a Colt .357 magnum and a strange single-shot pistol that looks like an old Barns .50 boot gun. There is a story to go with each of these weapons. Each of them was used, at one time or another, to try to put Jay Armes out of business —permanently.

I always lock my car doors, something I got into the habit of doing a long time ago. There have been a lot of assassination attempts on me, and I have no intention of making it easy for the next would-be killer. I own nine automobiles, including the Rolls and two special-bodied Cadillacs, and I employ a full-time chauffeur-bodyguard, Joe Dark Eagle Breedlove. Joe is a graduate of The Investigators Training Academy. He's over six feet tall, built like a Mack truck, part Sioux Indian, trained in the martial arts, a former field agent and a rough man to tangle with.

I'm often asked why I have a bodyguard, although the answer is really very simple. Although I can do as much as, if not more than, most people who have two hands, although I've been called "super-sleuth" and "man of steel" and other things less polite, there is one trick I've never been able to master. I can't see out of the back of my head—hence Joe Dark Eagle Breedlove. Incidentally, my using his full name is not an affectation. He is proud of his Indian heritage, and insists upon his full name—even on his paychecks. Joe is a superb driver, a damned good backup man and the best kind of friend there is—the kind who's right there when the lid blows off.

Once in a while, however, even a bodyguard has to have a day off, and frankly, I don't mind at all. It gives me a chance to practice my driving. I don't like to let myself get out of synch with any of the skills I have mastered—whether it be behind the wheel or underwater in scuba gear or unarmed combat. On Joe's day off I'll sometimes get into my Corvette Stingray and go way out to Hueco Tanks, where I own a patch of land I'm planning to turn into a safari park. There on the deserted dirt roads I practice helldriving: hand-brake turns, anticlockwise spin stops, double-heel-and-toe-declutching, rally cornering, the works. There are times when the ability to make your car do things that would turn a Sunday drivers' hair white can save your life. The ordinary man hitting a sharp bend far too fast will go off the road. If you can hit the hand brake and spin the car anticlockwise—providing that the road is both empty and wider than the length of your vehicle—you can stop, and stay alive.

The best drivers know that if you do get pushed off the road, the sensible thing is to steer only to avoid obstacles like trees or buildings until the car slows. Trying to hold the road until the bitter end will turn you over faster than anything you're likely to hit off the tarmac. This kind of driving is called ten-tenths driving, and it should only be done if you really know how. My Stingray, apart from its special equipment, has special shock absorbers, tires, lights, coil, battery, brakes, camshaft, carburetors and pistons, and is race-tuned to a hair. I don't allow anyone else to drive it.

I live about eleven miles from downtown El Paso, and one day, on my way back from practice, I decided to stop off in town and buy some linseed oil to treat a gun stock I was working on. I went to the paint shop and picked some up, together with resin and very fine sandpaper. I stopped off at one or two other stores before I came back to the car, which was in the parking lot directly opposite the Plaza. I noticed immediately that the door on the driver's side was not properly closed.

I didn't need to think about it. If the door was not closed, it meant someone had been in the car. Its a pretty conspicuous vehicle, so maybe it was some small-time thief trying to rip out my equipment, but a small-time thief wouldn't have circumvented the alarm system. I walked warily around the car twice, all my hackles raised. I checked through the rear window and from the passenger side. Everything looked normal, although on that side the special tracking equipment blocks your view of the seat well on the other side. I put down my packages and did a full check, flat on my back beneath the car, and then inch by inch along the body, front to rear. Finally I went back to the driver's side, and carefully checked the interior, scanning it inch by inch. You can do this very thoroughly by using three credit cards, or business cards, placing them across each other in a triangle, so that there is a triangular aperture in the center. Holding this about six inches from the eye, you squint through the hole and move your screen, slowly traversing whatever it is you're inspecting. It removes the distracting effect of peripheral vision, and it was by this method that I spotted a short piece of tubing, like a steel pipe, sticking up at an angle from the floorboards near the base of the steering wheel.

With the most infinite care, I opened the door on the passenger side and inched into the car. It was a warm day, but the sweat trickling down my back was cold. I checked the inside of the door for trip wires, cord, switches. Nothing. I opened it wider and looked more closely at the thing on the floor. It looked like some kind of pistol, but not any pistol I have ever seen. A wire-and-pulley device was rigged to the gas pedal. All I had to do was get in the car, switch on the engine and depress the pedal, and the trigger would be pulled. The barrel of the weapon was aimed just about where the driver's belly would be.

It took me the best part of an hour to unrig that murderous booby trap, and by the time I finished I was wet with sweat, my muscles were fluttering with tension and my throat was as dry as Kansas. The weapon was a single-barreled shotgun, carrying a twelve-gauge cartridge. When I showed it to a gunsmith friend of mine later, he shook his head and observed laconically that a thing like that could blow a hole in a man big enough to put a picture window in. It was an illegal and long-obsolete weapon once used to kill wolves and other predators. Once in a while I take it out of the gun case and look at it, and it still gives me a cold chill in the pit of my stomach.

I questioned the attendant at the parking lot, but he hadn't seen anyone near the automobile. I made some pretty strenuous efforts to find out who had rigged the device, and why, but I had nothing to go on and I came to a dead end. I still don't know who put it there, but whoever it was wanted to kill me very messily. Which is a further reason for my having a bodyguard. Now I'll give you another.

Julia Donaldson was a nice ordinary woman with a husband, two sons and a daughter, a little poodle called Fifi and a beautiful home in Coronado, one of El Paso's most exclusive residential areas. Although she was no longer young, she was still a handsome woman with a good figure who lived for her family and her garden, which was immaculate and colorful, even in the most murderous Texas summers. On this particular evening, she was puttering about in the garden, dressed in a blouse and shorts. Her husband Ernest had taken the three children to a ball game. In fact, there'd been a small family row over it, because Katie, the daughter, had said she would prefer to stay home with her mother, but Ernest Donaldson had insisted she go to the game, which began at seven. Julia Donaldson was planning to make them coffee and cinnamon buns as a peace offering when they came home. She looked at her watch: nearly nine. The ball park was only four miles away, and they'd be home soon. She went inside, put on a sweater and filled the percolator. As she put it on the stove, the front doorbell rang and she ran to answer it, thinking that perhaps Ernest had forgotten his key. When she opened the door, however, she found a young woman standing there. She was short, with cropped dark hair and none-too-clean denims, although she was nicely spoken. She was a complete stranger to Mrs. Donaldson, and when she asked to use the telephone, the older woman had some misgivings.

"Has there been an accident?" she asked the girl.

The girl said no, no accident. She seemed very much on edge, and repeated that she must use the telephone urgently. Mrs. Donaldson felt more uneasy than ever. It was almost dark, and there was not a soul in sight up or down the road. Where was Ernest, she wondered?

"I'm sorry," she said to the stranger on her doorstep. She began to close the door but as she did she felt something cold and metallic on the back of her neck. She knew, without knowing how she knew, that it was a gun barrel. She turned slowly to find a tall man with a nylon stocking over his head pointing a revolver at her. It looked as huge as a cannon.

"Open the door," the man snapped gruffly. He was wearing a Levi jacket and pants, scuffed dress boots and a T-shirt. He looked about thirty, but it was hard to tell because of the stocking mask. Mrs. Donaldson now realized that the dark-haired girl at the door had been a decoy to distract her attention while the man forced an entry in the back of the house. She drew in her breath, but almost as if he sensed her thought, the man cocked the gun.

"You scream," he hissed, "and I'll splatter you all over the house!"

The girl came inside now, closing the door behind her and leaning against it. She was breathing like someone who had run up a flight of stairs.

"What do you want?" Mrs. Donaldson said. She was frightened, but determined not to show it. Ernest would be home any time now, she told herself. "What is this all about?"

"You got a ten-thousand-dollar necklace," the man said. "Get it."

"I don't have any necklace worth that much," Mrs. Donaldson said, quite truthfully. "I haven't any jewelry worth that kind of money."

"We know all about it, lady," the man said. "The turquoise necklace with the gold clasps. You got about ten seconds to quit gabbin' and get it!"

Mrs. Donaldson led the way into the kitchen, wondering how the intruders could so accurately describe her necklace. She kept her jewelry hidden in a paper sack in a drawer in one of the cabinets, feeling that burglars would be less likely to look for it there. There seemed to be no point in telling the intruders that its value wasn't half the figure the man had named. She handed the sack to the man, who stuck it into his pocket without looking at it, as if he wasn't really interested in its contents. The poodle, Fifi, who had been locked in the kitchen, now started yipping at the feet of the strangers.

"Car keys," the man snapped. "Where are your car keys?"

"My husband has them," Mrs. Donaldson lied. She was playing for time, for surely her family would arrive home at any moment and end this nightmare. Fifi scampered about, barking furiously at the man.

"Yeah, baby," the man leered. "Look, we know Big Daddy ain't got the keys, so quite playin' games. Go get the goddamn keys before I get mad. And tell this yappin' ball of fluff to shut up before I shoot its damn head off!"

"Don't worry about the dog," the girl said. "You know he don't bite—he's chicken."

"I'll take him into the bedroom," Mrs. Donaldson said.

"Do that," the man said. "An' put your shoes on, Lucy, 'cause you're comin' for a ride with us."

How do they know so much about us? Julia Donaldson wondered. How do they know that Ernest hasn't got my car keys, how do they *know* that Fifi doesn't bite? She went into the bedroom and got her car keys, shutting the poodle in.

"Where are you taking me?" she asked. "You have my jewels. What else do you want?"

"Ask me no questions, baby," the man sneered, "an' I'll tell you no lies."

Julia Donaldson desperately tried to think of ways to delay their departure. She looked at the clock in the hall: 9:45. Surely Ernest and the children must be only minutes away from the house!

"Out the back," the man said to the girl. "You lead the way. Get the car started."

To Mrs. Donaldson's surprise, he started out after the girl, as if he expected his prisoner to follow like a puppy. As soon as he had gone through the door, however, she slammed it shut behind him and rammed the bolt home, twisting the key furiously in the lock. She saw the masked man freeze, and then turn, almost as if in slow motion. With a shout of sheer anger, he thrust the gun through the glassed upper half of the door, shattering it. It was terrifying.

"Open this goddamn door or I'll blow your goddamn head off!" he shouted, and the petrified Mrs. Donaldson obeyed, babbling that it had been an accident, an accident. She could see blood pouring from beneath the surgical glove the man was wearing.

"I'm sorry," she stammered. "I'm sorry. I'm sorry."

"I oughta kill you right here!" the man raged. "Go get a towel or sump'n, ya dumb cow! Make a bandage, for Chrissake!"

There were little blobs of blood on the off-white tiles of the kitchen floor. They looked like the seals notaries public use on documents, Mrs. Donaldson thought, as she wound a makeshift tourniquet around the man's forearm. It all felt unreal, as if she were in a nightmare from which she could not wake.

The man was holding the pistol in his left hand, but now he handed it to his accomplice while he went into the bathroom downstairs to have Mrs. Donaldson swab his cuts with merthiolate. As she was doing this, there was the sound of a pistol shot in the kitchen.

"What the hell?" the man said, running back into the kitchen. His woman accomplice looked at him with a sheepish smile.

"It's all right," she said. "I was just changing hands and it sort of went off."

Mrs. Donaldson looked around. The kitchen stunk of cordite and there was a jagged chunk of plaster torn from the wall. The big bullet had torn a hole in the door of the refrigerator and then ricocheted against the kitchen wall. There was broken plaster on the floor, broken glass, blood. Fifi was barking dementedly in the bedroom.

The man grabbed the gun from his girlfriend.

"Dumb bitch!" he snarled. "Let's get the hell outa here before you wind up killin' *me!*"

They hustled Mrs. Donaldson out of the house, and

told her to lie down on the floor in the back of the car. The man then got in back with her, and held the barrel of the pistol against her forehead while the girl gunned the engine and barreled the car down the road toward the highway.

"Where are we going?" Mrs. Donaldson asked, craning her neck so she could talk to the man. "What are you going to do with me?"

"Just a job, lady," the man said offhandedly. "Just another job."

They drove in silence for a while, and then the man asked the girl driving where they were supposed to meet.

"She'll be waiting in back of the apartments," the girl said.

She? Mrs. Donaldson thought. Another woman? About twenty minutes later, by her estimate, the car stopped in some kind of apartment development. Mrs. Donaldson could see tall buildings with lighted windows, and knew that at this time of night business premises would have been dark. The woman driver got out, and talked with someone. Then she slid back behind the wheel.

"She says we got to follow her," she announced, putting the car into gear. They moved off again, and this time they were traveling faster. Mrs. Donaldson could hear the tires squealing on the road as they cornered.

"Tell that dumb bitch to slow down!" the man snapped. "She want us to get stopped by some jerk cop?"

"You know Cricket," the girl said over her shoulder. "She's got a foot like a deep-sea diver."

Cricket? Mrs. Donaldson thought. It was the first name anyone had used, and she clung to it like a life raft. The car bumped off the highway on to a dirt road. After a while, it stopped.

"All right, lady," the man said. "Here's where you get off."

"I don't understand," Julia Donaldson said. "What

is this all about? Won't one of you please tell me what it's all about?"

"You know the saying, lady," the man said. "Money is the root of all evil."

He motioned her to get out of the car.

"We get the money," he said. "And you get the evil."

She was fumbling in the darkness, getting out of the car, when he hit her over the head with the gun, slamming her back half-conscious against the rear seat, blood spurting from her broken scalp. In a swimming haze of pain she heard the woman scolding the man for being so stupid, there was blood everywhere and now they wouldn't be able to use the car.

"Ah, go to hell," the man said. He was breathing rapidly, shallowly, as if he were excited. "We'll jus' leave her in it. Just another roadside murder, baby."

As Mrs. Donaldson sprawled face down in the dirt, the man put his knee in the small of her back. Using both hands, he twisted her head 180 degrees, breaking her neck as dispassionately as if he were killing a chicken. Mrs. Donaldson passed out, but astonishingly, she was not dead. When she came to, moments or minutes later, the man was holding her wrist as if taking her pulse, and he gave a short laugh of triumph as he let it go.

"She's as dead as she'll ever be!" he yelled to his companions. He then lifted Julia Donaldson's limp body off the ground and clumsily jammed it, doubled over, beneath the dash on the passenger side of her own car.

"Go on!" she heard the man call. "I'll follow you."

She heard the cars start up, but the bumpy movement brought on huge waves of pain and she passed out. It was like some insane horror film. She would become conscious for a while, then pass out again. Once she heard the man laughing and talking to himself.

"Why you doin' this to me?" he was saying, in a grisly mockery of her own voice. "What this all about?" Then in his own voice he replied. "For money, honey. That's what turns the wheels. Yeah, yeah, yeah."

After what seemed like an eternity, Mrs. Donaldson felt the car stop again. The man got out, locking all the doors. She heard his footsteps receding, heard the other car start up and drive off. Then there was only the immense empty silence of the desert night.

How long she waited Mrs. Donaldson had no idea. Ten minutes, an hour, several—she lost all track of time. Her world was a world of terrifying sweeps of pain, swooning mists of half-consciousness. She knew that she had to try and get out of the car to find help, but she could not bear the pain of moving. When she tried to, she found that she quite literally could not lift her head. She had to hold it, like a goldfish bowl, in both hands. Even like this, every movement sent spasms of pain shooting down her spine, drenching her chilled body with perspiration. Finally, she managed to maneuver her body around so that she could brace herself against the back of the seat. Infinitely slowly, she held her head in her hands and tried to turn it face forward to its natural position. She passed out again as soon as she had done it.

When she came to, she found she could see over the top of the dashboard. She inched forward until her chin was resting on the padded dash. She felt as if she had walked a thousand miles, but the tiredness disappeared like a dream when she saw the twin headlights of an approaching car. Sobbing desperately with weakness, she tried to roll down the car window so she could flag for help, but even as she did, she suddenly realized that she was not on a highway but on a deserted dirt road in the middle of nowhere. The only people likely to be passing this way were her former captors, returning for something they had forgotten. She got the window closed and slumped back into her former position, passing out from the pain as she did so.

It was just as well, for the car was indeed that of

her captors, and it was her would-be murderer who opened the door of the car and took something. A gun, she thought, somehow knowing what it was without seeing it. To her horror, he patted her back as if she were a sleeping dog.

"Sleep warm, baby," he said, and closed the door again.

Time passed. Mrs. Donaldson counted five hundred, and then tried to do it again, but she could not remember where she was up to. Her head was swimming, and in her fetal position under the dashboard, all her earlier efforts had been canceled out. Finally she decided that if she didn't move soon she was going to die. Inch by agonizing inch, she got herself upright once more on the car seat.

It took her what seemed like a hundred years to get the car door open without letting her head fall uncontrollably forward, setting off the agonizing chain reaction of pain throughout her body. She got out of the car.

The night was as black as the hinges on the doorway of hell and she hadn't the remotest idea of where she was. She heard a coyote yapping somewhere and shivered. She decided to walk in the opposite direction to the way the car was pointing, figuring that the nearest help would lie where they had come from, and not ahead. She set out, stumbling on the rutted road, holding her head upright by clasping both hands tight around her neck just below the jawline. She had no idea how long she walked or how many times she fell. Sometimes she would fall down and just lie there and think of going to sleep and not trying anymore, but then she would get to her feet again and stagger on.

It was a little after dawn that she came to the house of an allergist named Peter Engler. There was a sign on the gate: *Beware of the Dog*. Mrs. Donaldson was still game enough to smile. Cerberus himself, she told me later, could not have kept her from the door of that house.

She pounded on the door until the Englers opened up. Fortunately for Mrs. Donaldson the allergist had medical knowledge, and he did what he could for the battered, sobbing woman while his wife called the police and an ambulance. As soon as they had her story, the police dispatched a unit to the Donaldson house in Coronado to apprise her husband of what had happened. Mrs. Donaldson was meanwhile rushed into surgery, where they stitched up her lacerated skull and set her broken neck, encasing her from chin to hip in plaster. She also had a hairline fracture of the skull and concussion, together with multiple lacerations and contusions from the desert thorns and her many falls.

When the police got to Coronado they found the Donaldson house dark. It took five minutes of hammering on the door before Ernest Donaldson opened it, wearing a bathrobe and demanding to know what all the racket was about.

They told him about his wife, noticing that he took the news very calmly. They asked if they could come in, check the house against the story Mrs. Donaldson had told them. He agreed, and they found things pretty much as she had described them. The glass in the back door was broken, and there was a bullet hole in the refrigerator, while a hunk of plaster was missing from the wall. There was no broken glass or plaster on the floor, however, nor any bloodstains.

"Who cleaned up here?" the detectives asked.

"I did," Donaldson said. "Didn't want to cut my feet."

"You wipe up the bloodstains, too?"

"Right," Donaldson said.

"You found your back door smashed in, bloodstains on the floor, a bullet hole in your icebox and your wife missing—and you just cleaned up the mess? You didn't call the police?"

"No," Donaldson said. "What for?"

"You didn't suspect foul play?"

"No."

"What did you suspect?"

"Didn't suspect anything," Donaldson replied. "We came home from the ball game and went to bed."

"Before or after you cleaned up the mess?"

"That's a real dumb question," Donaldson said.

"Sheee-hit," the detectives said, and went to call it in. They were told to stay and grill him until he was cooked both sides, but they couldn't get him to change his story. He'd come home from the ball game, he said, found the broken glass and the blood and figured that maybe Julia had cut herself, taken the car and gone down to the hospital. They checked and found he hadn't called the hospital. He said there wasn't any reason why he should. He imagined Julia would be home before he went to sleep.

"And the bullet hole?" they asked.

Donaldson said he couldn't figure it out, it hadn't made any sense to him, either, but there was a gun in the house. Maybe Julia heard something, thought it was a prowler, broke the window, cut herself. It had to be some kind of freak accident, so he left it at that. He said he'd been tired, so he went up to bed, expecting Julia to wake him when she came in. The next think he knew the police were banging on the door.

His story was far-fetched, in fact bizarre, but they couldn't shake Donaldson, and they didn't have a thing on him. He had a fireproof alibi—his three children had been with him throughout the ball game; he was never out of their sight. He told his wife the same story when he went in to see her the next day, and she didn't believe it, either. The boys at the courthouse told me Donaldson could have given Ananias a head start and romped home. Donaldson knew he had them flimflammed; they could suspect any damned thing they liked, but they had to prove it to nail him. And proof was conspicuously absent.

As for Julia Donaldson's assailants, the police couldn't get any kind of line on them—although to be fair, her description of the man and the woman didn't give them a lot to go on, and in Texas there are enough girls called Cricket to start an association. They were no nearer cracking the case when the doctors took Julia out of the plaster cast and started her on physiotherapy than they had been the night it happened. The sole detective assigned to the case by the city kept calling her in the hospital, asking her whether she had heard anything. She wondered what he thought she would be likely to hear lying flat on her back in a plaster cast in a hospital, but he kept on calling every few days anyway.

Finally, a group of her women friends, who included the wives of golfer Lee Trevino and his manager Jesse Whittington, nagged Julia into taking private action to find out why she had been attacked and who had been responsible. She said she wouldn't know where to start, but they told her that was easy: call Jay J. Armes.

A few days later Mrs. Donaldson retained me. She told me everything she could remember, and said she realized that after all these weeks my chances of finding out anything were on the far side of remote.

I broke the case in exactly three days.

Julia Donaldson was a popular woman with no enemies. There was only one person who could possibly benefit from her death, and that was her husband. Since it was easily ascertained that she carried no life insurance and that he had not taken out any policies without her knowledge, Ernest Donaldson's only reason for wanting his wife dead had to be another woman. In investigative work, the old rule *cherchez la femme* is still a good one. Our only lead in that direction was the name "Cricket," and I found out fast how many women have that nickname in the Southwest.

Mrs. Donaldson had estimated that the time between her leaving her own home and arriving at the apartment house where they had met Cricket was about twenty minutes. I got a large-scale map of the area, did some figuring of probable car speeds and allowed an extra ten minutes either way on Mrs. Donaldson's estimate. I then drew three circles with her home as the axis, and we worked in from each circle, checking out any and every apartment house that fell within it. Process of elimination—it works every time.

While this method was delivering us a list of women known as Cricket, we put a round-the-clock tail on Ernest Donaldson. I also put a room bug alongside every telephone in the house, using Mrs. Donaldson's keys to get in while Donaldson was out. Another one was hidden in his office desk, and that was the one that gave us Cricket on a plate.

Donaldson was having an affair with her. Her real name was Bella Turner, and it was she who had hired the thugs to kill Julia Donaldson. She was living in an apartment house in east El Paso under the name of Bonnie Thompson.

I reported my findings to Julia Donaldson, who didn't seem very surprised. She asked me what I thought she should do. I told her that she could prefer charges against her husband, but that it was vital that Bella Turner not be tipped off. I was afraid that when she filed her complaint, the police would go over and lean on Turner, and she would flee the nest, leaving us with no case. I suggested we go to Frank Manning, the chief deputy sheriff, whom I know and like.

Manning acted fast when he had all the facts. He called in Ray Montez, a captain of the Highway Patrol, and assigned him exclusively to the case. Montez, Manning and I stood by while Mrs. Donaldson made a four-and-one-half-hour statement for Manning to present to the district attorney's office. They, in turn, would give it directly to the grand jury, who would hand down sealed indictments against Turner and her confederates. I marveled at Julia Donaldson's self-control, going over and over every point of that awful ordeal under the cold fluorescent light of the office on South Campbell Street. She talked about it as if it had happened to someone else.

Unfortunately, Deputy Manning wasn't able to bypass the usual channels, and in reporting the case to his own superiors, he perforce revealed Bella Turner's involvement. The sheriff's office reacted just the way I had feared they would. A unit was sent down to question Turner on the allegations contained in Mrs. Donaldson's statement and the report of my investigation that was attached to it. Within twenty minutes of that official visit, Bella "Cricket" Turner had disappeared and there wasn't a damned thing we could do about it.

Inspector George Wagnon of the EPPD started an investigation when I complained of the way the matter had been handled, but the damage had been done. No indictments were ever handed down. About a year later, after his wife divorced him, I heard that Ernest Donaldson had married Bella Turner. Everybody knows, of course, that a wife and husband cannot be made to testify against each other.

As for the two hired assassins—they're still out there somewhere, free as birds. It's unlikely they'll ever find Julia Donaldson, who remarried and moved to the Northwest, but they know where I am. They know I have a file on them and they know it's open. If I ever get a lead on them, I'll nail them, and they know that too. That's why my wife and children have a bodyguard. And one more reason why I do too.

9.

The Armes house—really more a mansion than a
house—is about eleven miles from the center of El
Paso, taking up the entire 8100 block on North Loop
Road. Like its owner, the house is a long way from
typical. Originally a small place Armes bought for his
mother and kept for sentimental reasons after her
death, the house has grown from its original eight
rooms to a twenty-six-room palace that can only be
described as constantly surprising.

The frontage on North Loop is an eighteen-foot-high
stockade into which are set two massive iron gates
bearing the shield and crest of The Investigators.
Twenty thousand volts course through the wires sur-
mounting the wooden palings, and closed-circuit TV
cameras inspect everyone approaching the gates, behind which roams a pack of trained-to-kill bull
mastiffs.

The gates can be opened only by someone inside the
house, or by the specially made electronic controls
carried in each of Armes' armored limousines. In the
highly unlikely event that the gates and walls are
breached, there are a number of other electronic
alarms and protective systems built into the driveway
and the ground around the house.

The front of the house is dominated by four planta-
tion-style pillars flanked by white-painted stone lions.
The downstairs windows are all barred. The glass is
backed by heavy metal mesh. A second-floor balcony,
vaguely reminiscent of the bridge of a ship, is deco-

rated with Chinese good luck signs. These are repeated
in other parts of the house and grounds.

Inside, the house seems at first to be one big open-
plan living area, but after a while it becomes apparent
that there are other, more functional living rooms,
bathrooms, kitchens, playrooms—all above or adjacent
to the main lounge, which is a low-ceilinged long, wide
room through which flows a bridged stream. There are
cane-lined walls, as in the office downtown, but here
they seem even more exotic because of the live trees
growing in pots and the fishing nets draped on the
walls. The effect is highly individual, highly unusual,
much nearer Macao than El Paso.

At the far end of the room there is a well-stocked
bar: Chivas Regal, Jack Daniels, Glenfiddich, Rémy
Martin, Beefeater, Harvey's, Stolichnaya—every kind
of liquor and two different beers on tap for thirsty visitors, although neither Armes nor his wife drinks. At
one side stands a grand piano, a Blüthner.

On the far side, across the bridge with its Chinese
motif spelling Linda Armes' name, there is a glassed-in
indoor pool and solarium, the water kept at a constant
67°F. Marble steps lead down into the shallow end,
and there is a line across the middle so the smaller
children won't go too deep. Up a small stairway to the
left is a brightly lit dining room with silver candelabra
on the table, and beyond it a gleaming kitchen in
which, as you might expect, there is a glittering selection of gadgets: juicers, toasters, microwave oven,
mixers, blenders, coffeemakers—"General Electric's
best friend," Armes calls himself.

There are no stairs to the second floor bedroom.
They were torn out, and a ramp was built to the investigator's design and specification. Like the rest of the
house, it is covered with a deep and luxurious carpet-
ing, and rises so steeply to the upper floor that climbing it is almost hard work, and when descending, it is
difficult not to break into a trot. Armes says it keeps
him fit, and the kids use it as a slalom sometimes.

The master bedroom—in which the furniture, like everything else in the house, was designed by Armes— is huge and roomy. All the unit-style furniture is ranged along the walls and there are no tables, no loose rugs, no knickknacks. Armes says there are two reasons for this: first, he dislikes clutter, and second, if he has to go into action in the dark, he doesn't want to have to worry about falling over anything. In one corner of the room stands an opulent twelve-foot-diameter circular bed, to one side of which, on the wall, flickers the omnipresent TV monitor screen. At the flick of a switch, every room in the house and various angles of the extensive grounds outside can be closely scanned. A kidnapper would have hard work here—there are closed-circuit cameras trained on each of the children's beds.

The kids have a room next to Armes' library, in which he keeps a staggering collection of weaponry and hardware. He's not afraid of their going in there and getting into trouble. Young Jay, seven, can already shoot handguns and rifles as well as most men, and to the other kids, weapons and gadgets are as commonplace as cornflakes. Young Jay has only to ask for something, and his ingenious father works out a way of doing it. The boy wanted a "hideaway" bedroom— with the other kids, yet separated from them. Armes knocked out a wall and built a room halfway up it— like a big box into which the boy climbs and looks slightly down on the other two kids. Jay Jr. said he wished he could go fishing sometimes. Dad decided to build him a one-and-a-half-acre lake. When the boy said that if they had a lake, he'd need a boat, Armes bought him a speedboat, and now the youngster hotrods it around the private lake his Dad built.

The lake holds about nine and a half million gallons, which is a hell of a lot of water in a desert town like El Paso, and Armes didn't have the easiest time convincing the city planning board that he was serious when he put up the proposal. They gave him the okay to build the lake because they were sure he"d fall flat on his face when he tried to tap a water supply. Armes put down a four-inch well that made them laugh out of the other side of their mouths. Again to his own design, he had a waterfall built at one end of the lake. It is two hundred feet long and the actual fall is twenty feet. Fifty thousand gallons a minute thunder into the lake, automatically aerating the water and moving it toward the far end, where it falls into an underground piping system of two twenty-four-inch pipes, which channel it back to the base of the fall. There, using a free-flow system boosted by two 65-hp pumps, it is taken to the top to repeat the process. Armes then stocked the lake with bass and catfish, added a spawning area so they could multiply, put a Chinese bridge across to an island in the center—with wife Linda's name, On Ting, emblazoned on it—and planted fig, pear and bamboo trees. In the evenings, the cascading water, backlit by colored lamps, shines like a beacon through the electrified fence that surrounds the estate.

At one side of the house there are tennis courts. Armes plays a good game although he's no Jimmy Connors. Beside the house stand the cars: the dull gold Corvette Stingray, the svelte Rolls, the sinister Cadillac limo with its winged angel on the hood. All of the cars bear the heraldic device of The Investigators. All of them are fitted with special equipment worth hundreds of thousands of dollars.

The Stingray is fitted with revolving license plates that give the car a new registration at the flick of a switch, plus closed-circuit television, radar-tracking console, hidden cameras, hideaway pistols and much more that Armes won't reveal. The big Caddy was built in Detroit to his specification and cost $65,000. Its extras include bulletproof glass and armor plating, plus a bombproof shield underneath the vehicle, video tape equipment and a closed-circuit television camera with a one-mile range that is fitted with a zoom lens that will bring figures or automobiles seventeen blocks *away up close on the monitor inside the vehicle. The rear compartment is soundproofed so that clients can talk to Armes in complete privacy—even the usual window behind the door on the passenger side has been removed, and the rear window exchanged for a smaller, bullet-proof one. There are controls for a siren and yelper, and a PA system that enables Armes to broadcast without leaving his seat. The car is equipped with a police radio, citizen's band and a stereo tape player. Its emergency equipment includes an Armes invention: he can reinflate a blown or shot-out tire by throwing a switch inside the car. There are a number of other secrets, deterrent or offensive. Armes designed a similar car for the family of King Faisal of Iraq.*

Beyond the parked vehicles and the tennis courts is the helicopter landing pad with a gleaming World Twin Rudder Trainer perched like some gigantic grasshopper. It is on several acres of landscaped grounds upon which once stood an apartment house that Armes bought and tore down to make room for it. He planted trees and fescue grass, and installed computerized sprinklers that retract when the helicopter is landing or taking off, and keep the grassy stretch verdant and fresh at all times. The grass is not a vanity. Keeping it green and lush insures that when Armes brings in the chopper, he doesn't kick up a duststorm. When he thinks a thing through, he thinks it through all the way.

In back of the house, the gardens turn startlingly into a fair replica of an African jungle village. It is as if in El Paso one had stumbled upon the location for a Tarzan movie. The same bizarrely familiar conical thatched huts stand in the same dusty compound, beyond them an impenetrable stand of bamboo. A small stream—diverted from the nearby lake and carefully designed to stay fresh by free flow—meanders through the village, and in one of the palm trees there is a concealed door behind which hangs a pushbutton telephone.

Between house and lake lies the menagerie, a fabulous collection of animals Armes has bought over the years against the day when he opens the safari park he's always dreamed of building. There are two hissing black panthers in a cage, a puma and a Siberian tiger that rolls over on its back like a big soft pussycat when Armes talks to it in a high-pitched wheedle. He goes into the cages of the big cats without turning a hair, petting them as casually as another man would stroke a dog. He says that he can tell just by the way the animals move what they are thinking and what they are going to do. He won't let visitors into the cages unless they truly are not scared. The big cats can smell your fear and they react to it.

In another cage is Gypsy, Armes' pet chimpanzee. He bribes her to do tricks with a stick of Care-Free Sugarless gum. There is a compound that has zebras, and ostriches haughty as rich old ladies peering over the fence. There are many more animals on his ranch in New Mexico, and they will all be moved one day to Hueco Tanks, the land on which he plans to build the safari park.

Armes has loved animals all his life. He takes obvious, childlike pleasure in owning them and being able to handle them. And in crossing a zebra with an Appaloosa because all the experts told him that it just plain couldn't be done.

People are always asking me why I work so hard. I tell them jokingly that a man has to work hard when he's got so many animals to feed. With the price of meat the way it is, giving those big cats two square meals a day is no cakewalk.

I've always loved animals, like to work with them. I guess it goes back to having had that smart dog, Butch, when I was a kid. I trained him to do all sorts of tricks on command. I enjoyed it, and the dog enjoyed it too. Animals respond to discipline as long as it is not cruelly imposed.

Later on, when I had the facilities to keep them, I
bought a few more animals. That was around the time
I designed the African village, just as I designed everything around the house. I set up the gymnasium on the
second floor, installed all the machinery, the matting,
the mirrors, everything. I also drew up the plans for
the sauna, and built in the electrically-operated clothes
rail for my suits in the walk-in dressing room adjoining
the bedroom. It is an adaptation of the ones they have
in dry-cleaning establishments and it can carry 750
suits.

When I got the African village underway, I got hold
of a very rare miniature white rhinoceros. He was as
cute as a cartload of monkeys, and we called him Gus.
He was really friendly, a pet. He used to love to have
me go over his hide with a stiff wire brush, a kind of
rhinoceros rubdown. He had gotten so that whenever
he heard my voice, he would come a-running, and believe me, when Gus came at the trot, you had to watch
out. He was a lot heavier than he knew, and if he hit
you it was like being sideswiped by a jeep. Giving him
his wire-brush rubdown was like a good workout in the
gym.

This particular day I was out in back with Gus when
I happened to look up toward the corner of the fence.
Why I did, I'll never know—I figure the good Lord
was looking out for me—but there, perched right on
top of the fence, I saw the figure of a man. Now the
front of my house is not much like your typical American suburban ranch-style, and it tends to attract sight-
seers. Something in people, I guess. Show them a
twenty-foot fence and they want to know what's on
the other side of it. Let them see the big cats prowling
around—they roam the grounds at will after dark—
and they want to come and have a closer look. Which
in those days I didn't mind at all. Animals are beautiful to look at, the kibitzers couldn't get into any
trouble.

So I thought when I saw the strange figure perched

up there that he was some kind of nut, because he looked like he had a bow and arrow in his hands. I thought he was maybe a Tarzan freak, and yelled at him to get away from there. I made an angry wave with my right arm and the movement saved my life. It wasn't a bow and arrow the man was carrying, it was a crossbow.

The bolt from it whapped between my arm and my body and killed Gus dead on the spot. You might think that the crossbow is an archaic weapon that belongs in a museum, but you'd be wrong. Today's crossbow is an enormously powerful and effective killing weapon. It has the range of a good middle-caliber carbine and is at least as accurate, while having the additional advantage of being totally silent. For this reason, it is much prized by deer hunters and other bold pursuers of our ferocious woodland wildlife. When we examined Gus afterwards, we found that the bolt had gone right through his neck just above the shoulder—which gives some indication of what would have happened had it hit me.

I ran toward the man on the fence, pulling out my .38, but he was already out of sight on the far side. I turned fast and ran for the controls operating the gates, throwing the switch and simultaneously wheeling back toward the gate. As I did, I heard the roar of a motor bike being started, and by the time I got onto the street, the man was already two hundred yards down the highway and still accelerating. I stood and watched him go, the gun still in my hand. I didn't have a snowball's chance in hell of catching him.

For the next three days, I tried everything I knew to get a lead on that would-be assassin. I checked every sporting goods store in five counties trying to get a line on anyone who'd bought or owned a crossbow. I came up empty. Whoever the man had been, he wasn't local —which meant he had been brought in with a contract to kill me. Why? I have no idea, never will. In my business, you're almost certain to step on some

tender toes—toes you often don't even know are there
—and antagonize one set of people in the very act of
satisfying another.

I've been involved in every kind of case there is: kidnapping, white slaving, drug trafficking, illegal immigration, forgery, extortion and murder, to name but a
few. I imagine I've made a few enemies along the way,
people who would be very happy to see me put out of
business for good, and it doesn't make life any easier
knowing that you are in constant danger. But nobody
said it was supposed to be easy.

So we electrified the fence, and installed a variety of
ultrasophisticated devices inside the perimeter. Any
intruder who manages to bypass the fence, elude the
dogs and big cats and stay out of range of the closed-
circuit TV cameras would still find himself up to his
elbows in big trouble if he moved more than five yards
in any direction unannounced.

In those days, there were other houses near mine,
and a small apartment block. Not all of my neighbors
thought that the Armes menagerie was delightful.
When my oldest boy was two (and he is as fascinated
with animals as I am), I went to India and brought
him back a baby elephant for his birthday. My idea
was to train the elephant to let Jay ride on his back. I
built a little howdah for the boy to sit in, and off he'd
go, cute as a pinto pony.

Kadumah—we called him that because it was the
nearest Jay could get to imitating the elephant's call—
drank about three gallons of milk with rice a day. His
first feed was very early in the morning, and he would
come close to the house and call to us, right beneath
the window. I can understand why our nearest neighbors didn't get the biggest thrill of their lives when that
little fellow started blowing his trumpet at 5 A.M., but
I thought they would understand that when he got
older he would stop doing it.

Not them. A petition was raised, claiming that the
animals were disturbing the peace, the lions were roar-

ing all night—and that even if they weren't, an El Paso suburb was not the ideal location for such beasts, which might escape and savage somebody. It was unreasonable and untrue, but that never stops people with their heads down and their eyes shut. They tried to use the courts to force me to get rid of the animals, but I fought them every inch of the way—and won.

Around about that time, we had workmen on the grounds, excavating and landscaping in preparation for the building of the African village. Naturally enough, we switched off the high-tension wires while they were around. I later worked out that one of our neighbors bribed a workman to "accidentally" leave a ladder leaning against the fence. Using another on the outside, this person climbed into the compound and put strychnine into the elephant's drinking water. It must have been done late in the afternoon, before all the alarms were turned on. Next morning when we came down to feed him, we found Kadumah dead. Little Jay was just heartbroken. I tried to console him, but all the time I was mad enough to eat beef with the hide on. I vowed to find out who had done such a heartless thing.

I took a sample of the animal's blood and made a chemical analysis of it. When I found it contained strychnine, I began an intensive check of all feed stores and pharmacies that sold the poison. Farmers often use strychnine for killing off rodents and other varmints, but it is a controlled poison—that is to say, the seller must keep a record of the amounts he sells and to whom he sells them. It didn't take me very long to discover that one of our neighbors had purchased enough strychnine to kill a horse—or an elephant. Proving that he had personally administered it was, however, another matter entirely. My case against the man was entirely circumstantial, and the DA's office was not about to accept a complaint without more proof. It isn't a hanging offense to possess strychnine, although you might wonder what a man who lived in a suburban two-story frame house would want with the stuff. So I backed off, although I was still mad. I decided to find another way to skin this particular skunk.

A reporter from the *Herald-Post* ran a story about the poisoning of the elephant, and it unleashed a deluge of letters and calls—more than seven hundred of them—from people asking me to name the person responsible. Every one of them had roughly the same idea in mind—to feed him some of his own "medicine." One man even suggested a Gilbertian punishment to fit the crime.

"I'd make the SOB *eat* the dead elephant," he said. "Raw!"

I told them all the same thing: thanks, but I had my own plans for paying off this particular debt. For some time I had been planning to add a feature to my house that I'd always dreamed of—a private lake. Young Jay triggered it afresh in my mind at this time by saying one day that he would love to go fishing, but that there was nowhere nearby he could go. It was then that I sat down and began to draw up the plans for the lake, and to work out the mechanics of the waterfall. I talked to an architect and he threw up his hands in alarm.

"Have you any idea how much a thing like that would cost?" he said.

"Some," I replied. "Is it feasible?"

"It's feasible," he said. "All it takes is money."

"If all it takes is money," I said, "do it!"

Acting with my attorney, he started quietly buying up the land that would be needed. Then they started working on the houses nearby, making the owners such handsome offers for their property that they fell over themselves to sell out and scat. One of them was the neighbor whom I suspected of killing Jay's elephant.

As soon as the purchases were completed and the papers filed, I brought in bulldozers and tore those houses down. They were gone, flat, razed, faster than you could blink, and people were appalled. I didn't care: I was determined to make sure nobody ever got the chance to kill another one of my animals.

I extended the perimenter to its present size, finished the African village, installed the cages and pens for the animals, built the lake and got the waterfall working. It really looks very beautiful at night. We get wild ducks stopping in on their way north or south, depending on the season. I installed tapes of mocking birds singing up in the trees.

Sometimes on hot summer nights Linda and I will go out there and sit in the basket swing under the cottonwood tree. It's very pretty, and sitting there, I reflect that the score was finally evened without there being any "revenge" involved. I read somewhere that "a man who studies revenge keeps his own wounds green" and I haven't got the time to waste on that sort of folly. My way was—I hope—a little more constructive.

10.

The lady was from New Mexico and she was beautiful. Cat-green eyes, honey-blond hair and the kind of figure that Raymond Chandler once said would make a bishop want to kick a hole in a stained-glass window. She was a former New York model, twenty-nine years of age, and her husband was the Onion King of America. A strange title, but an accurate one. Sixty-year-old Kenichi Matsushita was the country's—if not the world's—largest grower of onions. He had thousands and thousands of acres under cultivation, and his business had made him a millionaire.

I first met them both when Mrs. Matsushita called me and asked me to locate her husband, who had walked out without telling her where he was going. At first, she had thought he was just taking a short trip, but when the days lengthened into a week, she got worried. She told me they'd quarreled and now she feared that he might have left her. Business problems that called for his attention were piling up and she needed to know his whereabouts. I diagnosed a marital difference and knew I wasn't getting anything like the full story, but that's often par for the course. I had all I needed, however, to do what I was being paid to do, and I located Mr. Matsushita quite quickly. He was staying at the Sacramento Street home of his sister in San Francisco, and if he wasn't altogether delighted that his wife had hired an investigator to find him—especially since he had to pick up the tab—he said nothing out loud. He came on back home to New Mexico and that, I thought, was the end of that.

Then very early one morning, at 5:45, three or four months later, I got a frantic call from Helen Matsushita.

"Mr. Armes," she said, "can you get up here right away? My husband has been murdered!"

I didn't bother with any further questions. I jumped into my Stingray and burned rubber, covering the forty-odd miles up US 10 to Las Cruces in just under half that many minutes. That Matsushita house was a big, sprawling three-story place set in a shade grove of cottonwoods and worth $250,000 of anybody's money.

The police and ambulance had already been and gone, taking the body of Matsushita with them. The beautiful Mrs. Matsushita was red-eyed and confused. She told me she had taken a sleeping pill and a tranquilizer the night before, and felt "fuddly."

I asked her to tell me as much as she could, and she said that the day before she had argued with her husband over a check she had written for cash to the tune of $20,000. Her explanation that it had been for her brother to open a garage in Dallas had not convinced him, and he left the house still angry. He told her he'd be back around six, by which time she had better have a truthful answer ready. When he didn't come back, she didn't worry at first. He often reacted this way, sometimes even going to sleep in another part of the house and not speaking to her for days on end. It was then that she decided to go to bed early, taking a sleeping pill and a tranquilizer. The next thing she knew Manuel, the foreman, was hammering on the door, shouting for someone to call an ambulance because he had found Mr. Matsushita out in the fields, suffering from multiple bullet wounds. When the police came, they questioned her perfunctorily, but that was all.

Fairly straightforward. I knew the Matsushitas didn't have what you'd call an ideal marital relationship. She was restless and wanted to have a good time. He was a homebody, and knew nothing except hard work. Her story that there had been a family spat and that she hadn't seen her husband since the preceding morning had the ring of likelihood—but that was about the best that could be said for it.

My next series of questions established that Ken Matsushita was not in any financial or business trouble. He had not been away from the place for any length of time recently, and it seemed unlikely to me that he was the kind of man who would make enemies who'd want to kill him. Yet someone had. Someone had put five bullets into him.

I asked her how she had spent the preceding day. She told me she'd slept until one, and had a snack before going to the beauty parlor. She got back when the kids were coming home from school—there were three children, aged six, seven and eight. She watched TV for a while, and went to bed early.

I told her I would like to question the two servants, and she agreed, as long as she could be present. I told her the girls would be more relaxed if she wasn't there, and she acquiesced, although not enthusiastically.

The first maid slept above the garage. She told me that the preceding night she'd heard the sound of raised voices, breaking glass, then someone starting the car. It was about 1 A.M. The car drove off, and she heard several backfires. About twenty minutes or so later, the car came back. She could hear the engine iding in the garage for a long time, maybe an hour. Then it was turned off. As she told me this, the maid froze, and I looked up to see that Helen Matsushita had slipped quietly into the room. She asked me if I'd found out anything; I had a pretty shrewd idea why.

The second maid, who slept close to the children at the other end of the house, said that she had looked out the window after being awakened by the sound of an argument. She could see husband and wife standing in the beams of the car headlights, waving their arms and quarreling. She had no idea what time it was. Then they struggled with each other, and Mrs. Matsushita literally tore the shirt off her husband's back. He had gotten into the car and stayed there. After a while his wife got in and they drove off. The car returned about half an hour later, and she assumed that they had settled their differences and gone to bed. The next morning she had learned that Mr. Matsushita had been murdered.

I went out and talked to the foreman, Manuel Sedillo. He took me out to the fields and showed me where he had found the body. It was way over high noon, and it was hot and dusty out in the open. I could see the Organ Mountains off to the east, shimmering like a mirage. I spent more than an hour out there, hunting around until I found tracks where a body had been dragged on the ground. I took a cast of the tire tracks in the dust at the side of the road, checking later to find that they indeed matched the station wagon in the garage. Manuel added the final dimension to the picture.

He told me that Mr. Matsushita had been very depressed that day, and asked him if he had ever heard any talk about Helen in town. Manuel said he would just as soon not get involved in anybody's domestic problems. In fact, he knew that Mrs. Matsushita was having an affair with another man—it was common gossip in Las Cruces—but he didn't dare tell his boss. I asked him to tell me, promising that it would remain confidential. Manuel said that several men were playing footsie with Mrs. Matsushita, but the main one was a black professional football player who was seeing her regularly when Matsushita was away, even to the extent of visiting the estate and staying in the guest house about half a mile from the main residence.

I knew what I wanted now: a long, long talk with my client. Mrs. Matsushita was lying on a couch in the living room when I got back. She told me she had just taken two Valiums.

"I'm not sure I'd make too much sense if you asked me questions now," she said.

"Do your best with this one," I said. "Why did you shoot your husband?"

Tranquilizers or not, she sat up abruptly, her eyes wide. "Are you insane?" she snapped.

I didn't bother with that one. I asked her whether she and her husband had quarreled the preceding night. She said no, not really. Just a family spat over money, as she'd told me earlier.

"You didn't fight?"

"No."

"You didn't hit him?"

"No, of course not!"

"You didn't get into the car with him?"

"What is this, Mr. Armes?"

"You're lying to me," I said. "And you know it."

She got up off the couch and her eyes were flashing with anger. She pointed an imperious finger at the door.

"You're fired!" she screeched. "Get out of here!"

I told her not to waste her time with amateur dramatics. She knew she had shot her husband, and I knew it too. I told her how I could prove it.

"You told me you didn't see his body, didn't you?"

"That's right," she said.

"Then how come you knew he had five bullets in him?"

"Someone must have told me," she said. "Manuel. The police. Somebody."

"Nobody told you," I said. "You knew because you were the one who put them there. What have you done with the gun?"

"You're against me!" she said, slumping back on the couch, dramatically asprawl. "Everyone is against me!"

I got no chance to comment on that. The door opened and a couple of detectives from the Mesilla Park police came in with a warrant for Helen Matsushita's arrest.

"What's the charge?" I asked them.

"Attempted murder," they said.

Ken Matsushita was not dead. He had lain bleeding for nearly four hours with five separate bullet wounds in his body, and he ought to have been deader than a mackerel. But after intensive all-day surgery he had pulled through and given the police a statement.

"You're trying to frame me!" she shouted over her shoulder as they took her out to the car. "Everyone is against me!"

I made arrangements for the servants to take the three children to stay with Ken Matsushita's mother, and then went out to the hospital to see the wounded man. I didn't expect him to greet me like a long-lost brother, but that's exactly what happened. He asked me to tell him everything that had happened, and I told him about my investigation and findings. His fingers plucked feebly at the sheets as I spoke. His skin looked like paper, and his mouth was a bloodless line. But he smiled and nodded weakly as he listened to me.

"You got it almost exactly right," he whispered. "Does that conclude your involvement?"

"I guess so," I said.

"Good," he said. "Because now I want to hire you."

"To do what?"

"To get my wife out of jail."

I told him that wasn't as easy to do as it was to say. The state of New Mexico would probably be filing charges of attempted murder, or at the very least assault with a deadly weapon.

"No," he said softly, "not if I refuse to testify."

So, I was back on the Matsushita payroll, but this time the masculine side. I got out of there, thinking how unpredictable the reactions of people always are.

I went to the Criminal Division of the Las Cruces Police Department and advised them that Ken Matsushita was not going to file charges or testify against his wife, and that I proposed to take her before a magistrate and ask him to set bail.

The magistrate set the figure at $150,000, and I

volunteered to be the bondsman. I was told that as a
resident of the state of Texas, I was not acceptable.
The court wanted someone who had property in New
Mexico. I shrugged and told the judge that I owned
property in the state valued well in excess of the required amount and that I was prepared to offer it as
collateral. I signed the papers, putting my Radium
Springs property on the line by doing it, but I knew
that Ken Matsushita was an honorable man.

It was nearly midnight by the time I got Mrs. Matsushita out of there, explained everything and drove
her back to the house. When we got back the place
was dark and empty. She asked me to go in with her
because she was afraid to be in the house all alone. I
went in because there was still one loose end I wanted
to tie up. Helen Matsushita asked me if I would like
to stay the night. The tone of her voice was such that
I knew she didn't mean in the guest house.

"I'd rather know what you did with the gun," I said.

She said she would tell me if I would agree to stay.
Now I had been on the go almost continuously for
nineteen very eventful hours. I hadn't eaten and I
hadn't shaved and my clothes felt as if a bear had slept
in them. What I needed like a hole in the head at 1
A.M. was a romantic pass from a lonely and confused
woman, even one as undeniably beautiful as Helen
Matsushita. I told her I was heading back for El Paso
just as soon as she got the gun with which she'd tried
to kill her husband.

"What's the matter with me?" she said. "I'm pretty,
aren't I?"

I told her she certainly was, and I didn't have to lie
about it. I also repeated that as soon as she went and
got the gun, I was heading home. She looked at me for
a long moment, and then nodded.

"In the cellar," she said. She led the way down to
the car room and went straight across to a striker
switchbox on the wall. She unscrewed one screw and
took off the plate. There in the corner lay a .32 Brown-

ing automatic. I sniffed the barrel. It still stank of cordite.

"I'll take this along," I said.

"You're going?"

"You bet."

"Wait!" Helen Matsushita said, imperiously, "I'll hire you to protect me!"

"From what?" I said.

"Anyone," she said. "Anything that could happen. You never know."

I knew, all right, and I wasn't playing.

"Just lock all the doors," I said. "You'll be all right. It's already nearly morning."

"If you leave," she said, and her voice started up the scale, tense and shrill, "I'll kill myself!"

"No, you won't," I said. "You've got too much to live for."

I got out of there as fast as I could, and climbed into the Stingray, pushing her as fast as I could south toward home, and reflecting on how little gratitude there was in the woman. She had taken a lover, thrown her husband's money away, put five bullets into him and left him for dead in a dusty field, and he had forgiven her. Another man would have nothing on his mind but revenge, but Ken Matsushita had automatically, almost instinctively, sought to protect and defend his wife by hiring me to get her off the hook. And how did she repay all this forgiveness? By trying to get me to go to bed with her. I was glad to be away from there.

I realized now that I was dog tired. The car seemed to be thundering down an endless tunnel, and my eyeballs felt as if someone had been sandpapering them. I was just south of Mesquite when the car phone shrilled. It was my office in El Paso, asking my ten-twenty.

I gave them my location. They patched me through to the Las Cruces police, who had called to say that Mrs. Matsushita had just shot herself, and had been taken to the same hospital as the one her husband was in.

I allowed myself just one huge sigh of exasperation as I swung the car around and headed back. When I got to the hospital, they told me Mrs. Matsushita was in surgery. Shaking their heads, the medics said she'd tried to commit suicide by pressing a shotgun against her side and pulling the trigger. She was in a hell of a mess—but she was alive.

I was there all night.

The following morning, Helen Matsushita regained consciousness and told the police that she had shot herself after I left, and that she wouldn't have done it if I had stayed as she asked me to. That let me off the hook, and I went in to see the old man and tell him what had happened. He took it all calmly, the way some men take the news that everything they own has been wiped out in a disaster. He asked me to stay on the case until the charges against his wife were dropped, which I did. In the course of doing so, I tracked down that $20,000 check, the one that had started the whole chain of events. It had been used to buy a racehorse at Sunland Park down in Anapra, and the title for that expensive animal was in the name of the football player. There wasn't a damned thing I could do but tell the old man.

I wish I could tell you that after her release, Helen and Ken Matsushita were reconciled and lived happily ever after, but it wouldn't be true. They separated and were later divorced. He could forgive her for trying to kill him, but not for betraying him.

11.

Each morning around 4 A.M. the flat Hitachi speaker beneath Jay Armes' pillow emits its preset alarm signal, and he begins his twenty-hour day. Donning a karate gi—the sailcloth exercise suit of the expert—he pads through the house to the mirrored gymnasium on the second floor, designed and installed at a cost of $90,000, and containing every conceivable kind of keep-fit machine. Vaulting horses, padded mats, a hanging body bag, a rowing machine, barbells, and neatly-stacked circular weights—name it, it's there. For a solid hour, Armes works out like a dedicated Olympic hopeful—karate exercises, weights, eighteen hundred pushups. Yes, eighteen hundred! Those steel hooks and the metal prosthesis have given him a strength in his arms unlike that of ordinary men. With those hooks Armes can apply a pressure of thirty-eight pounds per square inch—three times as much as a man with normal hands.

After the workout he has a sauna in the lavishly fitted steam room he himself designed. Then, fresh and spruce, he may dictate some case notes on the portable machine, carrying it around with him as he moves, perhaps urging the use of a type of stationery he has perfected which is soluble in water and can be drunk without after-effects, or proposing that another subject be reported on in the special code he has invented.

Now down the curving ramp and into the subterranean shooting range, where he works out for another hour, using all kinds of weapons. Today he is firing a

9mm gun used by the German and Dutch armies and other military and police. After that he picks up his own snubnose .38, and fires from kneeling, standing and prone positions. Then he programs the computer by punching at the buttons with his eyes shut, so he won't know which way the targets will come at him. He shoots very fast, very accurately. He grins. One of the advantages of steel hooks is that you don't get sweaty palms.

Finally he practices a few times with the .22 magnum built into his right prosthesis, and then he reloads the .38 and puts it on one side to pick up on his way out. He hauls in his riddled targets and marks them with chalk rings so that tomorrow's hits will be easier to spot. He does not wear the earmuffs hanging from a hook in each shooting position; they are there for any visitor who may have what the shooters call "soft ears."

Armes takes off his shooting suit—tailored in exactly the same style as his ordinary workday clothes, but treated to resist the grease and oil endemic to a shooting range—and showers and shaves. Then he selects a suit from the electrically operated rack in the dressing room, lays it aside, presses another button and watches the shoes go by as on a conveyor belt until he sees the pair he wants. The dressing room is packed with custom-made shirts, ties, shoes, suits. All the shirts are monogrammed. Armes will not wear the suit he wears today for another year.

When he has dressed, he joins his family downstairs for breakfast. He eats a high-protein cereal, no coffee. Then he gets ready to go to work.

First he checks the .38 snubnose again. He slides it into the no-bulge holster placed in his waistband for a smooth, fast cross-draw. He checks out the .22 magnum and also the special equipment in the other prosthesis—no one, except him and the team that put it there, knows what it is. Armes won't even discuss it: because one day it might be needed to save his life.

Then he uses the house intercom to tell Joe Dark Eagle Breedlove to bring around the big black limousine. The huge metal gates swing ponderously back and Jay J. Armes is on the move. Ahead of him is the fat bundle of mail from all over the world that Joyce Peterson will have sorted into three piles on the desk: must-see, take-a-look, and only-if-you-want-to. There will be folders with reports from the hundreds of agents he has out in the field at any given moment. There will be a pile of question-and-answer papers from students in The Investigators Training Academy.

"I'm not trying to break records or prove anything," he says. *"I'm just trying to get everything out of life that it can possibly produce. The more I draw on myself, the more I find I have left."*

Mail and urgent matters taken care of, he now works his way through the long list of messages, neatly annotated by Joyce with time of call, name of caller and a return number. They come in all shapes and sizes, ranging from a request for polygraph tests— Armes, of course, has his own machine—on some restaurant employees suspected of dealing in pilferage, to a full-scale international investigation. Armes won't see his wife and children until at least seven, and if anything comes up, perhaps not for twenty-four hours or a week or six weeks. They never know what the next day is going to bring. Linda, a handsome woman who somehow manages the far from easy job of running Jay J. Armes' domestic life so that he doesn't have to give it a second thought, seems to accept this uneven life-style philosophically.

Linda's Chinese name is On Ting. She was the youngest child in a Chinese family of eight kids. Her parents brought them all up in the old-country way. They were, of course, allowed to have friends at school from outside the race, but not dates, no kind of permanent relationship with anyone but another Chinese. Marriages for the older girls were arranged by the parents. That was the way things were—and still are—in a great many Chinese families.

Mr. Chew owned a supermarket not far from where we now live. Still does, come to that. All his children helped out in the store, as soon as they were out of school. He believed in starting them young.

Once in a while he'd ask my advice. The biggest bane of the small storekeeper is the bad-check merchant. Usually, the businessman has little or no redress. If it's a small amount, the collection agencies don't even bother to try and get the money. If it's larger, they'll try, and keep 50 percent as a fee if they recover. If not, not. Any way you cut it, the storekeeper loses blood.

I'd help out where I could, but that was in the days before I had organized the Hot Check Detail of The Investigators, and most of my help was confined to making sympathetic noises. Once in a while I would see Linda at the store, and I got talking to her as well. When we got to know each other better, I asked her for a date, and she told me about the family rule. I told her that kind of thing went out with bustles and smelling salts, but she just smiled.

"You've convinced me," she said. "Now go convince my father."

I grinned and told her the motto of The Investigators: the impossible we do right away. Miracles take a little longer.

"Well, a miracle's about what it would take." She smiled.

"I'll just have to rear back and pass one," I replied. She couldn't know that I was (and am) a firm believer in miracles. They take a great deal of hard work and more than a little time, but they can be made to happen. The more I got to know Linda, the more I came to believe that this was one miracle I was going to make happen.

One night I went into the store and Mr. Chew was at the counter. He came over and told me that he'd

taken a real bad one that day. A man had come into the
store and bought about $100 worth of food, endorsing
his paycheck over and taking another $250 in change.
The check was solid rubber, and Mr. Chew was out
$350 and very sore about it.

"He was a soldier," Linda told me. It was she who
had cashed the 'paycheck.' "He showed me Army ID."

"You want me to try and find him?" I asked the old
man.

"Of course. I want you to find him if you can," Mr.
Chew said, testily. "Where will you start?"

"Fort Bliss," I said.

"Take Linda with you," Mr. Chew said unexpectedly. "She can identify this thief."

We get a lot of military in El Paso. Nearby are
Biggs Air Force Base, the Fort Bliss Military Reservation, Holloman Air Research and Development Center, and, not far away, the White Sands missile range
and atomic research establishment. Fort Bliss itself
dates back to 1868. It was established on the El Paso–
San Antonio road about three miles northeast of town,
and consisted originally of five rented adobe buildings.
These palatial quarters housed about a hundred troop-
ers, their officers, laundresses and horses. There was
also a schoolhouse and a hospital. Today tourists are
taken to visit a replica of the old fort (no trace of the
original one remains). The real military business at
new Fort Bliss is on a somewhat bigger scale than it
was a hundred years ago.

Linda and I drove up there. She was still surprised
that her father had permitted her to go out with me
at all. I said at least it was a step in the right direction.
Linda just smiled.

The provost-marshal listened attentively to Linda's
story, and from her description surmised that it was
the same man they were looking for themselves on
another, similar complaint. He pulled out a dossier,
and showed us a photograph of the man, a discharged
SP/5 named Chris Robertson. The provost-marshal

had been to the man's last known address but he was no longer there, and they hadn't been able to track him down, although they'd been looking for him since early May. It was now late July, so their APB wasn't getting any results you would have noticed. The provost-marshal promised to let me know if they turned him up. Some hope, I thought, and drove Linda back to Ysleta.

I guess every young man wants to shine in the eyes of the girl he loves, and I was no exception. I promised her that I would run that check bouncer down and get the money back, and then I went out and did it—in twenty hours flat.

The difference between the official methods of investigation and my own is mainly a matter of time, energy and, most of all, inclination. The average policeman is naturally as anxious as you that thieves be caught, criminals trapped, murderers sent to prison, but he is a civil servant and he gets paid if none of this happens. If your burglar or bad-check merchant slips through his fingers, *tant pis*. You can't win 'em all, he'll shrug, and move on to the next case in his book. He's got too much work anyway, as he'll happily tell you for hours if you've got the time to listen.

Me, I concentrate on amassing the information my client needs and is paying for. In this particular case, it wasn't money that drove me, but the desire to erase the worried lines from sweet Linda's forehead. I went to the last known address for Chris Robertson and began a neighborhood survey. The survey turned up the name of a pal of his who worked at a garage downtown. The friend at the garage told me Chris was living in a trailer court off post, and I went down there and camped on his doorstep until he came home. I showed him my credentials and told him who I was. I told him what I wanted, and said he should get into the car.

"What?" he said. "Are you nuts or something?"

"You talk to me," I said, "or you talk to the military police. I don't much care which."

"What the hell are you trying to pull here, mister?" he squawked. "I'm a citizen, I got rights, you can't—"

"Fish or cut bait, Robertson," I snapped. "You're stalling and you know it!"

He was and he did. All the starch went out of him and he said he'd rather talk to me than to the police—especially the military police. I put the car in gear and drove over to the Chew store. Linda's eyes were wide and surprised when I marched Robertson in, as if she'd seen me turn a pumpkin into a golden coach.

"This him?" I asked her.

"That's him," she said, and ran to call her father. Robertson looked like he wished the ground would open up and swallow him.

"Look," he told Mr. Chew. "I've got a couple of hundred. I'll pay you back the rest when I get it."

I told him he had to make good a check for $350, and that the provost-marshal up at the reservation had another, so a couple of hundred wasn't going to cut it. Robertson turned his pockets out and put every cent in them on the counter. It came to just under $180. Then I took him back to the trailer court, and he pulled a tin cash box out from beneath the bed. I don't know how much was in there, didn't care. He gave me another $170 and I left. About a hundred yards down the highway I stopped at a phone booth and told the provost-marshal where they could find Robertson. One good turn deserves another, but you have to get them in the right order.

Mr. Chew was most impressed and wanted to pay me for my time. I told him to forget it, he could do me a favor some time. He didn't know yet what the favor was going to be, but it was going to be a big one, because I had decided to ask Linda to marry me. I won't pretend to be a plaster saint. I've kicked around the world, and met a lot of attractive women. Linda was different from any of them, sweet, shy, warm, understanding. A few months later, when her parents were away visiting relatives in San Francisco, I cajoled her into having dinner with me. After they came back, we resorted to subterfuge so we could go on seeing each other. Eventually, of course, the inevitable happened. Someone who had seen us together mentioned it casually to Linda's father, and it hit the fan.

He forbade her to see me again. He contacted a sister in San Francisco and made arrangements to send Linda to live there, so there would be no more of this foolish talk of marrying me. Linda looked to her brothers and sisters for support but they were, if anything, more traditionally minded than she. In the end, Linda dug in her heels, and when my Linda digs in her heels you can expect fireworks. She told her parents that they either accepted their new son-in-law-to-be or —they lost a daughter. To her great misery they turned their faces from her. They told her that as far as they were concerned, they no longer had a daughter named On Ting. And she no longer had parents.

Linda and I were married without the blessing of her parents, and it was a sadder occasion because of that. Just the same, I didn't give up hope. I used to make jokes, tell her that her father still owed me a favor, one day he'd have to stump up, things like that. I don't know why, but I always felt sure it would come good, and gradually, over the years that we've been married, it has. Our children broke the ice, and it stayed broken. Nowadays, the kids chatter away like starlings in Chinese, and they've developed a new interest. Linda has a Portuguese nurse to look after Tracy, the baby, and the boys have already learned a lot of Portuguese from her—as has Linda. You know what they're doing? They're teaching it to old Mr. Chew. He may yet become the first Chinaman to sing *fado*.

12.

Most private investigators today work for somone else. There are innumerable small agencies, known in the trade as "mom and pop" outfits, but these do not generate the power of the big corporations. *Standard & Poor*'s lists twenty-one corporations whose main function is the provision of private investigation services, generating a gross income of well over $800 million and employing more than 110,000 people. Their most demanded services are in the field of security, although they also handle a lot of industrial espionage and counterespionage, electronic protection and vast amounts of credit checking. In addition to all these, there are, of course, the many more hundreds of insurance investigators and adjustors who are not listed as private investigators, but whose functions often overlap that field. So you see, there's plenty of competition, although I don't think too many of them work the way I do, or stick out their necks quite so far so often. I have the bullet scars to prove my contention.

I got the one that nearly killed me on a case I really didn't want. I was retained by a woman I didn't like to bring back a runaway I knew was a loser, and when you get into that kind of situation, you ought not to be surprised when it goes bad. All that notwithstanding, it's still a surprise to take a bullet in the chest, and no pleasure to be that close to a personalized toe-ticket and single-occupancy marble slab in the city morgue.

With runaways everyone loses. Parents call me all the time and ask me to locate their kidnapped child, and when I conduct my preliminary interrogation I discover in short order that no kidnap is involved—the youngster has simply run away. Boys often decide to take off just for the hell of it, seeking adventure, new sights, a new part of the country—or some other country. The girls are more likely to have run away with a boyfriend whom the parents disapproved of or did not know, and you find them closed up in some apartment, playing Mr. and Mrs. Parents often don't want to admit that their children have run away from home, and prefer to pay investigators good money to solve a "kidnapping" case rather than face neighborhood gossip. If I am asked to take on a "kidnapping" case that turns out to be a straightforward runaway, I usually turn it down. It's a waste of time. You bring them back, and the first chance they get, they run away again.

So when Marian Miller phoned me from San Francisco and told me she wanted me to locate her kidnapped daughter, I asked her the same questions I always ask. My evaluation of the case, based on her answers, was that this was no kidnapping, but a straightforward runaway; and I said so. She said she wanted me to look into it anyway, and I reluctantly agreed—mostly because a good friend of mine, Dick Gould, was with the Millers and asked me to take on the case. I told them I'd get out to the Coast as fast as I could.

The Millers were a very wealthy family; he was the chairman of a large electronics company, and she a leading social light in the city, a member of just about every preservation society and do-good committee extant. The Millers were ultrasnob. They skied only in Europe, drove only Mercedes cars, drank only imported wines. They read all the novelists approved by *The New York Review of Books,* liked Ingmar Bergman movies, had annual subscriptions to the opera and the symphony and were personal friends of Mayor Alioto and Governor Reagan. They lived in a beautiful mansion high on a hill above Sausalito, across the bay from the city and looking out toward Angel Island and

Tiburon. Mrs. Miller received me in an airy high-ceilinged drawing room full of antique furniture and what
looked like a Mondrian on the wall above the ornate
marble fireplace. She was about forty, a tall, slender,
handsome woman who could have stood in for Cather-
ine Deneuve in the Chanel ads. Her manner was assured and self-possessed. She was polite but somewhat
distant with me, employing that slightly-down-the-nose
stare that leaves you in no doubt that you are hired
help. In the world of the Marian Millers, there are
only two kinds of people: those like oneself, and the
hired help. I decided, for Dick Gould's sake, not to
find this offensive; but I had to chew on it quite a
while before I could swallow it.

We talked about Caroline's disappearance, the facts
of which were fairly straightforward. She had been
hanging around a disco in the city, grooving on the
musicians. When they had moved on, so had the girl.
I doubted that Mrs. Miller knew the word "groupie"
or that she'd appreciate it being used in connection
with her fifteen-year-old daughter even if she did, but
that was what Caroline sounded like. I explained to
Mrs. Miller that there was really no evidence of kidnapping. The most that the musicians could be accused
of was technical abduction, or, possibly, contributing
to the delinquency of a minor. And first, they had to
be caught doing it.

"I understand that," Mrs. Miller said frigidly, as
through I had challenged her intelligence. "I still do
not relish the thought of my daughter being involved
with those hippies." She said the word as if it were the
foulest one in her lexicon. She said she wanted me to
get started right away and bring Caroline home, and to
use whatever force was necessary to do so. Her eyes
glinted with malice and I made a mental note not to
get on her wrong side.

Sausalito is a pretty place, but whatever charm it
had in the days when it was a little fishing village
across the bay from the big city has long since been

buried beneath a welter of yachting marinas and cutesy-pie boutiques selling overpriced junk to the tourists. I had a couple of contacts, however. One was a guy who tended bar in a place called Ports O'Call. He steered me the right way, and I started my neighborhod survey on Caroline Miller. It took me from Sausalito to Berkeley, from Berkeley to North Beach, and from North Beach back to the city, and what it revealed was that Caroline Miller was running wild. The crowd she was with was into booze, pot, speed, anything that produced "kicks." The disco they frequented was called The Sands, and it stood on one of the sleazier blocks of Columbus Avenue. Caroline Miller's special boyfriend, I was told, was called Buzz, a drummer who played with a group called Independence Rock.

I eventually discovered from one of the musicians playing at The Sands that Buzz had a pad in Los Angeles, an apartment house off Hollywood Boulevard. It figured.

"He's anywhere except on the road, man, he'll be there," my new-found friend told me. During the twenty minutes we'd been talking in the club, he had hit me up for six straight bourbons. I signaled for a seventh, and he nodded, as if all I'd done was to anticipate his own intention.

"Like as not Caro will be there with him," he said. "She just grooves on Buzz. Swinger, that's what."

"Caro?"

"Yeah, man. She really swings, y'know?"

He leered in case I was in any doubt. I paid the check and got out of there. The diesel fumes from a nearby bus smelled almost sweet after the atmosphere inside. I checked in at the airport and flew down to Los Angeles. A taxi driver took me to the address on North Gower and on the way told me how much money he owed and what lousy pay he got pushing a hack. I agreed that times were hard but I didn't give him the big tip he was hoping for. His cab was filthy and I was glad to get out of it.

The apartment house on Gower was run down. It looked like it might have seen better days around 1935. Paint peeled from the corridor walls, and the floors were gritty with unbrushed dirt. There was that tenement smell of dirty washing and uncollected garbage and cats. If anyone ever asks you what happened to Hollywood, tell them to go to the Hollywood Boulevard area and look around.

I banged on the door of the second-floor apartment. The door opened and a barefoot bearded man in a dirty Levi shirt and jeans glared at me. I could see right past him into the apartment. Caroline Miller was sprawled on the bed smoking a cigarette. The smell told me it wasn't a Virginia Slim.

"I'm looking for Kitty Sansome," I said. "She live here?"

"No!" the man snapped, and slammed the door in my face. So much for the subtle approach. I hammered on the door again. The same man jerked it open, but this time I found myself staring down the barrel of a .22 Marlin repeater. It's not a big rifle, but its slug can ruin your digestion. I reacted without even thinking about it, smashing the beared man across the side of the head with my right hook. He slammed against the wall and bounced forward into my left jab that doubled him over, the carbine clattering to the floor. I chopped him down with another right and went over his sprawled body into the room, grabbing Caroline Miller by the right arm and dragging her toward the door. She started to scream bloody murder, and I shouted at her to stop, waving my ID in front of her befuddled gaze. I could have been showing her the top of a Wheaties box for all the difference it made. She screamed some more, and the bedroom door burst open. Through it came a second man, also bearded, but really big, around six foot and built like a heavyweight boxer. His hand was full of gun.

I saw it was a snubnose revolver, but that was all I had time for because he saw me and pulled the trigger. The pistol made that strange, flat, loud, boxed-in sound

guns always make in an enclosed space, and I felt
something like a big sting in my chest, as if I had been
stung hard by a wasp. The force of the slug slammed
me against the wall and down beside the bed, probably saving my life. The big man couldn't get in an
immediate second shot, but he was lining up for one
when my mind cleared. All this seemed to take no
longer than two heartbeats, but I knew without any
doubt that he intended to kill me. I had no choice. I
lifted my arm and fired the .22 magnum hidden in the
hook.

The big man went over backward as if some invisible giant had swatted him with a bat. He was killed
instantaneously, the bullet going right between his
eyes. The other man was groaning on the floor. There
were loud voices outside in the hall, hammering fists
pounding on the door as people demanded to know
what was going on. There was no telephone in the
apartment, so I opened the door and told the nearest
of the pop-eyed neighbors to go call the police. Then I
closed it again and waited for the law to arrive. I had
no fear of repercussions. I was a law-enforcement officer and I had been forced to kill in self-defense. But
taking the life of another man is an enormously trau-
matizing experience. TV shows make it seem commonplace, an everyday event in the life of a law-enforcement
officer, but it is not. When it happens you have to make
a whole new set of adjustments to who you are and
what you do. You have to learn to live with the fact
that you have ended the life of another human being,
no matter what the justification. It is not and never
will be easy.

After the police had moved in and taken statements
from me and the girl, I told them I would like to get
out of there and take her home to San Francisco. The
power of attorney given me by her parents was sufficient legal grounds for my doing so, and we were
allowed to leave with the provision that we hold ourselves available for the court of inquiry looking into

the killing. The medical examiner took a look at the hole in my chest and told me I ought to get to hospital and have a checkup, but it wasn't really bothering me so I told him I would get it done in San Francisco after I took the girl home. He shrugged, and gave me one of those "don't blame me" looks.

We got a ride to the airport in a police car, and a charter plane was standing by at my request to fly us up to San Francisco. Caroline Miller was anything but grateful to me or anyone else for this red-carpet treatment. She had already told me several times what she thought of me, and every time I tried to ask her a question, she told me again. Expurgated, it was to the effect that I was a louse, who had killed her friend Charlie. I was a dirty sneaking paid "pimp" sent by her unmentionable mother and inexpressible father to get her lover Buzz busted for contributing to the delinquency of a minor, possession of drugs, unlicensed firearms and various other peccadilloes that would ensure his staying in a penitentiary for a long, long time. She told me there was a name for people like me and she told me what it was. She said that since I was so interested she would tell me what she had been doing at the apartment, and told me in very graphic detail. Sweet little fifteen-year-old doll, that was Caroline Miller.

A few hours later, she was reunited with her frozen-faced mother. There were no hugs, no kisses, no tears. Caroline was sullen and unresponsive, and her parents had no intention of revealing their feelings while I was present. So I excused myself, which was no great effort, and headed back across the Golden Gate Bridge. Frankly, I wasn't in much of a mood to appreciate the beauty of the view. My head was pounding, and my throat felt dry and sore. I knew I was feverish, because once in a while long, racking shivers would course through my body. I stopped off at a phone booth on the Embarcadero and called 552-2155, the number of the FBI. A pal of mine, Gus Jorgenson, is an agent, and he phoned ahead for a specialist at the City and County Hospital to be standing by when I arrived.

I wasn't in the place more than three minutes before they had me scheduled for immediate surgery. I argued with the doctor, telling him I felt fine, just a little feverish. I told him I really didn't have the time to go into hospital unless it was absolutely vital.

"If you think having a bullet less than an inch from your heart isn't vital, fine," he said. "Go catch your plane and enjoy the last twenty-four hours of your life."

I was still trying to think of a good retort to that one when the anesthetic took effect. I simply had had no idea that the shot I'd taken was that dangerous. It had hit me high on the chest, to the left. There was hardly any pain. I'd traveled all the way to San Francisco, happily ignorant of the fact that the bullet had glanced off a bone and ranged downward, lodging within an inch of my heart.

They took the bullet out without complications, and twelve days later I was back in business, as good as new (almost). The Miller caper had nearly cost me my life, and I didn't have a great deal of hope for Caroline's conversion. First chance she got, she'd hit the road again, but that wasn't my problem; that one was for her parents to work out. I charged them the same fee I charge everyone else. You don't get extra for bullet holes.

13.

It's very satisfying to get into a caper and crack it open very fast, but you don't always get the breaks. The Calhoun case is a good example. It ought not even to be called a case, really, because it never got that far. It was the only time in my life that I found myself with a debt to a dead man.

It started with an evening phone call from a friend of mine, Ted Garritty, who is a special prosecutor on the staff of the district attorney of Albuquerque, New Mexico. Prior to holding public office, Ted had run his own law firm and I'd done a lot of work for him. He told me that he had a problem, and the problem was a man called Calhoun.

"Jay, I just can't figure this guy out," he confessed. "He might be nuts, he might be on the level. Either way, he keeps coming into my office with weird stories that someone is going to assassinate him."

I asked Ted what he wanted me to do. He told me that his office was powerless to act unless some attempt had actually been made upon the man's life. This is something that people often overlook about the work of a private investigator. Unlike the police, he can enter a case at any time or on any level. He is not bound, as they are, by city, county and federal restrictions, nor does he have to wait until a crime has actually been committed. In many cases, a good private investigator can forestall the execution of a crime, and Ted knew this. He told me he'd suggested to Calhoun that he contact The Investigators in El Paso, and that I'd probably be hearing from him shortly.

"Let me know what you think after you talk with him," Ted said.

"You think he's for real?" I said.

"Damned if I know," Ted said. "Use your own judgment."

About midmorning of the following day, Joyce buzzed me to say I had a call from a Mr. Calhoun in Albuquerque. I told her to put him on.

"Mr. Armes?" he said without preamble. "You know they're trying to kill me?" He said it the way you might say, do you know what day it is today?

I asked him who "they" were.

"That's what I want you to find out," he said. "I want you to find out who they are and keep them from me."

He might be genuine, I thought. He might also be as crazy as a bedbug. The kooks are often very convincing because they really do believe that the CIA has bugged their phone or the Russians are shadowing them or the FBI is recording their every movement or the Mafia has marked them for a hit. They are usually harmless, but you wouldn't want to spend your life trying to find their nonexistent bogeymen. I have a good test for the freaks.

"Where are you now, Mr. Calhoun?" I asked.

"In a phone booth near my home," he said. "I don't have a phone."

That meant he wasn't one of those telephone nuts who spend all day on the horn telling people that their receivers are hooked up to some unspecified listening post where everything is being recorded. I asked him if he could come down to see me in El Paso, because if I was going to take his case I would need a lot more information, would want to go over his life. I told him that what I'd like to have him do between now and tomorrow was to think of anyone who might have a grudge against him, or any reason for wanting to kill him. He said there was no one, no one at all.

I got him to tell me a little about himself. He told

me he was thirty-six, married, with two children, a girl sixteen and a boy thirteen. He had a steady job as a machinist, earned good money, seven-fifty an hour. His wife did not work.

I asked him what his outside interests were, and he said he had none. He didn't go to bars, bowling alleys, anywhere. He would go straight home from work, especially since his wife was often out, cook a meal, watch television, go to bed early.

I asked him if he was having any domestic problems, and he said no, unless you could count an argument with his wife over whether or not they should move to a farm about sixty miles from Albuquerque that had been left to him by his parents. He was a town dweller, and had no inclination to work a farm. His wife Josie was enamored of the idea, and they had quarreled—well, had had a heated argument, anyway —more than once about it. But that was all.

We ended our conversation and he said he'd be down to see me early the following day. I still wasn't quite sure about James Calhoun, or I would have gone up there to see him. My estimation of the situation was that if he were a phony, he wouldn't turn up the following day. Albuquerque is a long way to go wild-goose hunting.

The telephones of The Investigators are manned twenty-four hours a day, three hundred and sixty-five days a year. No matter where I may be, anywhere in the world, a call to that number can be relayed to me in minutes. At 1:30 that morning, I got a frantic call from James Calhoun.

"Mr. Armes," he said, and his voice was shrill with fear, "they're here! They're going to kill me right now!"

"Who?" I said. "Who's going to kill you?"

"They're parked across the street right now!" he said.

"*Who* is?" I shouted.

"It's them," he said.

"Where are you, Mr. Calhoun?"

"In the phone booth. Candelaria and Second, near my home. I was taking a walk when I saw them. I just ran in here to call you!" He had told me he lived on the north side of town, a couple of blocks off Second Street. My brain was racing. He was more than 250 miles away, and there was no way I could help him.

"Can you see the license plate of the car?" I said.

"No," he said. "What shall I do?"

"Can you see anyone, give me a description, anything?"

"No, Mr. Armes," he said. "I just know they're there. They're going to kill me!"

"Hang up!" I said. "Dial 911 and get the police. I'll try to get some help there!"

I had no option. I called Ted Garritty. He wasn't pleased about being awakened at 1:40 A.M.

"You remember that man Calhoun?" I said.

"Good God, Jay," he said. "Have you caught it, too?"

I knew what he meant. Calhoun had been telephoning Ted at all hours, in his office and at home. Now I was doing it. I just crossed my fingers—I mean hooks —and hoped Calhoun was for real. Otherwise I was going to look like the biggest chump in Christendom. Garritty said he'd check it out and call me back. It was about an hour before he did, and his voice was grave when he came on the line.

"We found him, Jay," he said. "He's dead."

Calhoun had started to call 911—the police emergency number—when he had been killed. The line was still open, the receiver dangling at the end of its cord. The phone booth was on an unlit corner not far from the AT&SF railroad tracks. Calhoun was lying half in and half out of the booth, shot through both the head and body. No trace of an assailant, no witnesses, nothing. Just another DOA for the morgue. Ted said he would contact the wife, and I told him to call me if there was any way I could help. After he hung up, I prowled around the house, unable to sleep. I blamed myself for believing that Calhoun had been some kind of nut, for not going up there and looking into his case as soon as he called me. Now he was dead in the street, and it made me angry. He had been blown away, callously and efficiently, and although he had not retained me, I decided to go up to Albuquerque and find out who had killed him.

My first stop was the police building on Marquette Avenue, between Third and Fourth streets. Ted Garritty's office turned over the autopsy report and the statement Calhoun had given to them when he had first come in with his strange story. The autopsy report was cold and brutal and short. Calhoun had been shot at close range with a .38 caliber gun. Death instantaneous, clues none. The statement was another matter, and it added sinister dimensions to what Calhoun had told me on the telephone.

He had told the police that on one occasion the brakes on his GMC '66 pickup had failed completely, and he had gone off the road. When he investigated the cause of the brake failure, he found that his brake lines had been cut. He also stated that he sometimes got violently ill with severe headaches after he ate meals at home cooked by his wife, although when he cooked for himself he did not. He said that he had seen his brothers-in-law following him, although when he confronted them they explained that it was just coincidence that they had met. He said that he feared for his life and requested police intervention. Action: none.

It gave me something to go on, at least. I put a team together and got them on the job of compiling a dossier on James Calhoun, with special emphasis upon his family life. We set to work questioning neighbors, co-workers, acquaintances, garage attendants, delivery-men, even the kids playing on the block. We checked out the records in the Bernalillo County Courthouse and the Municipal Building, and Calhoun's telephone company and bank records. When we were through, we had a background file that would have made the late J. Edgar Hoover green with envy. It told us everything there was to know about James Patrick Calhoun, born Duluth, Minnesota, June 22, 1935, who had been married on May 14, 1955, to Josephine Bradley, a good-looking local girl. He was well liked, a good worker, a regular saver with something like $8000 to his credit at the bank. He paid his bills on time, owned his car and had a $100,000 insurance policy with a double indemnity clause. It had been taken out three weeks before his murder and the beneficiary was his wife.

I put Josie Calhoun under round-the-clock surveillance. Two days later she left her house and went to a motel on Central Avenue where she spent several hours with a man. We checked out the lover, and found that they had been having an affair for several months. Armed with this information, I confronted Josie Calhoun and obtained a confession from her. She implicated her two brothers, one of whom was an ex-convict with a record from here to there. She and her lover had paid the two men to kill her husband, promising them $50,000 from the proceeds of the insurance policy. She said that Lolo had pulled the trigger, Lolo being the nickname of her older brother, Lawrence. The other one was called Theodore, Teddy. Both of them had taken off in a red Mustang for Los Angeles, where they planned to hole up until the insurance company paid out.

I handed the whole thing over to Ted Garritty: names, dates, addresses, everything. I knew I could rely on him to do the rest. He would swear out warrants for the two men, and bring in Josie Calhoun's lover. They were all party to cold-blooded murder, and they would all eventually pay the price for it. As for me, I was satisfied. I had paid my debt to a dead man and that was enough. I don't like loose ends one little bit.

14.

Since I paid my debt to the dead man I've never turned
away any caller, kook or not. It's worth putting up with
the sad souls who are simply crying out for attention
if, in doing so, I can prevent the death of another single person. However, by definition, accepting all calls
can sometimes leave you open to experiences you could
happily have struggled through life without. For one
thing, telephone calls can mask the identity of whoever
is hiring you, and even the check that I will usually run
on clients wanting anonymity can sometimes fail to
turn up any warning of impending danger.

One time I was retained by some people in Florida,
a legitimate business corporation working out of
Miami, with a good address on Biscayne Boulevard.
They wanted me to conduct round-the-clock surveillance on a subject in Chicago, and to report back,
daily, on where he went, whom he saw and, wherever
possible, what he said. They wanted me to understand
that they were retaining my personal services, and did
not want any other agents involved, no team, no associates, just me. The use of equipment and the expenses
I incurred were entirely up to me. In this matter,
money was absolutely no object. It seemed straightforward enough, and I agreed. They asked me where I
usually stayed in Chicago, and promised to have the
subject's photograph and other data waiting at my
hotel when I arrived, together with a cashier's check
to cover my retainer.

I made arrangements to fly to Chicago the following
day, and meanwhile used my own network to run a

rapid check on my clients. They came up smelling of roses, a diversified miniconglomerate with hotel, realty and offshore banking interests. Two of the firm's executive vice-presidents were also highly respected corporate lawyers.

Reassured, I flew to Chicago and checked in at the Regency Hyatt. I love to stay in Hyatt hotels, especially the ones that make you feel as if you have walked right into an M. C. Escher print. In a world where more and more hotels are like eggboxes for people, I treasure such individuality.

The envelope with the information I needed was waiting for me at the desk. There was no note, no salutation, not even a "with compliments" slip—just the photograph and data about the subject, Charles Salmi, who lived in an apartment on Lake Shore Drive, owned a Lincoln Continental, registration such-and-such. All perfectly straightforward and uncomplicated, and I got to work right away. Mr. Salmi was no trouble to find, but he was some trouble to stay behind. It was almost as if he expected to be followed, and took evasive action as a matter of course. Someone who suspects he is being followed can often shake his "tail" by going into a hotel lobby or a department store, losing himself momentarily in the crowd, and then leaving quickly by another exit. He can go into a movie theater, move around in the darkness, leave unexpectedly. He can hail a taxi, tell the man to drive like hell around the block, and almost be pulling up behind his pursuer just as the frantic man climbs into his own taxi and shouts "Follow that cab!" Professionals often wear reversible coats, and carry golf hats or caps rolled up in a pocket, so they can change their appearance in a pay toilet or men's room someplace. There are a thousand such tricks and the pro investigator knows most of them. I couldn't help wondering, first, how Mr. Salmi knew he was being followed, and second, if he didn't know, why he acted as if he did.

I soon found out. He was what people in the rackets call "connected," and I was hearing things on my parabellum microphone that were likely to qualify me for a cement overcoat. The only people who would be interested in knowing what Charles Salmi was up to were the federal government or people in the same line of business as himself. Which meant, no matter how clean they looked, that my clients were also "connected," and I was the patsy in the middle. I called Miami and told them I was dropping the case forthwith and mailing back their check and the dossier on Salmi by registered mail immediately. I never have and never will work for anyone I know to be involved in criminal activities, and even less will I let them maneuver me or my agents into doing their dirty work.

The man at the other end said he did not think that was either possible or advisable. He had a voice like someone tearing silk. He felt it incumbent upon him to remind me that I knew more than was good for me, and too much to back out at this stage. He was as polite as a Georgia lawyer.

"I've got a lousy memory," I said, "and I'm out. As of now."

"You won't reconsider?"

"Thanks, but no thanks," I said.

"I hope you won't regret your decision," Deep Throat said, and hung up. I shrugged and headed for the airport. If that had been a threat, it wasn't going to give me any sleepless nights. I've been threatened before. I wrote the trip off as a bad debt, and went about my business. Nothing happened to me. Nobody tried to shoot my head off or run me down with a combine harvester or any of those exciting things that happen to Joe Mannix every week as regularly as clockwork. Well . . . not for almost six weeks, anyway.

I got a call from a man named Walter Clare. He mentioned as a reference a former client of mine, and told me he would like to retain my services for some work in New Orleans. Once again, it was one of those occasions when only I would do—the client wanted the investigation handled by me and not by any of my agents, because of its confidential nature. In fact, it was so confidential that he did not want to discuss it on the phone except to say that it was a business investigation and involved the compilation of a comprehensive dossier on certain firms in and around the city. He asked me if I was prepared to fly out to meet him, and when I said yes, he told me to ask for him at the desk of the Royal Orleans in the French Quarter.

To tell the truth, I had been half-expecting a call like this, and yet on the face of it everything looked kosher. I decided to take the first step blind, and called Delta.

Next day I sauntered up Royal Street glancing in the windows of the antique shops, and arrived at the desk of the hotel right on time. I asked at the desk for Walter Clare, and the clerk told me that Mr. Clare had been called away but had left an envelope for me. In it, I found five one-hundred-dollar bills, all so new you could still smell the printing ink, and a note from Clare saying that he had been called urgently to Biloxi where his wife had suddenly fallen ill. Would I be kind enough to follow him there, and come to his home, the address of which was given, together with a telephone number.

By now, my intuition was starting to blip like the radar screen at Kennedy on a foggy day, so I spent the next half-hour making some telephone calls. Then I went over to the Budget office on Canal Street, rented a car, and headed up St. Bernard Avenue to the junction at Gentilly Boulevard that leads to US 90. Soon the city was behind me and I was driving along the Mississippi Sound, with the water off to my right gleaming in the sunlight as if someone had scattered it with millions of diamonds. I could see the white triangles of sailboats offshore, and once in a while a tanker or a freighter hull down on the horizon, en route to New Orleans.

Clare's given address was in a plush residential district, a nice-looking house with well-kept lawns and a double garage in which a Suzuki motorbike and a Dodge pickup were parked. There was one of those metal jockeys beside the front door, although it didn't look as if anyone had tied a horse to the ring he was holding for a long time. I rang the bell, and heard the Westminster chimes. A tall man opened the door, his face partially shadowed.

"Come in, Mr. Armes," he said, and stood back. I stepped over the threshold, ready for anything, my hand on the gun, which I had drawn from the holster and put into my jacket pocket. Nothing happened. The tall man, who I assumed was Clare, led the way into the lounge and I followed him. I never even smelled the guy who clobbered me but he must have hit me pretty hard. When I woke up I was at sea.

I felt the pitch and yaw of the boat, smelled the salt air and wondered if I was dreaming. My mouth felt as if someone had emptied a birdcage in it, and my head throbbed like an underground generator. I lifted my arm to move, and discovered that I was on the deck of a boat, shackled hand and foot with a steel chain that passed through a hasp in a metal collar fastened around my neck, wound around my arms and legs, and ended up fastened to a two-by-two-by-three block of solid concrete. Fragments of what had happened started to sift into my memory—it's amazing how you can recall the smallest details of such an ordeal afterward. I remembered being hit, and then nothing for a long time. I don't know what they knocked me out with, but whatever it was, it later took eight stitches to sew up the gash in my scalp. I had a vague memory of being dragged, feet trailing, across a concrete ramp, and then dumped on to something wooden and hard before I passed out again. I assumed now the something was the deck of the boat I was now on. I shifted so that I could see better. The sun was high in the sky: eleven o'clock, I judged. Had a day disappeared somewhere? It looked like it.

The boat was a big cabin cruiser, flush deck, about forty-odd feet, doubtless gas fueled. Custom-built by the look of her, with a flared bow and outriggers, but she had that look of careless ownership that anyone who loves boats hates to see: milky varnish, pitted chrome, bird droppings on the woodwork, frayed lines. There was no sign of my captors, but I could hear voices somewhere, and I told myself I was liable to be turned into shark bait in about five minutes if all my projections didn't intersect exactly as I'd planned them. Funny, I wasn't even perturbed, because it was all out of my hands. Either my plan would work or it wouldn't. If it didn't, I'd be dead, and that would be that. I remember distinctly that one part of my brain seemed to be saying why bother, give it up, let it happen. It was as if two parts of me were warring with each other, the will to live and the apathetic inclination to surrender.

Then the helicopter roared overhead. I was never so glad to see my agents in my life. Their call to surrender over the loudspeaker was sweeter music than ever Schubert wrote, and I lay there and watched as two men came running up the steps, pistols in their hands, and then threw in the towel without firing a shot. They had no stomach for a fight when their own skins were on the line, and that's exactly the way it was: one of my agents was positioned in the open hatchway of the chopper, a .30 caliber carbine with wire stock ready to blast them if they so much as raised an angry voice.

My telephone calls from the Royal Orleans in New Orleans had all been of the "Red Alert" variety. From the moment I picked up the car on Canal Street until the moment my captors sailed the cruiser out of the slip at Biloxi, they and I had been under constant and concentrated surveillance, ground and air.

Neither we nor the Mississippi State Police could get a peep out of the two men we'd captured. They were like the three wise monkeys. They had seen nothing, heard nothing and said nothing. The house had been rented by someone using a name that turned out to be as false as the credentials he had shown. Dead end.

The two men turned out to be cheap crooks with records as long as a good man's arm and the judge had no hesitation in sending them up for attempted murder. I ordered a neighborhood survey just on the off chance that we could turn up something on the elusive Mr. Walter Clare, but we got nothing that led anywhere.

The moral of that story might be that an investigator should always check out his clients—but that isn't always practical, is usually unnecessary and is always expensive. Sometimes you wish you had, though. As in the case of Mrs. d'Arblay.

She lived up in Kern Place, the very best part of town, and she called me one Friday with a terrible tale.

"Mr. Armes," she said, "my little girl has been raped!"

She proceeded to make the story not just terrible, but bizarre, by telling me that her little girl was only two years old. The rape had taken place just a couple of hours ago, she said. I told her it was a criminal matter, and that she should immediately contact the Crimes Against the Person Bureau of the El Paso Police Department.

"I've already called them," she said. "They have a report. But when I spoke to the district attorney's office, they said that if anyone could prove who had done this awful thing it was you."

I said that it was very flattering of the DA's office to say nice things about me, but rape was a police matter and she didn't have to hire a very expensive investigator to do something they were supposed to do as their duty.

"Mr. Armes," she said, "I want you to come up here. I don't care about the money. I want whoever did this punished."

I thought she sounded pretty controlled considering the ordeal she was going through. I went over to her house. It was up on the prow of Franklin Mountain, with a sensational view across the river and all the way down to the Sierra Madre. A maid answered the door and ushered me into an elegantly furnished living room with a Steinway grand piano in one corner.

"Madame will be with you in one moment," she

said, and left me there wondering if perchance I'd wandered onto the set of a movie that was being made from a vaguely familiar script. Then Mrs. d'Arblay came in. She was about forty-five, her graying hair beautifully coiffed, her skin smooth, her figure good. She was wearing about $10,000 worth of jewelry and a perfume that wouldn't sell at much less than $70 an ounce. She looked about as upset as a melon.

"How nice of you to come so quickly," she said. Her voice had a strong French accent. She offered me something to drink, tea, coffee, and I refused, thinking "curiouser and curiouser." I told her I would prefer to get started right away and asked her to tell me exactly what had happened, leaving nothing out, no matter how unpleasant.

She told me that she was a widow, and had been preparing for a trip to France with her little girl the following week. Then this shocking thing had to happen.

"That monster!" she said. "He will have to pay for this!"

"Monster?" I said. "You mean you know who did it?"

"Of course," she replied, "and I wish you to prove him guilty. He has been harassing me for a long time and now he has done this just to damage me."

Even making allowances for her fractured English, Mrs. d'Arblay was making less sense with every word she spoke. I asked her where the little girl was, whether she had been taken to the hospital or what. She looked at me as if I was some new species of moron.

"*Mais non,* she is in her room," she said. "Come with me and I show you."

She led the way upstairs and I followed. Mrs. d'Arblay opened the door of a prettily decorated bedroom. The blinds were drawn, but I could see there was a four-poster bed in the room. I couldn't see any sign of a baby crib.

"There she is," Mrs. d'Arblay said. "There is my poor baby."

Entrance to the Armes compound. Note automatic gate mechanism in foreground. The fence surrounding the property carries a 20,000-volt charge. *(Fred Honig)*

ABOVE: Overhang supported by massive pillars shades the front of the house. Several automobiles are always in the driveway, ready for action. (*Fred Honig*)

LEFT: A guard checks one of the many closed-circuit television cameras which constantly scan all corners of the Armes property. (*Fred Honig*)

The rather unusual living room features a well-stocked bar at one end, many tables and leather armchairs, palm trees, and a stream running along its length. (*Fred Honig*)

I am an exercise freak and do a great number of pushups every morning. (*Tony Korody/Sygma*)

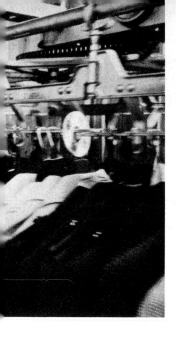

This closet—some would call it a room—contains 750 suits on a motorized, revolving rack.
(*Tony Korody/Sygma*)

Daily workouts with the punching bag, as well as karate, keep me in top shape. (*Tony Korody/Sygma*)

Here's how I solved the problem of having a waterfall on my lake. Two powerful pumps move 50,000 gallons per minute to the top of a 20-foot-high by 200-foot-long ramp from which torrents of water cascade into the lake. (*Fred Honig*)

My chimp Gypsy loves to grab hold of people to pull them through the bars of her cage. (*Fred Honig*)

One big, happy family. Here's my wife Linda with our friendly lion, Leo. (*J. J. Armes*)

You're never far from animals on my estate. Here is one of my zebras, which gets along very well with the pony in the back.

(Fred Honig)

My twin-rudder, 12-passenger helicopter in temporary storage. It will soon be stationed on the new landing field (foreground).

(Fred Honig)

This display case in my study contains some of the handguns connected with cases I have solved. Each gun was responsible for at least one death. (*Fred Honig*)

I don't spend too much time in my downtown office because I'm usually on the move. I have all the necessary facilities and equipment in my limousines, and I can be found most often in the back seat of one of these cars. (*Tony Korody/Sygma*)

ABOVE: I like the Corvette Stingray for its speed and maneuverability. Among its special features are a rear mounted closed-circuit TV camera, revolving license plates, and full-range communications equipment. (*Tony Korody/Sygma*) BELOW RIGHT: I make use of many items of specialized equipment, some of which, for obvious reasons, I can't discuss. Here, in my study at home, I'm adjusting an infra-red sniperscope which is useful for nighttime surveillance. (*Fred Honig*)

Quick on the draw, the special gun built into my right prosthesis is guaranteed to outdraw even Wyatt Earp. *(Tony Korody/Sygma)*
BELOW RIGHT: Here is the lethal-looking specially built shotgun that nearly took my life. It was rigged up below the steering wheel of my Corvette and was meant to put a sudden stop to my career. *(Fred Honig)*

Here I am on one of my capers wearing cosmetic hands and arms for disguise.

I also carry a police special, which I'm loading here prior to my daily target practice. (*Fred Honig*)

My underground target range has computer-programmed targets which can perform a vast variety of movements to sharpen my reflexes in coping with unexpected situations. (*Fred Honig*)

ABOVE: The Jay Armes-designed underground range contains the latest equipment and has been compared favorably with the most modern police ranges. BELOW: Three booths enable my assistants to practice along with me. (*Fred Honig*)

ABOVE: In addition to the three forward and backward moving targets shown, the range contains five pop-up figures and six pop-down targets that are controlled by the computer for random action. BELOW: Spent bullets are collected in the slanting racks at rear of range. (*Fred Honig*)

The Marlon Brando kidnapping caper was one of my more celebrated cases. ABOVE: Brando congratulates me after I had testified at the trial. BELOW: National television networks interviewed me about details of the case.

She drew back the canopy of the bed. On it lay a small black French poodle.

Well, Armes, I said to myself, you asked for it and you got it. Now that my eyes had adjusted to the gloom of the bedroom I could see that one wall was covered with certificates and silver-chased shields and rosettes and plaques testifying to the inordinate length and exclusivity of the poodle's pedigree. She was champion this and champion that, and one way and another, just about the most exclusive dog in the entire Southwest.

"My poor darling," Mrs. d'Arblay cooed to it, "debauched, *n'est'ce pas*? She is worth twenty-five thousand dollars you know," she said, turning to me. "And that beast next door, he has raped her!"

"There's a dog next door?" I ventured.

"Dog?" she said scornfully. "That mongrel brute a *dog*?"

There was no stopping her. She told me about the man next door, an attorney by profession, who had deliberately lifted his mongrel hound over the fence between the houses so that it could "rape" her beloved poodle. When she had complained to the police, they had been sympathetic but nothing more. She had then called the DA, who had told her that the only man who could help her was the world's greatest investigator, Jay Armes. Once in a while the boys down at the courthouse like to get one in at me, and once in a while I get in one of my own. Overall, the score is about even, but I had to admit they'd given me a good one this time.

"That man next door is a beast as well," she sniffed. "He not only helped his dog to rape my baby, he insulted me as well when I complained to him. He demeaned me, Mr. Armes!"

"Demeaned you?" I said. "How?"

"He told me it was a pity his dog didn't get to me as well," she said. I managed not to laugh until after I got out of her house.

15.

The calls never stop coming in, no matter where Jay Armes may be. He never knows what the next caper will involve. The wife of a very important Southern politician wants Armes to look into the background of the man who tried to assassinate her husband, because she is sure there was a coverup. She asks Armes to contrive a code for communicating with her, so that nobody will know she has retained him to investigate the murder attempt. A woman telephones while he is in his car on the way to his home, wanting to know if he can sell her a chimpanzee. He tries to talk her out of it, telling her that monkeys can be fun but they aren't babies. She persists and he says he will see what he can do. They want him to give a speech to the Kiwanis Club. He agrees and tells them to arrange the date with Joyce.

A business executive calls him long distance and asks him to undertake some industrial espionage. It transpires that what he wants Armes to do is find out what his competitors are bidding for a federal road-construction job; Armes won't touch it.

There is a call from the mayor's office. A woman in France has written to His Honor asking him to forward her request that Armes should contact her. Jay calls her immediately. She tells him that her son has been kidnapped, she thinks by her former husband. The police are doing nothing, the boy may have been taken out of the country, she does not know what to do, can he help her? Armes says that he will have

*someone with her in about forty-five minutes. She re-
minds him that she is in Paris, France, not Paris,
Texas. He gravely acknowledges that he knows that,
and asks her to call him back as soon as his agent ar-
rives. Forty minutes later she is on the telephone again,
her voice excited.*

*"I cannot believe it," she says. "When my son was
taken, it was twenty-four hours before the Police Judi-
ciare arrived from the city. You are on the other side
of the world, yet you have someone here within an
hour!"*

*"I work a little differently from the police, ma-
dame,"* he says.

Next, an attorney he knows calls. He is having
trouble with a client known to Armes. The client wants
to take the attorney off his case and appoint a new one
because he's afraid that the prosecuting attorney is too
hot for his man. They are halfway through the hearing, and the attorney says he doesn't know whether to
cry or spit. Armes tells him that the client has already
worked his way through half a dozen other attorneys
on this case, and right now there isn't one in town
who'd touch him with a ten-foot pole. He suggests the
attorney have his client call him, and he will talk to
him.

The client calls. Armes talks to him for maybe five
minutes and pulls no punches. The man takes Armes'
advice and says he'll stay with the present attorney.
The attorney calls back to say thanks, and Armes ad-
vises him on how to handle the case, suggesting he go
for a change of venue. How? The judge trying the case
was given his job by the present prosecuting attorney,
so the attorney should present a plea for change of
venue due to conflict of interest. The attorney says he
doesn't know what to say except thank you.

"Then say it and get off the line." Armes grins.
"You're costing me money."

A woman telephones him. She says she wants to
come and see him about the death of her husband, who

*was killed in an auto wreck. He says he will send a car
for her, asks where she is and how he will recognize
her. She says she is downtown at the Civic Center, she
is Oriental, wearing a brown coat and slacks. Joe Dark
Eagle Breedlove is sent to fetch her, and when she
comes into the office, she is very nervous, very edgy.
Slowly, haltingly, she tells him about her husband,
killed in a crash involving an Army truck. The police
reports state categorically that her husband went
through a stop sign and her lawyer has advised her that
the Army has no case to answer, but she is being
troubled by bad dreams. In these dreams, she finds her
husband, who never smoked, smoking pot. When she
asks him where he got it, he tells her he got it off his
friend, a soldier. He keeps bringing the soldier to the
house. It is the soldier who was driving the truck that
killed him. It is as though her subconscious is trying to
tell her that drugs were involved. Maybe the soldier
was a user, maybe the crash wasn't an accident, maybe
the famous Jay J. Armes could investigate it and come
up with the truth?*

*She has begun to cry as she talks, fingers plucking
nervously at the edges of the four-page police accident
report with its diagrams and measurements and chilling
details of injuries. She holds it as if it were a memento,
last tangible evidence of the fact that she had a husband whom she loved, whose children she bore and
whose death she has been unable to comprehend or
accept. There has to be a reason. "So'y," she keeps
saying, "so'y, so'y," sorry for crying, sorry, sorry.*

*Armes is all business. He tells her what such an in-
vestigation would cost and tells her to go home and
think it over. He also tells her that if she does not have
the money, she must not consider borrowing it or selling anything she owns to raise it. The little Oriental
woman with the work-worn hands sits there with her
head bowed, thinking of all that money, her fingers
still trembling. After a while she leaves; he will never
see or hear from her again.*

I honestly don't know how many there have been over the years like Mrs. Usami. I lost count a long time ago. I think they come in to see me because they have to talk to someone, someone they think may be able to effect the miracle of proving that people don't just die like chalk being wiped off a blackboard, needlessly and senselessly; even though, deep down, they know it happens all the time. They just can't accept the idea that it has happened to someone they love. I sympathize, believe me. I know a lot better than most people what it's like to look up at the sky and wonder if there is a God up there at all, and if there is, why he had to let what happened happen to me. But I have to be cruel to be kind. If I'm objective about their problems, they straighten up their shoulders—metaphorically speaking—and face reality. It's not easy for me. Many of the stories I sit and listen to are unbearably sad, but it isn't going to help anyone, least of all the client, if I sit down and bawl as well. The best way is to keep clear of any possible emotional entanglement. The "honest thief" caper is probably as good an example of the wisdom of my attitude as anything.

It began soon after an article about me had appeared in the magazine *Newsweek*. Late one night, the operator called my unlisted home number and said she had an emergency call from a Jeanette Black in New York City, and asked whether I wanted the call put through. I told her instead to get a number and I would call back.

The operator was only trying to be helpful, and it probably never occurred to her that the "emergency call" routine is one of the best ways there is of ascertaining an unlisted number. Armed with that, it's a short step to getting an address to go with it. Ask any movie star, any pop artist bedeviled by fans. In my case, the "fans" are liable to want my blood instead of my autograph, so I take extra precautions.

Using another telephone, I called the New York number through the call-back operator.

"You're very efficient, Mr. Armes," Jeanette Black said when she answered the phone. Her voice was cultured and well modulated.

"You said it was an emergency," I reminded her. "What's the trouble?"

She said that very simply it was that she was a thief. Not a dime-store shoplifter, but a thief on the grand scale. She told me she was also a fraud and a liar and a cheat and that she had gotten to the point where she was ready to take her own life, and had even bought a gun to do it. Then she happened to read the article about me in *Newsweek* and thought that there was just a faint chance that I could help her. She had started crying while she was talking.

"You're my last hope," she said. "Please don't turn me down."

I encouraged her to keep on talking, to tell me about herself. She revealed that although she practiced in Manhattan as a doctor, and had been doing so for almost nine years, she was a fraud. She hadn't even been to medical school. She told me she had two Mercedes cars in the driveway of her house in Connecticut, both stolen, and a private plane in a shed at La Guardia that did not belong to her. She had even obtained her pilot's license fraudulently.

I listened with growing amazement as she went on to say that she had purloined the deed to the building in which she rented an office, and used it as collateral to raise $150,000 from the bank with which to buy her house. There was a whole string of other frauds and embezzlements. They had netted her large amounts of money and valuables. She was simply unable to do anything honestly.

"I even conned you into paying for this call," she said. "It's just the way I am, Mr. Armes."

I told her the bad news. I had called back through Operator Six, and the hour-long conversation between New York and El Paso had been charged to her, not me. Charity begins at home, right?

"Oh, I knew I was right to call you," she said, as if delighted to have had the tables turned on her. "I'm so glad I did. I want you to help me give back everything I've stolen."

"You can do that yourself," I said. "You don't need me."

She demurred, saying she was frightened that she would make a slip and they would send her to prison. I told her that I would help her on one condition, and only one condition—that she implicitly obey my instructions, without questions, arguments, ifs, buts or maybes. She was not to challenge my judgment no matter what the circumstances.

She agreed instantly. I told her to get together every penny she possessed and put it into the form of a cashier's check. Then she was to get on a plane and bring it to El Paso, where I would take control of it. I sensed her hesitation and waited.

"It would be nearly sixty thousand dollars," she said. "I'm not sure . . ."

"No questions asked, remember?"

"All right," she said.

I instructed her to bring with her the records of any transactions she had made, anything with which we could document the people or firms she had swindled. She said there were so many, she could never remember all of them. I told her to do her best, and be in El Paso no later than Friday. Actually, there wasn't any need to bring her all the way down to Texas, but I wanted to be sure that she would do what I had told her to do.

Friday afternoon, she called me from El Paso International. She'd flown in her "own" plane, a twin-engined Beechcraft. I went out there to meet her, and found her to be a strikingly elegant woman in her early thirties, with raven hair and stunning blue eyes. I told her that I had booked her a room at the Plaza. I added that I had told them at the hotel that she would be paying in cash, in advance, in case she had to leave the hotel "unexpectedly."

"Mr. Armes," she said, "I think I'm going to like you."

I got her settled in, and told her the ground rules. No collect calls, no room service, nothing charged and no sending out. It was to be cash on the line from here on in. I was going to make her go straight even if it hurt.

Later on, we talked for a long time in the hotel lounge. She was wearing a lemon-yellow blouse and a Pucci suit that complemented her jet black hair. She drank a vermouth with ice, while I treated myself to a Coke.

"I'm a fraud, Mr. Armes," she confessed. "My whole life is like a charade played inside a nightmare. I'm thirty-two years old and everything is built on lies and deceit. I'm not even a woman in the true sense. I've never been to bed with a man. Other women, yes, but never a man."

"They can't hang you for that," I said, more to encourage her to go on talking than out of any interest, one way or another, in her private life. She told me that her parents had wanted her to go to medical school, but that she had used the fees to pay for the courses at a different kind of educational establishment—a swindler's school in New York.

"A what?" I said.

"A con artist's college," she said. "They teach you all the tricks: bunco, swindling, forgery, con tricks, the lot."

She told me the name of the place and where it was. It sounded like a very respectable address, and I wondered how the other occupants of that famous building would feel if they knew what was going on beneath or above them. I asked her how long she had gone there, and she told me four years. She had never attended one session of medical school, but had graduated top of her class at the other "college."

I tried to picture the graduation ceremonies at that

most unusual establishment, but my imagination wasn't up to that kind of stretch. You'd need a John Collier or a Ray Bradbury to do it justice. Jeanette Black was now telling me how she had established a residency at a big New York hospital on the Upper East Side, using fake diplomas obtained through her alma mater in midtown Manhattan. Then she had set up her own practice uptown with more. I asked her how she had managed to practice medicine for nine years without killing anyone.

"God knows," she said. "Luck, I guess."

The practice had grown quite large, and was very successful, she said. She had purchased some books, studied them: a Gray's *Anatomy,* Joan Gomez' *Dictionary of Symptoms,* medical encyclopedias, another book called *A Dictionary of Drugs.* When in doubt with a patient, she would excuse herself for a moment, check the symptoms in one book and the appropriate drugs in the other, come back with the correct terminology and diagnose accordingly. She said it seemed to work, and there had never been any complaints.

In a lot of cases where patients complained of vague pains, she would prescribe diuretics. Diuretics induce polyuria, the frequent passing of urine, which in turn creates dehydration. The pills were labeled something else, of course, and there were plenty to choose from: theophylline, aminophyllin and theobromine, for example. Potassium citrate and ammonium chloride also induce diuresis by altering the salt content of the blood. Then there are the organic mercurial substances and the various forms of chlorothiazade and hydrochlorothiazade. People on crash diets are the most frequent users of diuretics, but they're dangerous drugs to fool with, and I said so to Jeanette Black.

"I know," she said, "but I didn't take any chances. I'd prescribe three or four pills a day for a week. Patients had to call and tell me the result daily. If it was too severe, I'd have them reduce the dosage."

I thought of all those unsuspecting New Yorkers running to the bathroom twenty or thirty times a day

—because that's what three diuretic pills will do for you. In addition, they were paying for the dubious pleasure of it all.

"After a few days, the patients would usually complain of pain in the kidneys or the bladder," Jeanette continued. "I'd have them come into the office, diagnose a mild infection, and 'treat' them for that."

I asked her how, and she said she simply gave them a placebo, or sugar pill, containing no medicine whatsoever. At the same time, she would reduce the dosage of diuretics over a three- or four-day period. By this time, the patients would have run up a doctor bill of $300 or $400. Which, I reflected, was a lot of money to pay for fifty cents' worth of pills and a great deal of inconvenience. I asked Jeanette about the complaint that had originally brought the patient to see her.

"Most of them are psychosomatic anyway," she said. "After the diuretics, they have had enough pain and trouble for a while. They've either forgotten the original trouble or it's cured itself of its own accord."

"And if they weren't psychosomatic?"

"I referred them to another doctor. A real one. I never treated anyone once I discovered they were really sick."

"How many patients did this involve?" I asked.

"Oh, fifty, sixty at a time," she said.

I began to see how she came to have so much money in the bank and on her back. The diuretic game is only one of half a hundred that an unscrupulous quack can play on unsuspecting patients, and I had no doubt that Jeanette Black knew all of them. Surely she had been ashamed of what she had been doing? I said.

"Not then," she told me. "I think they left out the shame when they made me."

"Tell me about the cars," I suggested.

She told me she'd gone to a Mercedes showroom in uptown Manhattan and asked them to demonstrate various models. While they were showing her the cars, she made wax impressions of the ignition keys. She then took these down to a keymaker patronized by the swindler's college, had keys made and waited for the weekend. She had her eye on not one, but two cars: a white 280SE and a dove-gray 350SL convertible.

On weekends, when the showroom was closed, the cars were kept in a garage in back. Jeanette had been talking to a cute little blond friend of hers about these fabulous cars, and bet her that if they went up to the coffee shop where the lot attendant took his break, they could get him to give them each a ride. The girl-friend—completely ignorant of the real purpose of Jeanette's visit to the Mercedes showroom—went along with the lark, and the attendant fell for it like a ton of bricks. While he was out with Susie, Jeanette calmly got into the cars of her choice and drove them out of the garage, parking them nearby. Later in the day, using license plates she had bought from a wrecker also patronized by her fellow con artists, she drove the vehicles to her home in Connecticut, where in due course she registered them in her own name. With the title secure, she was free and clear. The cars were parked outside her home right now.

She told me how she had conned her way all over Europe and never paid a cent—an airline had footed the entire bill. She did a tour, shopping at all the expensive boutiques in Florence, Rome, Zürich, Frankfurt and Paris. She had gowns by every couturier, made to order—Yves St. Laurent, Dior, Balmain—Pucci blouses, Hermès scarves, a dozen pairs of hand-made alligator shoes from Gucci, purses in rich Florentine designs, silk blouses, wispy underwear. She was careful to get detailed receipts for everything. Her final fling before boarding the transatlantic plane was to buy a beautiful matched mink coat from a furrier in the Düsseldorferstrasse in Frankfurt. She insured her matched leather luggage, bought en route, for $25,000 and flew in to Kennedy with her companion, who had the same number of cases, packed with both her own and Jeanette's original clothing. They simply exchanged luggage. The confederate stacked all Jeanette's expensive cases on a trolley and called a redcap. She declared

all her "purchases" and happily paid the duty before
waltzing off in a taxi. Jeanette meanwhile stayed behind until it was obvious that "her" luggage wasn't
going to appear on the traveling ramp. She then went
to the airline desk and said her luggage was missing.
Airline people don't get too excited about missing luggage, no matter how valuable the passenger claims it
to be. They know all about missing luggage. They also
know that nowhere near as much as people think actually gets lost. Bags can be put on the wrong plane,
they can travel around the world six times, but they
seldom get permanently lost. They told Jeanette that
they would send her luggage to her as soon as they
could locate it. She smiled and went home and thirty
days later put in a claim for $25,000 to the insurance
company, using the airline's official letter admitting
that the baggage had gone astray, and the receipts she
had carefully collected in Europe for what she had
bought to support her claim. The insurers paid in full.

"All right," I said, stopping her. "I think I've got
the picture. Now let's start thinking of ways we can
set it all straight."

We started with the cars. Jeanette and I flew back
to New York in the Beechcraft, a Turbo-Baron model
56TC with two 380-hp Lycoming turbosupercharged
engines, fitted with four seats. Her cruising speed at
25,000 feet was almost 300 mph, and she had a very
effective range, allowing for warmups, takeoffs, land-
ings and a forty-five-minute reserve of fuel, of over
one thousand miles. I decided not to think about how
much the plane was worth, or ask Jeanette how she
had come into possession of it.

Once we were settled in New York, I rented space
in a garage owned by a friend of mine on the water-
front below the United Nations building. Then I went
over those two Mercs like a scientist looking for a new
microbe. I removed every fingerprint, every scrap of
paper, every inspection sticker, mechanic's chalk mark,
tar stain, footprint. I used a powerful industrial vac-
uum cleaner to siphon out every particle of grit, sand,

gravel and dust, and removed every foreign body lodged in the tire treads, washing them afterward under the jet of a powerful hose. By the time I got through, I would have defied the FBI Crime Laboratory to tell me where those cars had been and who had driven them.

Next I worked out the mileage that Jeanette had driven, and checked out the cost of leasing two such vehicles. Prorating the results, I came up with the amount it would have cost her had she leased both cars legitimately. It was a sizable chunk of money.

I rented a portable typewriter and bought some plain typing paper at Woolworth. I typed two notes thanking the owners of the cars for the use of the vehicles, enclosing the appropriate rental fees in used notes. Then Jeanette and I each drove one of the cars uptown. We parked them, almost as good as new, just around the corner from the showroom. Then, using an assumed voice, I called anonymously from a coffee shop—the same one Jeanette's parking attendant had used to take his break in—and told them the cars were there. We watched through the window as the staff of the agency ran out and discovered the cars. Their expressions when they found the notes and the money had to be seen to be believed. They were pounding each other on the back and hooting with delighted laughter. They must have phoned the story to the *Daily News* because that evening's edition ran an item about the return of the cars. It was headlined THE HONEST THIEF.

"Now we have to pay back the bank loan," I told Jeanette, "and retrieve the deed of the office building."

She did the first part of it herself. It meant she had to put the house in Connecticut on the market, but it was an attractive property and she had no trouble making an almost immediate sale—especially since, with a nice ironic humor, she offered it at a "give-away" price. She took the money for the house to the bank, paid off her loan and then brought the deed back to me. That evening I called in a technician specializing in locks and safes who works on retainer for me, training my agents how to open doors of all kinds, windows, suitcases, combination locks, safes, automobiles. He is a quiet, mousy little man who looks like an unsuccessful bookkeeper, but I have yet to see the security device he cannot by-pass. With his assistance, we went into the office of the lawyer from whom Jeanette had purloined the deed, and replaced it in the safe. I doubt that he ever realized it had been stolen.

I won't relate chapter and verse in grinding detail for every one of the reverse swindles that we pulled. I could see that in a strange way, Jeanette was beginning to enjoy this slightly criminal honesty almost as much as her former swindling. After three weeks, we had given back just about everything that could be returned. The Beechcraft was returned in much the same way the cars had been, with another untraceable anonymous note written on untraceable anonymous paper on our untraceable anonymous machine. A refund to the defrauded insurance company in untraceable used notes was handed in by a kid I paid five dollars to do it. I didn't know him, he didn't know me, and the company would never trace either of us. One by one, we worked off all Jeanette's misdeeds until, finally, inevitably, we ran out of money.

"Now what do I do?" she asked.

I told her she had to get herself a job, something she was actually qualified to do. She said she had no real qualifications of any kind. She said I would have to help her.

"No," I said. "This time you've got to be like Amelia Earhart: you have to fly all by yourself."

"I can't," she said. "I can't."

I told her she had to. I told her that if she didn't, if anyone else did it for her, it wouldn't be any achievement. She would find herself able to ditch the job and justify her actions much more easily. If she got it on her own, she would be involved in it.

It took her a little while, but before the last few hundred dollars ran out she got a job as an insurance clerk, and soon afterward applied for and got a transfer to the branch in Seattle. She learned how to type hunt-and-peck. She got a raise. And she found that she was enjoying being a law-abiding citizen.

Once in a while I get a progress report from her. She says she's very happy, making $125 a week now. She bought some clothes on layaway, and just put a $40 deposit on a telephone. She says when she gets some money saved, she'll pay me too. That's a hangover from the last time I saw her, just before I left for El Paso.

"I have one big problem left," she told me. "You used up all my money. I'm broke. I can't pay you."

"It wasn't your money to pay me with," I reminded her.

"There is one way," she said, looking at me for a long moment, as if trying to decide something. "Would you like to go to bed with me?"

"Jeanette, that's not my style," I said. "And you know it."

"You'd be doing me a favor," she said. "I'd like to know what it's like with a man."

I told her she would, one day. I said either she'd find the man, or he'd find her, but it would happen.

"Not to people like me," she said. "Not bad people."

"You were bad," I said. "But you've come good."

Her face lit up at my words. "You think so?" she said.

I told her I was betting on it—betting what I'd have charged as a retainer for the kind of caper we'd been involved in. I told her that I considered I was holding her promissory note, but that if she stayed straight, I wouldn't call it. If, however, I heard she was up to any of her old tricks, I'd come looking to collect—with interest.

"It's a deal," she said, and she's kept it, too.

16.

*Although nowadays El Paso sprawls all over the valley
of the Rio Grande—together with Juarez, El Paso
forms an "integrated metropolitan area" with a population of 888,000 covering 160 square miles—the place
retains a frontier flavor. It's still got a cowtown atmosphere, and the people walking its streets look the
way people expect Texans to look. They live that way,
too. It would be safe to bet there are more handguns,
carbines and rifles per head around these parts than
almost anywhere else on earth. El Paso isn't New York
or Chicago, or even Houston—murder capital of the
world—but it has its muggings and rapes and burgla-
ries, and many of the other dubious benefits of big-
town-dom. Even so, El Paso has tamed down considerably since the 1880s, when, to quote one eyewitness, El
Paso Street was like the midway at a world's fair.*

*Today, as then, El Paso Street goes roughly north-
south, with San Antonio running into it as the upright
of a T joins the bar. In the '80s, the main drag was
roughly west on San Antonio, from Neal Nuland's
saloon on the corner of Mesa as far as El Paso Street,
then south about three blocks. This L-shaped "run"
was where the action was, where the sporting men
hung out.*

*Among the leading lights of this fraternity were John
Wesley Hardin, Dallas Stoudenmire, and the brothers
Manning, who ran the Coliseum Theater and owned a
saloon roughly where the El Paso del Norte Hotel now
stands. There were Jack Doyle, who ran a "variety"
theater, Uncle Ben Dowell, Jim Gillett—men who, as*

the old Texas saying had it, would charge hell with a bucket of water, and if that didn't work, would spit on the fire. Men and women "made" the town at night: you had to come in early if you wanted to get near the gambling tables.

Right on the corner of Mesa, where the Coliseum and Billy Coffin's Old Boss Saloon once stood, is the scene of a legendary gunfight. Following an inquest in which he didn't like the way interpreter Gus Krempkau was translating the evidence, Gus Hale, manager of a ranch owned by the Manning boys, shot Krempkau dead in the street. City Marshal Dallas Stoudenmire promptly iced Gus and also a Mexican bystander who hadn't had the sense to hit the dirt. Hale's pal George Campbell decided to get in on the fun, whereupon Dallas blew him away as well. The whole thing took about five seconds, and earned Stoudenmire the sobriquet "The Butcher." If it bothered Stoudenmire, it didn't show. He was as big as a skinned horse, and so tough he had to sneak up on the dipper to get a drink of water. As his feud with the Manning boys grew, Dallas got even quicker on the trigger. When a man he believed they sent after him came at him with a shotgun, Dallas put enough lead into the man to sink a cruiser. The undeclared war came to a head when Stoudenmire's brother-in-law was shot shortly after declaring that he was going into the Coliseum to clean out that nest of snakes once and for all.*

Seven months later Stoudenmire was dead and it was the Mannings who killed him. He had been drinking heavily, maybe drowning his sorrows at losing his city marshal's badge to Jim Gillett. Although his face had been saved by an appointment as a deputy U.S. marshal, Dallas still had blood in his eye, a formal signed "truce" with the Manning boys notwithstanding. After a heavy session with the bottle at the Acme—where Wes Hardin would one day be shot in the back of the head—Dallas went across to the Coliseum and all hell broke loose.*

"Doc" Manning shot him twice in the body before

Stoudenmire could unlimber his own gun. When he did, his shot broke Doc's arm, making him drop his gun. Doc, with enormous presence of mind, grabbed Dallas around the body so he couldn't lift the gun to fire again. Roaring with rage, wrestling with Doc to try to shake him so he could shoot his head off, Dallas staggered out onto the sidewalk, about where the Capri Theater now stands. At that point, Jim Manning came running to his brother's aid, and put a slug into Stoudenmire's brain, bringing the festivities to a close. Jim was later tried for the killing—and acquitted, on the unassailable premise that if a man is trying to kill you, it's no sin to kill him first.

Well, of course, it's not like that today, but the sense of loyalty to one's own people, the sense of being among men who take pride in killing their own snakes, is still strong. It's still a place where education is one thing and "savvy" is another. After all, it was in Texas that they used to say when a man could count to a hundred he was ready to teach school. So perhaps Jay Armes' larger-than-life style goes over better in El Paso than it would in some other places. Perhaps it also stirs the same mixture of loyalty and dislike that fanned the old frontier feuds. You can sense a little of it when you go downtown to the courthouse or into police headquarters at 109 South Campbell. Everybody downtown knows the big black Cadillac, the uniformed chauffeur, the familiar figure with the hooks crossed in front or behind his body. He says hello, stops and talks with people he knows: Mrs. Valenzuela from the Herald-Post, Ruben Tellez and Danny Flores in the Hall of Records, people in the elevator on the way up to see George Wagnon, chief inspector of police. Nobody questions Armes' right to wander anyplace he cares to go in headquarters, although if anyone off the street tried to do it he'd find out how fast things can happen.

Armes walks along the corridor saying hello to almost everyone he passes. Behind a doorway in the

*room with a sign taped to the window that says "Vice"
a uniformed man with a paunch is sitting in an upright
chair reading a newspaper. He looks up as Armes
passes, and his expression changes to one of those
I'm-just-looking-I'm-not-looking-at-you looks, but his
thoughts are as plain as if they were printed on his
forehead: what's he doing here? They always want to
know what Armes is working on, what he's come in
for, what he's asking about—even if he's just dropped
in to say hello and have a Coke. Armes continues
along the depersonalized corridors, Crimes Against the
Person Bureau on the left, Narcotics on the right, a
half-open door where a young patrolman and a middle-
aged woman in civilian clothes are poring over some
documents.*

*Inspector Wagnon's office is way over in back.
He is defended from intrusion by a secretary in a
bullpen with a railing and a swing gate, but she just
smiles Armes right on in. George Wagnon is a big,
burly blond man with thinning hair, hornrim glasses,
rolling vowels. He looks a bit like Emil Meyer used to
look when he played tough cops. He is explaining
something complicated about an impounded automobile. A lieutenant of the department sits on the
opposite side of the desk, nodding and grinning as
Wagnon grimaces while he's talking. He and Armes
started off hating each other without ever having met.
Wagnon was told by people that you had to watch out
for Armes, he was clever, everybody knew about him.
They told Armes about Wagnon: You don't know that
guy? You ever heard what he says about you? Finally
they met through being members of the same church,
and have become fast friends.*

*"Jay's been very successful," Wagnon says, "and
that always makes for a certain amount of sour grapes.
If I didn't like him so well, I'd have to envy him myself. In the movies, the private eye steals all the glory
and makes all the locals look bad. Jay's never done
that as long as I've known him—and that's getting on*

twenty years. From what I've observed first-hand over those years, I've got to believe that he's one of the best detectives in the country."

The principal of the Ysleta elementary school, Rudy Resendez, remembers Jay getting fitted with plastic hands so he could participate in the school boxing program. *"I know Jay as someone who had it a lot rougher than most people, and made it big. I feel proud of Jay and what he's done for El Paso, proud to tell people he's my friend."*

Tom Price, comptroller and secretary-treasurer of the Jetco Company of El Paso, which manufactures electric boat motors, metal detectors and a host of similar products, recalls that Armes was called in to investigate an alarming loss of valuable products through in-house thievery. *"It's hard to believe, but Jay had it all wrapped up in a day,"* he says. *"He spent all night interrogating suspects, and the following day he had enough evidence to call in the sheriff's deputies to haul the thieves away. He put in a security system that has all but eliminated pilfering here."*

Bill Burgess, president and owner of Continental Water Conditioning, has known Armes for fifteen years, and has retained the investigator to handle *"highly personal"* matters as well as business-oriented investigations for the company throughout the United States. *"He is a totally competent, thorough and complete investigator,"* Burgess says. *"Those of us who don't achieve tend to dislike those who do, and I think this is Jay's biggest problem. Everything he's ever done for me has worked out the way it should. I know a lot of people who have had the same experience."*

Chris Cummings, owner of one of the oldest quality hotels in El Paso, refers to Armes as a super person and an excellent detective. *"He lives in a style that doesn't match the rest of El Paso, so people wonder about it,"* Cummings adds. *"He's a little bit eccentric, but I say this in a complimentary way. Jay is unusual, he does an unusual job. He's like no one else I know.*

We've been friends for twenty years, and I know Jay as someone who does things the way he says he will.[1]

His clients readily acknowledge that the investigator is expensive to hire, but add that it depends on your definition of expensive. Merchant Tom Dula, who operates the Del Norte department store, points out that a $10,000 retainer is not expensive when it results in your saving a quarter of a million dollars in recovered merchandise. "Jay's record for recovering stolen merchandise is truly remarkable," he says.

The Honorable Tati Santiesteban, state senator from El Paso's District 29, who knew Armes at Ysleta High School, estimates that he has retained the investigator on more than a hundred occasions in connection with his legal practice, and that where ability is concerned, there is no comparable investigator. "Jay Armes is in a class by himself. If the client can afford it, and the magnitude of the case justifies it, I would not hesitate to hire him."[2] Like many of the others, the senator believes that Armes' no-holds-barred courtroom style has made him some powerful enemies. "They know he's a fierce competitor. They know he does everything he has to do to win."[3]

Attorney Jim Cook concurs. He says Armes is expensive, fast and effective. "He's gutsy,"[2] Cook adds. "If it involves a certain amount of risk, that doesn't seem to bother him. It's his forte. You have to remember that in our business we're dealing with real people, real property, real children, real relationships. The stakes can be very high. Jay Armes is someone you hire for the difficult cases. His survival instincts are the no-nonsense kind. When the case is difficult, I definitely want someone like him on my side."

There are, Armes acknowledges, some lawyers in El Paso who pay him a retainer fee, and, for one reason or another, rarely use his services on a case. What they are buying is a form of insurance. They don't want to go into court with Armes in an adversary role.

Andy Bolton, an attorney with a thriving practice in El Paso, called me one day and told me he had a pressing problem. He was representing one Daniel Johnson in court, in a case concerning the custody of Johnson's children. Johnson was alleging that the mother was failing in her proper duties as a parent, smoking pot, drinking and seeing other men. The trouble was that Johnson didn't have any hard evidence that would convince a jury, and when his wife got up on the witness stand, Johnson just knew she was going to lie her head off, deny everything and anything thrown at her, just so she could hang on to the kids. She didn't even want the kids. She just didn't want her ex-husband to have them.

"This Johnson," I said, "is he on the level?"

"Honest as a looking glass," was Andy's reply.

I said in that case I would appear in court that morning for thirty minutes. My fee would be $1000.

I heard Andy take a deep breath while he got used to the idea, and waited until he asked me what it was I thought I could possibly do in half an hour that was worth that much money. I said I would guarantee a favorable result for his client. If the decision went against him, he wouldn't have to pay.

"Then he's got nothing to lose," Andy said. "What do I have to do?"

I told him how I wanted him to play it. He was to open his case exactly the way he had originally planned to, but during the first hour I would come into court and hand him a dossier containing documents and photographs. As soon as he had looked through it, surprised but obviously delighted, he was to ask for a ten-minute recess while he conferred with his client about some new evidence that had just come into his hands that could materially affect the course of the case. Which would be nothing less than the gospel truth.

"Okay," Andy said. "Then what?"

The woman's attorney would almost certainly recognize me, I told him. Seeing me, he would know—or think he knew—that what I was handing Johnson's attorney was a dossier on his client. The woman's attorney, fearing that we know all about her private life, will advise her that she had better tell the truth and nothing else on the stand, or she'll be sent up for perjury. All Andy would have to do would be to ask her the right questions.

"You think it will work?" he said.

"See you in court, counselor," I said, and when I walked into court later that morning, I wasn't surprised to see Diana Johnson giving a bravura performance as her attorney asked her about her life with her husband. The lace handkerchief, the stifled sobs and the drama of it all would have done credit to F. Lee Bailey. All the same, heads turned—including her attorney's—when I made a production out of leaning over the railing, handing Andy Bolton the dossier and whispering in his ear. I sat down as Andy opened the dossier, did a double-take that looked as if it had been stolen from *East Lynne,* and shortly afterward jumped to his feet to ask for—and get—a ten-minute recess from the puzzled judge. Mrs. Johnson's attorney, a man called George Henderson, came bustling across the courtroom and grabbed me by the arm.

"You working on this case?" he snapped.

I said I was indeed, and had been doing for a month or so. I could have told him I had been working on it with Sam Spade and Miles Archer if I'd wanted to—I wasn't under oath. He glared at Andy Bolton, mad enough to kick his own dog.

"How come you didn't tell me about this new evidence before now?" he demanded. Andy gave an eloquent shrug.

"I just this minute got it myself, George," he said. "You saw Mr. Armes bring it in."

"What's in there?" Henderson demanded.

I told him that I couldn't tell him what was in the dossier. At that moment the clerk preceded the judge back into the court, Henderson went back to his table

and his client, and I got out of there—fast! I knew
that Henderson was going to try to serve a subpoena
on me immediately so he could establish the contents
of that dossier. I would then have to admit, under
oath, that it contained the plans for a plastic airplane;
a photostat; some eight-by-ten glossies of a proposed
housing development in Mission Hills; and a half-dozen
carbons of letters snatched off Joyce's desk at random
that morning. I went "missing" and I stayed missing,
while Henderson fumed. Andy Bolton put Mrs. Johnson on the witness stand and began his cross-examination. He reminded her first of the laws and penalties
for perjury, rubbing it in. Then, using the "information" in the dossier he took her apart like a filleted
haddock. He made her admit to having sexual relations
with men in front of the children, smoking pot in the
house, giving wild drunken parties and a whole lot
more. By the time he was through, the jury was looking at her as if she were Messalina, and it took them
no more than five minutes' deliberation to award custody of the children to Daniel Johnson.

He took them back to Houston, happy as a heifer
with a fence post, and neglected to do only one thing:
he paid neither Andy Bolton's fee nor mine. After a
week, I called him, and he was profusely apologetic.
What with the court case, and all the excitement, he'd
had hardly a moment to himself. As for me, why he
hadn't stopped talking about me since that day in
court. I told him I'd as soon have a little less talk and
a little more do. I didn't raise my voice, shout or
threaten, because it's not my style. I told him I really
didn't want to have to take the time to travel to
Houston specially to see him, but that if there wasn't a
check on my desk by the following morning, I'd just
force myself to do it.

I got the check. Andy Bolton, however, is still waiting to be paid, and I wouldn't want to hang upside
down until it happens. It's one of the perils of certain
professions—doctors, lawyers, consultants and private
investigators included. People come to you in distress,

in pain, in fear, in trouble. Once the problem has been solved, the worry evaporated, the pain gone, the trouble settled—people forget who helped them. They don't need you anymore, so they don't think about you anymore. My business is based on mutual trust. An investigator has to take people on trust, whether it be over money, action or words. The big Colt automatic, a .38 on a .45 frame that hangs in my display gun case at home, is there because I took someone on trust. Her name was Nancy Gray.

It gets so you hardly even blink when a strange woman calls you in the small hours of the morning and whispers desperately into the telephone that her husband is trying to kill her. Nancy Gray was a little different in that she added that her husband was also trying to kill their children. She begged me to help her get out of town without his knowledge. I don't know why I assumed she was calling from El Paso, but I said I would come to see her the next day when her husband was not there if she would give me the address.

"1418 Holland Park Crescent," she said.

I repeated the address and then frowned. I didn't know any Holland Park Crescent in El Paso, and I said so.

"I'm not surprised," she said. "I'm calling from London."

I told her in that case, I'd have to revise my estimated time of arrival, and made an appointment for the following day for my London agent to call and see her, while I set to work on a schedule that would take me to England. I figured I could use the long flight to catch up on all the sleep I wasn't getting.

I rendezvoused with my agent, Paul Napier, in the Dorchester Hotel on Park Lane. He briefed me about the Gray family. They were very wealthy paper merchants with extensive timber holdings in Scandinavia and Canada. Nancy Gray was a sweet young woman of about twenty-eight; the two girls, Samantha and Sara, were four and six, respectively. Peter Gray, the husband, was a physically big man, thirty years of age, who earned his living as a sort of upperclass tout for a gambling club. He was deeply in debt, a heavy drinker and renowned in dozens of London pubs and clubs for his foul temper and even fouler vocabulary.

"In other words," Napier drawled, "a real sweetie."

He had been attached to Gray's coattails on my orders since I'd called him from El Paso, and we already had a general picture of our man's movements. He would rise around eleven, eat a leisurely breakfast and then wander across to his club in Pall Mall. He usually lunched at the club, emerging around four to find his way into Soho, where he was a member of a drinking club called the Colonial. British licensing laws decree that pubs may not serve alcoholic beverages between the hours of three and five-thirty, or after eleven P.M. To circumvent these laws, the inventive British came up with clubs, which can serve drinks—to "members" only, of course—at any time. So when the pubs close, the serious drinkers move on to places like the Colonial.

Gray used the Colonial for the same reasons he used his own club, to scout gamblers for the evening's games. By six he would be at the gambling establishment in the Edgeware Road, a casino operation that Napier said was perfect proof, if proof were needed, that all casinos are the triumph of infinite contempt over infinite greed. He would stay there until two or three in the morning, depending upon business. He was given free run of the place, drinks and food; and he usually managed to scare up enough money from somewhere to play the tables. Baccarat was his folly. Napier said he was a terrible player.

I told him to pick Gray up again and stay on his coattails no matter what, keeping me advised by radio-phone if for any reason at all the man looked as if he might be returning to his home, which was in a fashionable part of west London opposite a small park with a children's playground in it.

While Napier was getting a fix on Gray, I called

another agent of mine, Anne Irving, told her my problem and asked her to get over to meet me at the Dorchester instanter. By the time she arrived, Napier had called to say he'd picked up Gray, who was walking down St. James's Street, on the way to his club by the look of it. I told him to call again as soon as he knew for sure, and meanwhile telephoned a friend of mine in the security section at Heathrow Airport. I asked him if he could make special arrangements for a party of three, a woman and two small children, flying to Washington D.C. on British Airways that evening. Nancy Gray's parents lived in Annandale, Virginia, a short distance from the captial. They would meet her at the airport and take her by car to their summer home on Fire Island. It was highly unlikely that Peter Gray would think of looking for them there, even if he found out they had crossed the Atlantic.

Napier checked in again: Gray was in his club, so Anne Irving and I jumped into the waiting limousine and sped across town to the Gray home. Nancy Gray was a sweet-looking woman with cropped dark hair and high cheekbones, real pretty. It seemed bizarre that anyone should want to kill her, but she told us as she packed her clothes that she was sure her husband was going insane. He had sworn to kill her and the children, said they were "dragging him down." We had absolutely no reason to doubt her word, because she was clearly frightened. I asked her about her husband's family, and she said they had refused to believe her when she told them about their son's threats.

Before she left, I had Nancy Gray write her husband a note saying she was going away and taking the children, that she hoped the Mediterranean air would do them good, that sort of thing. If Gray decided to give chase, this might throw him off the track for a while. She was still putting things into her bags when the phone bleeped. It was Napier, telling me that Gray had left the club, jumped into a cab and was heading in what looked like the direction of home. He must have forgotten something, but whatever his reasons for coming back, they meant we had to get out, and fast.

We threw the rest of Nancy Gray's things into the cases any way we could, and hurried out of the house, tossing the luggage into the trunk and telling the driver to head for Heathrow Airport. I just hoped Harry Simons had laid on the facilities I had asked for, because the minute Peter Gray read his wife's note, he was going to come after her. If he caught us trying to get her out of the country, there would be hell to pay. Nancy Gray didn't make us any more comfortable by telling us that, contrary to the stringent British firearms laws, her husband had a Webley .38 service revolver that he had threatened to use on her.

Harry Simons was waiting for us outside Terminal Three, and he hurried Nancy Gray and her children through, bypassing the check-in area, and taking her along what I later discovered was the route used by Queen Elizabeth whenever she is flying from London. There was still some time before the big British Airways 707 was due to leave for Washington. Harry had arranged for the Grays to use the VVIP lounge—for very, very important persons, he said with a wink. Nobody could get in there without a very, very special pass, so they would be quite safe until plane time. Which was just as well, because Napier had already signaled frantically that Gray was en route to the airport.

"Let him come," I said, and gave him further instructions. I asked Harry Simons to show me the shortcuts from one terminal to the others, and when Napier bleeped again to say that Gray had driven to the entrance of Terminal One, which is the departure hall for British Airways flights to Europe, I grinned. Our delaying tactic had worked, and now I could spring the trap.

We hurried across to Terminal One; myself, Harry Simons and two very hefty security police. Napier picked us up immediately, and his signal indicated

Gray. He was leaning over one of the check-in counters, questioning the assistants, showing them what looked like a photograph. I nodded to the security police. They went across to Gray and tapped his shoulder. They asked him to accompany them quietly, and for a moment, I held my breath. Those British police were taking quite a chance, because it was a sure thing that Gray was armed, while they were just as obviously not. I saw one of the two policemen say something to Gray, and the man shrugged and nodded. He reached into his raincoat pocket and pulled out a revolver, which he handed to them. Then they took him away.

We all went back to the VVIP lounge, where Anne Irving was keeping an eye on Nancy Gray and her children. I told her what had happened, and she leaned forward impulsively and kissed me, her eyes dancing with excitement and relief. A little while later we stood on the viewing platform on the Queens Building and watched the big bird climb into the darkening sky. We all went back to Terminal Three, feeling very pleased with ourselves. Mrs. Gray and her children were safe, the murderously-inclined husband had been outwitted and all was well with the world. All except for one thing: when I finally presented it, Nancy Gray's check bounced about seventeen feet high.

Muttering to myself about damn fool private investigators who act like knights on white horses in an era when all knights on white horses are good for is selling sink cleanser, I tried to contact my client.

No dice.

Nobody at the address in Annandale. The operative I sent over there to check told me the apartment in Banner Court was closed down, and the manager said the Atkinsons—Nancy Gray's parents—had left for a European vacation. I tried the Fire Island address, a cottage in Ocean Beach. Mrs. Gray was no longer there and had left no forwarding address. It didn't seem likely that she would have returned to Britain,

but on the off chance I called Paul Napier and had him
check. Back came the reply: nobody at the house on
Holland Park Crescent. Neighbors supplied the information that the Gray family had moved away, lock,
stock and barrel.

Family? I said.

Napier confirmed my guess. Nancy Gray had returned to her husband and they had gone to live somewhere else—together. His skirmish with the police at
London Airport had resulted in no more than a fine
and confiscation of the pistol, Napier added. He suspected that the whole thing had been hushed up by the
Gray family, whose paper holdings gave them powerful
press connections in London's Fleet Street.

I felt vaguely annoyed about the whole thing. Like the
man in the joke: it wasn't the principle, it was the
money. That had been one hell of an expensive caper,
and it wasn't as if the Grays couldn't afford the bottom line. However, the trail was cold and four or so
months old. There was no point in throwing good
money after bad, so I wrote it off to experience and
let it go at that.

It must have been about seven months later that I
got a call from my office late in the evening. I was up
in Las Cruces on some business connected with the
ranch, but they patched me through to a Mrs. Jean
Carroll, who told me that she wanted to retain my
personal services immediately. I explained that I was
out of town and suggested that I send one of my people along to see her. That was not possible, she said.
Anyway, she wanted me to handle the matter personally. I asked her what it was, and she told me that
her husband had disappeared and she wanted him
traced. It was a confidential matter and she did not
wish to discuss it at length by telephone. When would
I be back in El Paso?

I told her I would be returning about nine that
night. She asked me if I could meet her in town some
time later, say ten o'clock. I said that would be fine,
and suggested she come by the office.

"No," she said. "I know too many people in El Paso. I don't want anyone to know I'm in town. Can't you meet me somewhere?"

I asked her where she had in mind, trying to place her accent, which was odd. Bostonian? Canadian? European, speaking learned English? It was hard to tell on the phone. She said she would meet me outside the American Furniture Company building downtown at ten, and asked me if I knew where it was—which is like asking a movie director if he has ever heard of Warner Bros. AFC owns one of El Paso's more noticeable buildings, and I wondered how someone who claimed to know so many people in town would imagine any native not knowing where the AFC was.

"Ten o'clock, then," she said. "I'll explain everything when I see you."

"How will I know you?"

"Look for a blonde wearing a white dress," she said. "Will you be coming by taxi or what?"

"I'll be in a gold Corvette Stingray," I said. "You can't miss it."

"Good," she said, and I thought I heard her chuckle. Right then, I put it down to a bad connection. Later, I realized how macabre her little laugh had been.

I passed the time driving back to El Paso putting one and one together and getting nothing. Mrs. Carroll didn't sound quite right, but there wasn't enough wrong to label her a phony. That accent—what was it? Canadian, British, European? She called a cab a taxi, which is the way the British say it—but then, so do lots of Americans. There was her choice of rendezvous. To say the least, it was unusual.

El Paso isn't up to big-city standards when it comes to muggings and rape, but that doesn't mean it doesn't have its share. Yet here was a woman who claimed to know the town, a blonde in a white dress prepared to stand around on a deserted downtown street at ten o'clock at night. I finally decided I'd better take out some insurance, even though my evidence for doing so was circumstantial. Some circumstantial evidence is pretty solid—for instance, as Thoreau said, when there's a trout in the milk. I made one or two phone calls from the car, and hoped I was not sticking out my neck too far. I turned into San Antonio Street at five to ten, and coasted to a stop outside the AFC building.

Nobody in sight, and I shook my head ruefully. Then, from a shadowed doorway, I saw a flash of white and, unbelievably, a blonde in a white dress hurrying across the sidewalk toward the car. I leaned over and opened the door for her.

"Mrs. Carroll?" I said.

"Yes, Mr. Armes," the women said as she slid into the car. As she did, a faint bluish glint caught my eye, and I realized she had a gun in her hand. I acted without conscious thought, striking out at the weapon as she pulled the trigger. There was a hell of a bang and the bullet blew a gaping hole in the windshield of the Stingray. Before she could fire again, I hit the woman with my left hook, stunning her. Her head jolted backward, and as it did, the blond hair tilted askew. Beneath the wig I recognized the face of my one-time client, Nancy Gray. I took the automatic away from her as an El Paso Police Department prowl car screeched to a stop alongside mine, siren growling and dome lights flashing. I had felt certain I was heading into some sort of setup, and I'd called to ask the EPPD to be there, or thereabouts, in case I needed backup.

I told the boys some cockamamie story about Mrs. Gray showing me the gun and its going off by accident. They didn't believe it any more than I did—try firing a Colt automatic accidentally, and you'll see why. They have a trigger pull like a rusty door hinge. However, if I wanted to shoot out the windshield of my own car, that was okay with them. They got back into the growler and took off.

I punched out the splintered windshield and fitted the emergency plastic one I always carry, then took the sullen, silent Nancy Gray back to my office on Montana, about a ten-minute drive from downtown.

She didn't speak, either on the way or when we got there. She sat looking around her like a kid in a strange house, eyes wide and unblinking, while I made long-distance telephone calls.

It was five in the morning in London, and the phone rang a long while before Paul Napier mumbled his number into it. Americans say hello, the Italians say *pronto* and the Swiss give you their name, but for some reason I've never quite worked out, the British always answer by quoting their phone number. It took Paul less than an hour to do what I wanted done, and track down Charles Gray, Nancy Gray's father-in-law.

I told Mr. Gray what had happened, and he begged me not to prefer charges against Nancy, but to have her placed in hospital under observation. He would fly out to El Paso and arrange for her to be put under psychiatric care.

"She needs help desperately," he said. "She's really not well."

That masterly British understatement again. A woman travels more than seven thousand miles to kill someone for no apparent reason, and the Englishman says she's not well! I asked him if he had any idea why she wanted to kill me, because it made no sense to me.

"Nothing Nancy has done for quite a while has made much sense, Mr. Armes," he said. He told me that his son and Nancy had separated, and that Peter had been mixed up in a mess involving the mistress of some London underworld figure who had been found murdered. Although there had been no arrest, the police had asked Gray to surrender his passport. More understatement. The British police never say a suspect is being grilled. They say "a man is helping the police with their inquiries."

"I think somehow Nancy may have got it into her head that you were responsible for her splitting up with Peter, which, in turn, led to his problems with this other woman. I'm guessing, of course. Who knows what has been going on in the poor child's mind?"

Three days later, Charles Gray arrived in El Paso,

and quietly and efficiently arranged to have his daughter-in-law flown back to Britain. There, arrangements had been made to have her committed to what they quaintly call a "nursing home."

So that was that. To the original cost of the unnecessary caper in London, I now added several transatlantic calls and the price of a new windshield. To offset the debit, I added to my special collection the big .38 automatic on the .45 frame. That makes it the most expensive gun I own, and a permanent reminder of another close shave. Some people have them in automobiles or with fork-lift truck or oxyacetylene burners. I have them with deranged women carrying guns.

17.

*A Jay Armes investigation can be local or interna-
tional, normal or bizarre. One day, someone will want
to retain him to locate a stolen bus, even a missing
rabbit, and the next, he will be talking half a million
dollars to find someone like Patty Hearst. He never actually got started on that caper, but long before Patty
was finally brought in, he was seriously discussing it.*

*It started when the late Leonard Freeman, then the
producer of the television show* Hawaii Five-O, *called
Armes and asked him whether he thought he could
find Patricia Hearst. Her sensational disappearance, the
Symbionese Liberation Army's gunpoint robbery of the
Hibernia Bank in San Francisco and her parents' an-
guished television appearances had made the Patricia
Hearst case front-page news all over the world.*

*Armes said he was sure he could locate her. There
was no bombast in it. The fact that every law-enforcement agency in the world could not track her down
didn't mean a thing to him. When Freeman pointed
this out, Armes just shrugged and said he doesn't work
the same way the FBI works. Freeman asked him how
much he thought it would take.*

*"Half a million," Armes said laconically. "Up
front."*

"You'd guarantee to find her?"

*Like the Chinese say, no tickee, no laundry. The
money could be paid into escrow, and paid over when,
and only when, he delivered.*

Freeman signed off, and came back a few days later.

He was acting as an intermediary for a national magazine, one of the household-name variety. They wanted to retain Armes to locate Patricia Hearst, and wanted to know what, exactly, the investigator offered for their $500,000.

Armes said he would provide them with her address and guarantee her physical presence there, and that they would get it simultaneously with the FBI and the police of whatever city he found her in. They agreed to this, and Armes told them to contact his attorney, J. William Hayes, who has offices in Beverly Hills, and work out a contract. A few days later, Hayes called Armes. He said he'd just received the contract, and it was so one-sided that it took his breath away.

"This isn't just chutzpa," Hayes said. "It's downright effrontery! They not only want you to locate the girl, they require you to produce her to them exclusively, and to guarantee them the time to obtain a thirty-thousand-word interview prior to the arrival of any law-enforcement officer other than yourself."

Armes called the prospective client. He said he was a man who ran his boot heels down avoiding trouble, and what they wanted was so much trouble he'd still be trying to get out of it in nine hundred and ninety-nine years. He told them he wasn't going to guarantee any interviews or TV appearances or photographs or guest shots on the Today *show or anything else they had in mind. The offer—take it or leave it—was to locate the girl and take them to her at the same time as the FBI and everyone else.*

Of course, that wasn't what the magazine people had in mind. They had a world exclusive in mind, and their busy little brains were already computing the income from selling the right to reproduce it in newspapers and magazines all around the world. Armes' $500,000 fee would be chickenfeed compared to what the story was worth, if they got it. They tried for several hours to get him to reconsider, but he was adamant.

"I don't need the money badly enough to do time

*for it," he said. As a law-enforcement officer himself,
he knew it would be his clear duty to report Hearst to
the proper authorities if he found her. To locate her
and not do so would have been to flout the law he is
sworn to uphold. And, he observed with a wry smile,
he'd also have been busted for about eighty things, the
very least of which would have been obstruction of
justice.*

*Well, as everyone knows, they found Patty Hearst,
and they found her, according to Armes, right about
where he planned to look. Easy for him to say he can
do better than the FBI—after the fact—you say?
Armes is doing better than the FBI all the time.*

Karl Bauer was a German diplomat working at the
United Nations in New York. A native of Munich, he
had a beautiful Bavarian wife and three sons, the
oldest of whom, Frederick, had just graduated from
college. As a graduation present, Bauer gave his son a
Mercedes sports car and the money to realize one of his
dreams—a trip across the United States from east to
west.

Frederick was a good boy, very close to his parents.
Every two days, no matter where he was, he would
call his parents in New York and let them know where
he was, how he was doing and where he was going next.
Then without warning, the calls stopped. After eight
days, Karl Bauer called the FBI. A check was run on
the boy's last location, San Antonio. He had said he
was heading for Mexico City, and after eight days of
frantic waiting, the Bauers were told that Frederick
had indeed crossed into Mexico—at El Paso—but then
he seemed to have vanished into thin air.

The Bauers were out of their minds with worry.
They had heard all those stories about Mexico, about
how you can get killed down there for fifty cents
(which is true if you're stupid or careless) or robbed
and thrown into a river or buried on the faceless desert
or thrown into some stinking *calabozo* and forgotten.

All those things can happen, and do. Life is a lot cheaper in wilderness Mexico, and a rich kid in a shiny new automobile would be a tempting morsel for some of the *cabrones* roaming the back streets of the mining towns on his route.

They contacted the German Embassy, the El Paso Police Department, the Mexican Federal Police and anyone else they could think of. Still no trace of the boy, and now it was ten days since he had last been heard of. Karl Bauer decided to fly down to El Paso. He'd read about me in some German magazine, and he and his wife had got to the stage where they were ready to clutch at the faintest hope: Even an El Paso detective with no hands!

"I want you to find my son," Bauer said to me in faultless slightly-accented English. "These other people all say a great deal but they don't appear to be doing much."

He told me the whole story, gave me photographs of the boy, details about the car. He asked me whether I thought Frederick was dead. I said there was no reason to suppose that. There were no reports of an abandoned car, an unidentified body, so there was every chance the boy was still alive. I said it to reassure the man, who was intensely worried.

"When can you start looking for him?" Bauer asked me. He was a handsome man, about fifty, dressed in a dark business suit of the kind you hardly see outside a bank president's office in El Paso, where the sun has failed to shine only twenty-one days since 1961. Bauer had short dark hair with gray, almost white patches at the temples and behind the ears. There were deep, dark shadows beneath his eyes that betrayed sleepless nights, and he got through the best part of a pack of cigarettes while we were talking, crushing them out after one or two puffs. I said I'd start right away.

I found Freddy Bauer in exactly eight hours, without even leaving El Paso. Risking overkill, let me repeat again that I do not work like the official law-

enforcement agencies. I work through local knowledge,
my chain of agents and a host of friends and contacts
all over the world—and especially in Mexico. The boy
had said he was heading for Mexico City, and if he was
like any other tourist who has never been to Mexico
before, he would fill up his gas tank before he crossed
the border. I worked out his range in the 350SL he
was driving. The car does around twenty miles to the
gallon, and the tank holds twenty-one gallons, so his
filling stops had to be at four-hundred-mile intervals.
If the boy had been planning to make his usual call to
his parents, he would have had to aim for one of the
larger cities, which meant he was somewhere between
Chihuahua and Torreón when whatever happened to
him happened, since I figured it highly unlikely that
he'd have covered more ground than the 582 miles
from San Antonio and the 497 from Juarez to Torréon
in that time. I put agents on the job of checking out
garages, filling stations, roadside cafes and motels.
Mexico isn't the United States, and a German boy in a
white Mercedes convertible isn't an everyday sight
down there. If he'd stopped anywhere, they would remember him, and they did.

Frederick had taken a second-class road leading up
into the Sierra del Tlahualilo, and his car had broken
down in a tiny little village just across the Coahuila
border. They had to send down to the nearest town for
a mechanic—there wasn't even a telephone in the
place—and while he was waiting overnight, Frederick
came down with a murderous case of dysentery. Nobody had warned him about the drinking water, and
he was a real mess. He couldn't even get out of bed
when my agent Herbert Ruiz found him. Frederick
was as effectively stranded as if someone had dropped
him on a Pacific atoll from a balloon.

Ruiz took the boy down to Torreón, and I sent my
plane down there to fly him back immediately to El
Paso. Ruiz would arrange for the automobile to be
driven back to the United States. A few hours later,

wan and thinned down by his illness, Frederick Bauer was reunited with his beaming father.

"I've seen those television detectives do things like this," Karl Bauer said to me, "but I never realized there was a real-life Mannix." He went out into the sunshine with his boy, smiling and looking ten years younger now that the weight of his worry had been removed. Five minutes later, he came back in, still smiling.

"I forgot," he said. "I had an appointment set up tomorrow to meet the FBI agent here in El Paso and discuss my son's disappearance. Do you think you could cancel it for me?"

18.

I think it was Henry Ford who said "Money is like an arm or a leg—use it or lose it." He might have been speaking directly to Joseph Costigan, a very prominent Denver dealer in highly-expensive audio equipment and electronic calculators, whose wife Ruth came to me with a most unusual request. She wanted me to help her burglarize the business in which she and her husband were partners.

She told me that the business was sound and highly profitable. It had been started up twenty years before, with $100,000 that she had inherited, and she and her husband had worked extremely hard all their lives to develop and expand it. Today they had branches all over Colorado, New Mexico, northwest Texas and eastern Arizona, and specialized in equipment in the $500-to-$800 range. Turnover was close to $3 million a year, which was pretty good for that kind of business. Suddenly, without warning, her husband had given her an ultimatum: her participation in the business was to be limited to operating one downtown store and nothing else.

"I couldn't believe it, Mr. Armes," she said when she came to my office.

She was not a young woman, well on her way to fifty, but still handsome, with an attractive face and figure. "He told he didn't want me to come to the office. I can't get in the safe or the files. He won't even let me near his desk. Something is going on, Mr. Armes, and I want to know what it is."

I asked her if she had observed any changes in her husband's personal habits, and she said she had, quite a few. He had taken to wearing Ivy League suits, bright-colored shirts on weekends, was letting his hair grow fashionably longer and was using aftershave lotion and a deodorant after years of not bothering.

"He never used to give a tinker's cuss about his appearance," she said. "I think he's got a girl someplace, if you want to know the truth."

I told her that it wasn't necessarily so. Maybe her husband was just enjoying a little late in life the things he hadn't been able to afford when he was younger. She said she'd just as soon believe that, but she still couldn't understand why he was trying to close her out of the business. That was why she wanted me to help her to break into the office.

Breaking and entering is, of course, a felony, but Ruth Costigan was a full partner in the business, which was called Audilectronics. I told her that if she would sign a power of attorney giving me permission to enter the premises, then—and only then—would I help her. Otherwise, under the law, I would be aiding and abetting her to commit a criminal act.

"Don't worry," she said, producing a sheet of paper from her purse. "I already talked to my attorney and he told me all that. Here's your power of attorney."

I asked her about the layout of the offices, and what exactly she wanted to do when she got in there. She said mostly she wanted to get into the safes. I asked her the make.

"One is a walk-in safe," she said. "A Mosler."

"Go on," I said, thinking this was going to be a tall order. It got a lot taller, because Mrs. Costigan was just getting warmed up. She told me there was another safe under the floor beneath the desk. She wanted to get into that, too, and open up all the drawers of the desk and any cabinets that might have deeds, bonds or other documents in them. She stopped, and I let out a sigh of relief. For a moment, I'd thought she was going to ask me to pick her husband's pocket as well.

I asked her about alarms, and she said the premises were protected by an ADT installation, which is an automatic alarm system linked by radio to a security firm. If the circuits are broken, lights flash on the coded panel in the offices and the security officer immediately dispatches a patrol, simultaneously informing the police.

Tall order didn't begin to cover it, I thought, as Mrs. Costigan sat back and folded her arms like a fresh kid who's just bet the magician he can't pull *another* rabbit out of his hat.

"It can be done," I told her. "But it'll be expensive."

"More than a hundred thousand dollars?" she asked.

Not that much, I said, and she smiled. She said she figured that she was out that much anyway, and if she got the information she wanted, she could fight to get it back. I then explained our procedure to her. I told her we would put her husband under surveillance, and asked her to make a list of his friends and the places he visited regularly. Once we established his pattern, we could make plans for our entry into the office, secure in our knowledge of his whereabouts. She said that Wednesdays he pretty nearly always played poker with his friends, but that his other outings were to no set routine. I told her we would call her when were ready to move. There were still a few things that had to be done. One was to find out what the code was for the Audilectronics office at the security firm.

All security systems must have a bypass. You lock up the premises, switch on the alarms, head for home. Later that evening, you remember a file you need is back at the office. You call in your code to the security firm, and they don't react to the signal flashing as you go in. When you're ready to leave, you just call them again, and that's that.

It was necessary to get into the records of the security firm and extract Costigan's code, and we did it quite easily. Naturally, I cannot give precise details of how, but this much I will say: you've got to have a contact. Once again risking repeating myself, contacts make a lot of the wheels go round in my business. The more you have, the more successful you will be. It's that easy, or that difficult, depending on where you're sitting. Everyone—especially in the United States—is an armchair detective. Shade-tree attorneys, they call them down El Paso way. There's some distance between that and the real thing, and if you don't have the contacts, you're dead in the water. I had one in Denver, and got the magic "Ajax" in twenty minutes flat.

I know I am bending the rules. You have to, to get the job done. If Joe Costigan had been playing fair with his wife—who was, after all, his partner in every sense—we wouldn't have needed to work that way. Ruth Costigan would have known the code, and we'd have been in like Flynn. As it was, her power of attorney was our justification for bending the rules, but that was about as far as I will ever go. I'm not in the business of obstructing justice or breaking the law.

The following Wednesday Ruth Costigan called me to say her husband was planning to go out that evening. He said he had a meeting downtown, and then he was going to have a drink with the boys, maybe play some poker. He told her he wouldn't be home until late, so she shouldn't wait up. When he left home that evening, he had one of my agents on his tail, and we got his report about half an hour later. Whatever Joe Costigan was planning to play that night, it wasn't poker. He was in the Mountain View apartment of a twenty-five-year-old blonde named Julia Watson. An hour later the agent called again to report that the couple had driven downtown and were presently having a candlelit dinner *à deux* in the Palace Arms at the Brown Palace Hotel on Tremont. I told him to go in and have a meal so he could keep an eye on them.

"You know what dinner costs up there?" he said.

"I know," I said. "Try the Rocky Mountain trout—it's great."

With Costigan safely out of the way, I called Mrs. Costigan and arranged to pick her up as we headed for the office. Ironically, it was only a stone's throw from the Brown Palace, in a building opposite the Lincoln Towers on the corner of Nineteenth and Sherman. I used the radio phone to call the security company.

"This is Ajax," I said. "I'm just going into the building to work on some books. I'll call you when I leave."

The security firm acknowledged, and told me not to work too late. I promised I wouldn't and we went into the place. We had already picked the lock and made a key, so we had no trouble getting in—myself, Mrs. Costigan and the technician who was going to pick the locks on the safes. Mrs. Costigan had what looked like a gray blanket under her arm and I asked her what it was.

"A duffel bag," she said, "in case I have to take away any papers."

As she had told us, the safe was in a walk-in closet. The closet itself had a double lock and a Yale deadbolt, But Henry Clarke, my technician, opened them up in less than four minutes. Mousy and unimportant though he looks, Henry's the best in the business, and when I saw him look at the door of that big old-fashioned Mosler safe in the closet and shake his head, my heart sank.

"This one will be a brute," he said, dumping his little canvas carryall on the floor. I could see what he meant. It looked as if nothing short of an atomic bomb would open that huge steel door. Henry was looking at it the way Sir Edmund Hilary must have looked at Everest the first time he saw it.

"Hold on, Henry," I said. I had an idea, and asked Mrs. Costigan how many times her husband had changed the combination of the safe that she knew about.

"Never," she said," and we've had it twenty-odd years."

"Why never?" People usually change the sequence of

numbers or letters on safes at regular intervals, for
security reasons. She told me that Costigan had the
worst kind of memory for numbers of anyone she'd
ever known. He couldn't even remember the number
of the post office box they rented at one time. She said
the only thing he could remember was not to give her
enough money. I asked her how long they'd been married, and she told me thirty years.

"Does he remember your anniversary?"

"No, nor my birthday nor Mother's Day nor Valentine's, either."

"How about his own birthday?"

"That he remembers," she said waspishly. "That he
always remembers."

"Tell me the date," I said.

"May 5, 1909," she said. "What's this all about, Mr.
Armes?"

"Try 551909," I said to Henry. He nodded, turned
the dial and smiled as he heard the tumblers sliding.
He swung open the door and made a little bow. Mrs.
Costigan looked at us as if we'd just turned lead into
gold. It turned out that was almost exactly what we'd
done, because that safe had enough paper money on
the shelves to pay off the national debt.

There were bundles of Mexican currency—Audilectronics did a lot of business south of the border—and
even more bundles of large-denomination American
notes. In addition, there were German marks, Swiss
francs, Swedish kronor and English pounds.

"Stand aside, young man," Ruth Costigan said, and
opened her duffel bag into which she proceeded to stuff
pile after pile of the money.

"Mrs. Costigan, what are you doing?" I said.

"I told you I worked hard to build this business,"
she said, puffing slightly from exertion. "I put up the
money to start it. Now you tell me Joe is gallivanting
around with some little spring chicken. Well, she can
have that dried-up old galoot. I'll just declare myself
an extraordinary dividend!"

Extraordinary was right. She finished stuffing all that money into the sack, and then came over to where Henry was just lifting up the floor door of the safe beneath the desk. On the top was a velvet-lined box with what looked like a coin collection in trays inside it. I only got a brief glimpse of it, then *bang!* into the sack it went. In fact, everything that looked remotely valuable went in. If I had been watching a movie, I would have found the sight of that little lady socking all that stuff away hilarious. Bonds, more money, jewelry and I don't know what else—all went into the bulging duffel bag. By the time the safe was empty, it was all Ruth Costigan could do to lift the thing.

"Now the desk," she said, panting. She was just getting warmed up, no more. I told her she wouldn't be able to carry the bag if she put any more into it.

"That's no problem," she said. "I got two healthy men to help me."

She cleaned that place out. Deeds and titles and contracts and money and valuables—I lost count. She stripped Joe Costigan like a piranha working on a chicken bone, and all the time she was doing it she had a little smile on her face and she was humming a tune, happy as a housewife with a white wash in a TV commercial.

It took Henry and me both to lift up that sack and put it outside in the hallway. Mrs. Costigan stood guard there while Henry helped me dust the place off, close all the safes, check out with the alarm company and call up the agent tailing Joe Costigan. No problem there: he was still playing footsie with the blonde.

We took Mrs. Costigan—and her bulging duffel bag —back to her home by the country club. When we got there, she took two big bundles of bills—they looked like fifties in the poor light of the street lamps—out of the bag and held them out to me.

"Here," she said. "A bonus for you and your colleague."

I shook my head and told her I didn't work that

way. She could send me her check like everyone else.
I also suggested that she put that bag away somewhere
real safe, because that was her ace in the hole.

"I know a place," she said. "I'll take it to—"

"Don't tell me!" I said quickly. "I don't want to
know."

I explained to her that if for any reason I was called
upon to state, under oath, whether I knew what had
happened to the money and documents she had taken
from the office, I would prefer to be able to say no and
be telling the truth. Henry and I took the bag inside
for her, and then we left.

I drove Henry across to the airport to catch his
plane home, and all the way there he was chuckling
to himself about Ruth Costigan, or "that spunky little
lady," as he called her. He allowed that she hadn't
really needed us at all. He said he was willing to bet
that if she had marched up to that big old Mosler and
commanded it to open, it would have popped like a
champagne cork—wouldn't have dared not to, according to Henry.

Next morning Ruth Costigan came down to the Hilton, where I was staying. If her expression was anything to go by, she was having more fun than an ant
at a picnic. She told me that shortly after her husband
went to the office, he'd called her to tell her that both
the office safes and his desk had been cleaned out.
Every penny, every document, every deed that had
been in the office was gone. She told him to call the
police. He said she ought to know better than that: he
had a lot of money in the safe that he hadn't reported.
She said she still thought he ought to call the police.
She said she knew what a terrible head he had for
numbers, so she gave him the phone number.

"You sound awful strange," he said. "It's like you
think this is funny, or something."

"Well," she said. "Something, anyway."

She let him stew in it, she said. Meanwhile, she had
been real busy. She had a man up at the house chang-

ing every lock in the place. She had taken her car to
the garage to have new ignition and door locks fitted.
And she had just come from seeing her attorney,
whom she had instructed to serve Joe Costigan with
divorce papers, and also to get an injunction prevent-
ing him from telephoning her, seeing her, visiting the
house or even writing her a letter.

"I keep imagining how he'll look when they serve
those papers," she said, a broad smile on her face. She
was enjoying herself while she kicked that poor man to
pieces. "Every time I think of it, I break up."

Still giggling, she handed me a cashier's check for
$20,000. I asked her what it was supposed to be for,
and she said it was a bonus for making her so happy. I
told her it was very generous, but I couldn't accept it any
more than I'd been able to accept the cash she'd
offered me the preceding night. I don't take bonuses,
tips, handouts, gifts, donations, windfalls, backhanders,
bribes, hush money or anything else. Nothing personal
about it. I state my fee and that's it. No hidden extras,
even for someone as obviously open-handed as Ruth
Costigan.

About a week after I got back to El Paso, Ruth
Costigan called me and told me there had been hell to
pay when the papers were served on Joe Costigan. He
had immediately deduced that it had been his wife who
had cleaned out the office, and restraining order or
no restraining order, he went up to Englewood and
broke down the door, mad enough to eat the front
sight off a sixgun. Mrs. Costigan told him that if he
didn't leave she would call the police. He told her to
call the police, call the FBI, call out the National
Guard if she wanted to, he wasn't about to leave until
she told him what she had done with the money. She
reached for the telephone and he ripped it out of the
wall and threw it across the room. Then he grabbed his
wife by the throat and banged her back against the
wall, shouting, "Give me my money! Give me my
money!"

By fortunate chance, the Costigans' grown son drove by to say hello, saw the splintered door and came up the drive on the run. He pulled his spluttering father away, and got him quieted down. Ruth Costigan explained the fight by telling him that she had filed for divorce. The son persuaded the father to leave with him, and Joe Costigan stormed off, swearing a terrible revenge.

I asked Mrs. Costigan if she wanted me to come back up to Denver, but she said there was no need. Costigan had been warned by the police that any repetition of his attack would lead to his being arrested, and her attorney had assured her that he was already discussing an out-of-court settlement with her husband's attorney. And in time, it turned out exactly that way, so Joe Costigan never got his revenge.

Ruth Costigan was awarded half of all the properties owned by the company, and half of all bank credits in the company's name. Since she also had all the floating cash she'd "stolen" from the firm, she did very nicely indeed.

About a year later, I had to be in Denver again on business, and as I was walking along Welton Street by the J. C. Penney store, a woman suddenly ran up to me and threw her arms around me and kissed me. I'd like to tell you that it's the sort of thing that happens to me all the time, but the plain truth is that it doesn't, and it threw me.

"Don't you recognize me?" the woman said. "I'm Ruth Costigan!"

"Mrs. Costigan," I said, "you look like a different woman!"

She did, too. She'd had her hair style changed, gotten a nose job and had reduced her weight by twenty or thirty pounds. She looked about ten years younger, and she was dressed in a very expensive Chanel suit with a zigzag pattern. She was stepping higher than a blind dog in a wheatfield.

"I've really been living, Mr. Armes!" she said. "That

whole business opened my eyes, and I owe it all to you!"

She went on to tell me that I'd probably be getting an invitation to a wedding before long—she was planning to remarry. She told me she had decided that two could play that game just as well as one, and she'd done better than Joe all the way down the line. I asked her what she meant.

"Well, that spring chicken of his, she was twenty-five." She giggled. "The boy I'm going to marry is only seventeen!"

19.

Can you state with certainty where you were on March 11, 1973, at 12:30 P.M.? For me, it's easy. I had just stepped down from the witness stand in the 34th District Court in El Paso, after a three-and-a-half-hour cross-examination by the attorney defending two men who had been apprehended by me after they hijacked a truck belonging to the Arden Motor Freight Line. Normal procedure is to recess court at midday for lunch, but the judge knew I had another court appearance at two, where I was testifying in a criminal matter involving a woman charged with murdering her husband and teenage stepson for $20,000 insurance money. As I was walking out of the courtroom, a man stopped me and asked if he could have a moment.

He told me his name was William Simpson, and that he was the accountant of the Superhighway Motor Freight Line, which was headquartered in New York but which operated nationwide. His son-in-law, Allan Lang, was president of the company, and had sent him down to El Paso when he heard I was testifying in the Arden Motor Freight Line case, to ask whether I would consider taking on SMFL as a client. Mr. Simpson was a thin, scholarly-looking man of about fifty, wearing tortoise-shell framed glasses and a dark business suit. I invited him to come and have lunch with me so we could discuss it more fully.

"They do a very good seafood salad at the El Paso Club," I said. "How does that suit you?"

He said that would be fine, so we went to the El Paso National Bank Building and took the elevator to the top floor. On the way, Bill Simpson told me something about Superhighway. I knew the name, of course —SMFL is one of the largest trucking companies operating out of New York, which makes it among the ten biggest in America. The loading dock at their freight warehouse is large enough to load three hundred trucks simultaneously, using enormous conveyors. They had a reputation for being very reliable.

Over lunch, he told me that they were being ripped off at an enormous level—losses of up to $100,000 a day were being incurred, and the insurance companies were only paying ten cents on a dollar. SMFL was heading for bankruptcy faster than one of their own juggernauts, despite the fact that the FBI had been working on the hijackings for more than four months. They had on one occasion set a trap inside a crate of guns destined for California, part of a shipment to sporting goods stores around the state. The thieves not only stole the guns, but disconnected the alarm and stole that as well—while the FBI actually had the consignment under surveillance. Disgusted, Lang had sent his father-in-law down to El Paso to retain me.

By the time lunch was over, we had a deal, and I had SMFL's check for a fairly large retainer in my pocket. I made arrangements to meet Simpson and his principal in New York the following day, and then made tracks for the 65th District Court. I was on the stand from 2:05 until 5:00 P.M., at which time the court was adjourned.

My limousine was waiting outside, motor purring as I bounded down the steps of the courthouse. We sped off toward Montana. Pausing only to pick up the equipment that I would need in New York (which had already been laid out on my instructions), I piled back into the car. We made the flight connecting with the New York plane from Dallas with literally only minutes to spare.

Lang and Simpson met me in one of their business offices overlooking the docks on the North River, as real New Yorkers call the Hudson.

It was gray and cold, a blustery Atlantic wind snapping the shipping line flags flat and horizontal on their poles. The office would not be open for business for another hour, and after we had our council of war, I asked Lang to show me some crates—preferably containing guns—which were due for shipment that day. Lang and Simpson checked through piles of yellow shipment manifests until they came up with something that fit the profile, a shipment of sporting goods scheduled for loading at two that afternoon. I placed microtransmitters in several of the cases, and then all three of us went back up to the office, where I began to synchronize my receiver with the transmitters. While I was doing it, three men walked into the office.

I had no idea who they were, but since the whole idea behind the stealth in placing the bugs had been that no one except myself, Lang and Simpson would even know I was on the case, it looked like my cover— and my planted bugs—were well and truly blown. But no, the intruders weren't employees, they were FBI agents! They were keeping the office under surveillance, and when they saw all the activity they had decided to investigate. They asked who I was and I told them.

You'd have thought I was trying to steal their wallets. They told me I had no right to interfere in their case. They told me it would be pointless for me to try catching these thieves, who were real pros and not likely to stumble into the clutches of amateur detectives. They told me that because the shipments were all interstate, the case was within their jurisdiction and theirs alone. They complained that they had put in a lot of hours, a lot of manpower, and lost a lot of sophisticated equipment in pursuing this case, and so on and so on. They stomped up and down like prima donnas until I told them to shut up because I was getting a signal.

The agent called Coke looked at me as if I had gone insane. Only fair, I guess. He couldn't see any receiver, for the one I was using was so small that anyone who

didn't know it was there would never have been able to
detect it with the naked eye. Nonetheless, it was beep-
ing like mad, and I told Lang that someone was loading the crates we had bugged. The FBI men looked at
each other and laughed nervously. Boy, what kind of
nut have we got here? their expressions said. I ignored
them and beckoned Mr. Lang to the office window. A
truck was pulling out of the warehouse below, although no truck was scheduled to do so.

"That truck has the guns on board," I said, and used
the radio-phone to whistle up an agent waiting nearby
in a car. The FBI agents asked, with elaborate polite-
ness, whether they could come along to see the big
catch. I told them sure; I was looking forward to
watching them eat a sizable helping of crow.

The big semitruck slogged up north through the
traffic and on to the Major Deegan Expressway. We
crossed the Hudson at the Tappan Zee Bridge and then
bore north on the New York State Thruway. I had no
fear of losing that huge vehicle, so we hung back, far
enough behind so that the driver wouldn't wonder
about the big black limo that seemed not to want to
overtake him.

The hijackers swung the rig off the Thruway at the
Modena exit heading west, and I asked my agent, Al
Davies, if he had any ideas. He was checking his map
and said that there was a private airfield a few miles
ahead. I nodded. An airfield was a perfect place to
stash stolen loot. Those big hangars could hold large
shipping crates for months with nobody asking any
questions. Private planes could fly the stuff out to anywhere in the country. They could almost claim to be
able to offer better service than the truckers.

The big truck turned off at the airfield exit and
backed up to a loading ramp at one of the hangars. I
noticed that the plane on the apron in front of the
building was a big Fairchild-Hiller short-haul twin-
turbofan transport. That baby had a 12,500-pound pay-
load, and a 540-mile range at best-cost cruising speed.
These men were kitted to shift anything they wanted,

anyplace they liked. There were eight of them now, busy as ants, unloading crate after crate from the big Superhighway truck. The FBI men were jumping about like hens on hot bricks, itching to make the collar. I persuaded them to wait until the truck was completely unloaded, and then we made our play.

We rushed the hangar and the Feds arrested everyone in sight. Lang and Simpson identified their own goods, and a lot of stuff that didn't come from SMFL's warehouse. The truck driver and his eight confederates were part of a huge ring, countrywide, that was literally stealing to order. They had men visiting stores and asking the buyers what they needed and what they'd like to pay. Once they had the "order," they went out and stole the goods, shipping them in to the customer and laughing all the way to the bank. This hangar had over $300,000 worth of goods in it, and by the time the arrested men had sung their songs, more than sixty people were apprehended, and $3 million worth of stolen goods recovered.

I was later invited by Superhighway Motor Freight to attend the Truckers' Association meeting in Las Vegas, and spent a pleasant three and three-quarter hours answering questions from the floor after my speech on pilferage prevention. Since I was scheduled for only twenty minutes, Allan Lang told me he counted my appearance as big a success as my work for him. I said the only thing I was sorry about was that I had not asked FBI Agent Victor Coke how he liked the taste of crow.

Not that I really had to: I had to eat my own share a long time ago. Believe me, it's a chastening experience to be nearly bludgeoned to death through your own carelessness.

I had been away for some weeks on a caper in Venezuela, and an enormous pile of letters, messages, progress reports and inquiries was waiting for me at the office. I had my secretary bring the most urgent and important ones over to the house, and started in on them immediately. By about ten that evening I had finished with all of it, and decided to run over to the office and pick up the rest in order to have a clean desk the following day.

Linda entered her usual comment: that I was out of my mind.

I gave my usual reply: I know, but I'm going anyway.

She said what she always says: Can't it wait until morning?

And I said what I always say: Yes, but why should it when I can do it now?

Whereupon she smiled like she always smiles and kissed me and said drive carefully, and I smiled and kissed her and said I would. Then I got into the Stingray and headed for the office. I was nearly at the Geronimo exit on Gateway before I realized that I hadn't strapped on my gun. No point in turning back, I thought. Anyway, I didn't plan to be out of the house more than three-quarters of an hour. And frankly, it never occurred to me that I would need it that night. This was only a couple of years after I had set up my organization. I didn't take half as many precautions in those days as I do now.

I picked up all the papers on the desk, neatly stacked in the usual piles. I sifted them and left the things that really could wait until morning, and stuffed the rest into my briefcase. It took me no more than fifteen minutes to cover the distance between the office and my home, and I swung off North Loop onto the ramp in front of the gate, reaching over for the control box to open it. It was a little awkward. I was wearing my seat belts—as always—and the gizmo had slid over to one side of the seat. Just as my hooks touched it, *wham! wham! wham!* two men came out of the shadows wielding baseball bats, one of them smashing in the windshield while the other whacked away the window on the passenger side.

One bang and two and then there was glass everywhere except in the window frames. I was pinned to the seat by my safety belt, and couldn't do more than

reel back a little. The man on the passenger side
reached in to try and grab me so he could pull me
where the bat would reach. I hit him with a right hook,
and I do mean hook. He fell back, his mouth a sudden
mess of bloody flesh; then he lurched at me again. I
hit him once more, and he reeled back out of sight,
making a broken, coughing sound. That was the best
lick I got, because in getting it, I'd given the second
man, who'd whacked away the windshield, all the time
in the world to get his shot just right. He smashed me
over the head with the baseball bat and I went back
against the seat and then came forward just in time to
receive his second one. Then 99.99 percent of all the
lights in the world went out. I fell forward against the
wheel, my broken head spouting blood like a stuck pig
and jamming the car horn so that it bellowed one long
continuous note. That very fact may just possibly have
saved my life, for it stirred up the dogs inside the
fence, and they started kicking up all sorts of noise.
Linda had been watching the whole thing on the
closed-circuit TV. She slammed all the lights on and
was running out to open the gates.

The assailants were long gone by the time she got
outside and found me sprawled in a bloody mess in the
driver's seat. She ran back inside, called an ambulance,
and I was whisked off to the hospital.

When I came to, I looked like I'd been in a fight
with a wildcat in a briar patch. I had an impressive
turban of white bandages, and my forehead down to
my eyebrows was one blue-black-yellow bruise. Both
my eyes were blacked, and the top of one of my torn
ears had been stitched back on. All that, however,
didn't bother me. What did was the fact that one side
of my body, opposite to the side of my head where I
had been hit, was completely numb. I could use every
muscle quite normally, but there was a strange dead
feeling when anything touched my skin, as though my
sensory perception had been deadened. Eventually, the
doctors gave me a program of tests and various shots,
but for four months after I left the hospital, the sensa-

tion persisted. Finally, I decided I would just ignore it, act as though there was nothing wrong with me. After a little while, there wasn't.

Besides, I was busy. I put some feelers out in certain underworld circles, and one of my informers—let's call him Lefty—came up with the information that a contract had been put out on me, and that it had been picked up in Seattle. I am not normally a vengeful person, but in this case I was more than willing to make an exception, so I flew up to Seattle. It took me a week of intensive work, but I managed to track down one of the hit men. I tailed him to a bar at the foot of Jackson Street near Pier 47, and when he saw me, he looked like a man who would have given all he had to be anyplace but where he was. I told him I'd like to discuss something with him, outside. When we were through, that cheap hoodlum had just about enough strength to crawl to the casualty ward. He would have told me the moon was made of creamcheese if I'd wanted him to, but I had to make do with the fact that what he had told me didn't give me any handle on the other man.

He had been recruited in a bar opposite the Trailways Bus Depot on Seventh Avenue by a black man, who asked him if he was interested in making some money messing up a guy who was running around with his buddy's girlfriend. "One thousand dollars now," the man told him, "and another thousand afterward. Fifteen hundred if the job's done well." He said he understood what "done well" meant—dead. He and the black guy had flown down to El Paso and attacked me, and flown back the same night. That was all he knew, except that the man's name was Sam something and he'd shipped out on a freighter for Yokohama.

I tried every way I know how to track down that character, but I ran into a dead end in Singapore, where he jumped ship. Nobody knows where he is right now, but I've still got an open file on Sam. One day I'm going to close it.

Permanently.

20.

For all his charisma, Jay Armes remains diffident about telling the full story behind all his capers, his many adventures and the attempts on his life. He can be, when he wants to, what one newspaper accurately described as "purposefully vague." When he is, there's usually a good reason for it. The reason he won't talk about the time a marksman with a high-powered rifle and a telescopic sight tried to pick him off at his own doorway as he was saying goodbye to some friends is that it would embarrass the couple concerned. He doesn't go into detail about the occasion when someone tried to assassinate him in his office, although the bullet holes in the windows and the pockmarks in the walls are still there. Why? Because he tracked down the would-be assassin and had him committed to a mental institution, and to reveal the man's name would be to give his family grave distress. He refuses to tell the story of how someone nearly kidnapped Tracy, one of the Armes children. It upsets Linda, and Armes will walk a country mile barefoot to avoid doing that.

He will once in a while mention his famous clients by name—Elvis Presley, Elizabeth Taylor, Frank Sinatra, the president of a South American republic, an internationally known financier, a famous politician, the chairman of a multinational corporation—but insists that they have a right to their privacy, and that he respects it. "No one would ever trust me again," he says, with justification, "if I revealed all the details of a confidential investigation I had carried out for them

on coast-to-coast television or in some book or maga-
zine. It wouldn't be fair to my client, and with me, the
client's interests take priority over everything else."

So all we know about Armes' work for King Faisal
is that it involved security at the royal palace, and all
we know about the Mexican prison helicopter escape
said to have inspired the Charles Bronson movie
Breakout is that it happened. Other people are at risk
if Armes tells it like it was, and there are more than a
few people waiting around hoping that he may just do
that so they can pay off some old scores. No chance—
the United Nations Plaza jewelry caper, the Miss Uni-
verse caper, the glider flight into Castro's Cuba, these
and many others involve confidences that may not be
broken without endangering the lives of people who
trust and rely on Armes, just as he implicitly trusts and
relies on them. "Maybe I'll tell these stories one day,"
he promises, "but not yet. Too many people could get
hurt." And what about Jay Armes? Couldn't he get
hurt? "Sure," he says. "That's part of the risk I run."
He shrugs. "And I accept it."

Judith Castleton was a handsome and intelligent
woman of perhaps seventy-five summers, although if
you had met her on the street you wouldn't have said
she was a day over sixty. She had that indefinable
something that the French call *chic,* the culture and
grace that derive from charm, wit, self-assurance, education and—sometimes—great wealth. Her father had
been a director of the de Beers organization in South
Africa, one of the world's largest producers of diamonds. He had moved to the United States when he
retired, and bought a beautiful house in Georgetown,
that much sought-after section of Washington that
was, in fact, a self-contained and lovely village long
before Pierre Charles L'Enfant's visionary city began
to rise out of the Potomac swamp.

Mrs. Castleton's father had been of Syrian descent,
and over the years he worked for de Beers, he invested

every penny he could scrape together in buying fine stones. Some of these were mounted in rings or bracelets, others in necklaces. At the time of his death, in the late 1940s, they were worth a quarter of a million pre-inflation dollars. He left everything to his only daughter, who had married the son of a Middle Eastern diplomat, and they divided their time between Washington and Paris, taking their summer vacations in an apartment in Menton on the Mediterranean coast of France. It was during such a vacation that Mrs. Castleton's jewelry was stolen from the Georgetown house, and its disappearance almost broke her heart. The loss was not discovered for a while, not until Mrs. Castleton flew back to the United States and noted her jewelry was gone. She called in the police, but break-ins in Georgetown are not exactly a novelty to the local cops. They took statements and descriptions of the missing jewelry, made a check of the premises and departed. The statistics for big-city burglary are frighteningly high, as any insurance assessor will tell you. He will also tell you that the odds against finding the culprits are much higher. The family was summoned to Washington by Mrs. Castleton's oldest son, James, and a council of war was held. The police were treating the case as a pro job, which meant they held out little hope of recovering the jewelry. The family's decision was to contact me. James flew to El Paso and came to my office.

"It's not just the value of the jewelry, Mr. Armes," he told me. "I guess the family could get together and buy replacements if we had to. But no replacements we could buy would ever have the sentimental value of her own things. You know how it is when heirlooms have been in a family for generations."

I could hardly say that my family hadn't had $800,000 worth of jewelry locked up for a century or so, but I understood how he felt. I asked him for a description of the stolen goods, and he provided me with a copy of the insurance adjustor's report. Included in the list were two marquise rings, one with a seven-karat and another a five-karat stone. One pear-shaped stone set in a platinum ring was worth $85,000. I asked him to describe in detail how the house had been broken into, and he said there had been hardly any damage at all. Nothing else had been stolen, although there were a number of valuable paintings, antique furniture and silverware in the house.

I asked him if he could provide me with a list of every single person who had access to the house or who would know about the jewelry. He said the list would run into hundreds of names, and I said I wasn't worried how many names were on the list; what mattered was that no one was left off it. I then asked him for a separate listing giving details of every member of the family who had access to the house. He was appalled at the inference. He told me his relatives were Syrian Orthodox, a close-knit family in which any thought of stealing from another member was unthinkable. He said that anyone who contemplated such an act would be beyond the pale, cast out by the rest of the family forever. He told me that I must look elsewhere for the thief.

I said I understood how he felt, but that his reaction was standard. Pretty nearly every client I've ever had says something along the same lines: it couldn't be him, or her, or them, it just couldn't be, they wouldn't do that to me. Sometimes, alas, it later becomes "how could they?" So I told James Castleton that I had to do things my way or not at all, and that my way was by process of elimination. I told him that I didn't automatically assume some member of the family was guilty, but that everyone would feel better knowing he or she had been checked and eliminated, and so would he. He nodded, reassured by what I said.

In fact, my immediate inclination, gut feeling, intuition, call it what you will, was to see the robbery as an inside job by someone close to Mrs. Castleton. Pro thieves are rarely tidy—they just don't give a damn for your house or your property, only the speed with which they can go through it. They rip out every drawer, fling open every closet and strew its contents on the floor, invert and empty every box, turn every suit inside out, rip up carpet, turn every picture askew and—usually—take everything worth anything. Cameras, TV sets, hi-fi equipment in the ordinary house. In a house like the one Mrs. Castleton lived in, with all the time in the world to make their selection, it seemed more than likely to me that pros would have stripped the place like buzzards working on a dead rabbit. Yet all that was gone was the jewelry.

It was still possible, of course, that it could have been a pro job, and that all they wanted was the ice. But jewelry—especially stones so identifiable—is hellishly hard to fence, and the rewards are small, sometimes only ten cents on the dollar. Why would pros pass up silver, carpets, paintings, a valuable coin collection that would be easy—much easier—to unload at a good price?

Finally James Castleton provided me with the lists I wanted, and I set to work checking everyone mentioned on them. I ran two kinds of check. On the random visitors to the Castleton home, neighbors, local people well known in the area, spot checks, what we in my organization call a QC/1—a quick check by one person, taking an hour—give or taken ten minutes. On the family members (there were ten of them) I ordered DC/24's—deep checks taking a minimum of twenty-four hours for each person. Everyone came up clean. None of them had any apparent motive for stealing the jewelry. They were a wealthy family, and no one was in any kind of financial or personal bind.

I still trusted my gut feeling, somehow sure that I was right. I piled all the reports in front of me and sat reading them over and over trying to find something I could put a handle on. My agents had all done thoroughly professional work, giving me detailed information on every member of the family, his or her routine,

habits, anything and everything that would present me
with a rounded picture of the person under surveillance. All but one: a granddaughter of Mrs. Castleton's, Joan Heathcote, twenty-year-old daughter of
James Castleton's sister Rose, a student at Georgetown
University, majoring in art, who was presently on vacation in Paris. There was nothing out of kilter about her
background or the checks my agent had been able to
run, but my vibes got stronger. I checked on her more
carefully, and discovered that the girl was a regular
visitor at her grandmother's home, and had been to see
her shortly before the grandmother had departed for
her European vacation. Joan and her grandmother
were very close. In fact, Joan was even now using the
Castleton apartment on the rue du Faubourg St.-
Honoré as her vacation home away from home.

I called my Paris agent and then sat fuming while he
collected the information I needed. I told him to work
as fast as he could, but not to rush it, and I had to
contain my impatience until he got what I wanted.
When he got back to me twenty-four hours later, I
knew my gut feeling had been right. Joan Heathcote
was visiting museums and libraries in Paris, and asking for information about cutting and shaping diamonds.

I'd used the time spent waiting for Claude Bonnetain's call to order a TBC—total background check—
on Joan Heathcote. I had it all with me as I boarded
the Washington-bound jet: habits, hobbies, friends,
scholastic records, interests, daily routines, even which
childhood diseases she'd had (scarlet fever and chick-
enpox). In Washington, I met with James Castleton
and told him I wanted a family power of attorney giving me permission to act in what I considered at any
time to be in its best interest, and that I wanted the
signature of every member of the family on it. He said
it would take some time to get that, and I told him he
had until nine o'clock that night, which was when my
plane was due to leave. I didn't tell him where I was

going, or what I had in mind. All I did was to tell him to have the paper ready when I returned from New York.

I grabbed the shuttle to Fun City and went to see a friend of mine who owns a business in the diamond center on Forty-seventh Street. I told him I wanted a crash course in diamond salesmanship, and that I would need to borrow a sample case full of top-class specimens of fine jewelry, which I would be taking out of the country. I left there at four in the afternoon, my head buzzing with all the new information I'd soaked up, and the slim attaché case padlocked to my left hook. I was in no doubt as to the quality of the merchandise I was carrying. My friend Lionel Leventhal had asked me for a check to cover the value of the jewelry, and I still had a cramp from writing all those zeros.

I hurried back to Washington and picked up the power of attorney from the still-puzzled but cooperative James Castleton. Then I dashed out to Dulles International, to be finally shunted aboard the 747 by one of those Afrika Korps troop carriers they use instead of buses up there.

Next morning I was in the City of Light. I contacted Claude Bonnetain, and then telephoned Joan Heathcote, telling her that I was from New York, and that Johnny Clarke, a mutual friend of ours, had suggested that I look her up when he heard that I was visiting Paris on business. My cover was carefully worked out, and fireproof. John Clarke, a fellow student of Joan's at Georgetown U., was presently vacationing with his family in the Virgin Islands. No way she would be able to check with him whether he knew Jay Armitage, a salesman for Leventhal Gems, Inc.

She sounded friendly enough on the telephone, and I asked her if she'd care to meet me for lunch. She said she would love to, and I said I would call for her at noon. On my instructions, Claude had rented a Rolls, and with him decked out in a chauffeur's uniform, I rolled up outside the door of the apartment house on the Faubourg St.-Honoré dead on time.

There's no getting away from it, the Rolls-Royce people know how to make a car that makes an impression. Joan Heathcote got in and I told my "chauffeur" to take us to Aux Lyonnais in the rue St.-Marc. It's an old and unpretentious bistro that I like very much, and it serves some of the best Lyonnaise cooking in Paris—which means just about the best there is. Monsieur Viollet, the *patron,* is a bit of a bully when it comes to ordering, but his heart is as soft as his roast duck. On the way, I weighed up my companion.

Joan Heathcote was almost startlingly pretty. High cheekbones and wide, generous lips, silken blond hair that hung straight—probably ironed—down to her waist, and eyes as blue as Delft china. There was a faint sprinkle of freckles across the bridge of her nose, and she had a beautiful smile.

She said she was surprised that Johnny Clarke had never mentioned me. I said maybe she'd forgotten, and she said she wouldn't be likely to forget his mentioning a friend who had two hooks instead of hands. I changed the subject, and over lunch I told her about myself. I said I was the European vice-president of the Leventhal organization—a cover Lionel was ready to back up verbally should anyone check with him in New York—and that I was visiting wholesalers and large retail establishments in Paris for a few days. Then I would be moving on to Zürich, Geneva, Lyon, Marseilles, Madrid and back home to New York.

"What a shame you'll only be in town for a few days," she said. "I could have given you my special conducted tour of the Louvre!"

I said I had to put work first and fun later, but that I'd just love to take her to dinner one evening if she was free. I knew she'd been impressed with the car, just as she had been impressed with my choice of restaurant and my obvious—or so it seemed to her, anyway—wealth. Most of all, of course, she was interested in my "profession," and during our return journey to the apartment, she asked me if I carried samples of my jewelry with me. I said that I did, but that unfortunately they were locked in the safe of the Hotel George V right now.

"Oh, I'd just love to see them," she said. "It sounds as if you have one of the most interesting jobs in the world."

"Well," I said, and it was no lie, "what I do does have its moments."

"Do you think I could see your samples?" she asked.

I said, of course, why didn't we have dinner that night, and I would bring my sample case with me? After a momentary hesitation, Joan agreed, and asked what she should wear.

"Dress up," I said. "We'll go somewhere extra nice."

At seven that evening Claude slid the Rolls to a stop outside the Castleton apartment. I saw the concierge peeping from behind her lace curtains as Joan Heathcote came down the stairs, and I didn't blame the old lady one bit. Joan was something to see. She was wearing a long white satin evening gown that bared her slightly tanned shoulders and back and a beautiful velvet cape over the dress. Two clusters of diamonds shone on the lobes of her ears, and on her left wrist was a bracelet fit for a queen. She was no longer an attractive girl, but a stunningly beautiful young woman.

"Where are we going?" she asked me as we got into the Rolls.

"Surprise," I said. It was a beautiful evening, warm and springlike. Claude took us down the Rue de Rivoli, past the Jeu du Paume and the Louvre and across the Pont Neuf. On the right I caught a glimpse of the Square du Vert Galant, where Ernest Hemingway used to go fishing when he was a young man in Paris. Then we bore left and along the Left Bank, past the floodlit grandeur of Notre Dame, and the car stopped.

"Quinze la Tournelle," Claude announced grandly.

15, quai de la Tournelle is one of the most famous gastronomic addresses in Paris, if not the world, for it houses la Tour d'Argent, that superb culinary establishment in the Fifth Arrondissement, with its fabled view across the Seine toward the dreaming spires of the great cathedral. I had reserved the corner table in the window alcove, and our fine view was only one part of a superb meal. We began with champagne, and followed the suggestions of François, the maitre d'hotel, regarding food and wine. Filet of sole cardinal, duck cooked as only the Tour d'Argent knows how, a soufflé so light that it literally melted on the tongue. And the wines! A fine, dry stony Sancerre with the fish, a burgundy with the duck, and Cognac Grand Fine Champagne with the *café filtre*—glorious. I was only sorry that I was on business—which meant that I had to make sure that my companion drank most of the wine, and that I led the conversation into the areas I wished it to go.

I asked Joan what had got her interested in jewelry, and where she had obtained the pieces she was wearing. She said they had been left to her by her grandmother, and that because of that she was thinking of designing her own jewelry. She said she had a lot of ideas for modern settings instead of the old-fashioned ones in which her present jewels were set. We talked about everything under the sun before, during and after I learned that salient set of facts, but it confirmed what I needed to know. As the coffee came, I sent a message down to my "chauffeur" to bring my sample case upstairs. Claude came in, delivered it, clicked his heels like a Prussian and went out, and it was all I could do not to grin. I went into the patter I had learned at the diamond exchange, and showed Joan some of the beautiful unmounted diamonds in my case. She was most impressed with them—so was I, for it was the first time I'd seen what I was carrying!— and after a while she asked me if I knew how to value jewelry.

"I can make a fairly close estimate of value for insurance purposes," I said. "Is that what you mean?"

For answer, she delved into her purse and brought out a ring, slipping it onto her slim finger and wriggling her hand so that the stone caught the candlelight and flashed like burning ice.

"It looks very nice," I said. "Is it real?"

She handed it to me, and I looked at it carefully through the jeweler's glass in the case, making a production out of it, turning the ring this way and that, pursing my lips like a pawnbroker. It was a seven-karat marquise ring, and it fitted perfectly the insurance description I had read in my office the day James Castleton came to see me.

"How much would you say it's worth?" the girl asked.

"An estimate? Around a hundred thousand. In my opinion."

"Is that all?" she said. "I thought it was worth a lot more than that." There was real disappointment in her voice, and I trotted out my pat speech in reply, which was to the effect that the value of jewelry and the price you get when you sell it are nothing like one and the same thing. I said I was talking about resale value, and its resale value was not more than $100,000, tops. I handed the ring back to her and, not much to my surprise, she handed me another. It had a flawless pear-shaped stone.

"What about this one?" Joan asked anxiously.

I repeated my routine of examining the ring and the stone, and then handed it back to her, saying that I estimated it as worth between $75,000 and $100,000. I told her it was difficult to be precise, because specially-shaped stones, unless they can be recut, are often harder to sell than the standard shapes and sizes.

"Now it's my turn to show you something, Joan," I said, and reached into my pocket. I laid my credentials on the table in front of her, and she stared at them as if I'd put a cobra there.

"An investigator," she said. "A private investigator?"

"That's right, Joan," I said, "and you know what I want, don't you?"

She sat there stock still, her face as white as flour, sudden tears in the beautiful blue eyes. More than ever, I was glad that I had specified the corner table, far enough away from the other diners so that they could not see us or hear our conversation.

"Where's the rest of it, Joan?" I said.

"At the apartment," she said listlessly. She looked at me with a frown wrinkling her forehead, and asked me how I had found out that she had taken the jewelry. I shrugged; that didn't matter at all, I said.

"But you got me to wear it!" she said, as if I had betrayed her. "I hadn't even touched it, taken it out of the box since I took it. You got me to wear it!"

I suppose I could have congratulated myself upon my powers of auto-suggestion, and the need of a pretty young girl to impress the Big Spender from New York, but I didn't. Too many people in my business have got round shoulders from patting themselves on the back, and I don't plan to join the club. I told Joan I wanted to go and get the rest of the missing jewelry. She said she would be glad when it was gone, glad the whole thing was out in the open.

"You don't know how badly I've felt about taking it," she said.

I didn't answer that, either. Quite a lot of thieves say exactly the same thing—after they're caught.

"I'll give everything back," Joan said, "but please, please, don't tell my parents, don't tell Grandma. They . . . they will just disown me."

"I'm sorry, Joan," I said. "I'll have to name you in my report. I don't have any choice."

"No, please!" she said.

I shook my head, and called for the bill. There really wasn't anything I could do to alleviate the girl's distress, and she was crying as she got into the Rolls. I told Claude to take us to the apartment on the Faubourg St.-Honoré.

After a while the crying stopped, and Joan Heathcote was silent as we wove our way through the late evening traffic.

"I'll do anything," she whispered after a while. "Anything. I'll be your slave. My father is rich. I'll get money. I'll give you anything you want, anything!"

I told her she didn't have anything I needed, and that the best I could do for her was to promise to recommend no prosecution. After that she was silent again. We got to the apartment and I told Claude to come up with us. The maid let us in, and watched with wide eyes as I followed Joan across the hall and into her bedroom. She turned to look at Claude in silent demand for an explanation of this strange intrusion, and Claude gave a huge Gallic shrug.

Joan had a velvet box on the dressing table in the beautiful high-ceilinged room. I checked the contents against the list I had with me. Everything was there. I told her to pack a bag.

"You can't be going to take me back?" she said. "You can't! I won't go!"

I told her that if I had to, I would arrest her and take her back in handcuffs. The Power of Attorney given to me by the family was all the authority I needed to do just that.

"You don't know what you're doing to me," she said, her eyes filling with tears again.

"Do you know what you did to your grandmother?"

She shook her head angrily, as though to shake away the tears, and dragged a suitcase from beneath a wardrobe. She threw things into it any damned way, and I did nothing to stop her. Let her work off the venom on the clothing. Better that than me.

We left the apartment an hour later. Joan Heathcote held her head high, and her face was cold and disdainful. She looked like Marie Antoinette going to the guillotine, with Claude and me the sansculottes who had brought her to the tumbrel. I'd checked ahead to Orly

Airport and discovered that there was a midnight flight to Lisbon that would connect with a Pan Am departure early the following morning for America. Late that afternoon, we touched down on the last leg of our long flight. Steve Dean, my agent in Washington, was waiting for us at the airport.

Joan Heathcote had hardly spoken the whole way home, just withdrawn into herself like a Baja California turtle going into his shell. I checked into the Watergate, and had Steve hold her in another room of the suite while I called James Castleton and asked him to come over and see me. He was knocking on the door in twenty minutes, and when he saw the jewelry spread on the velvet cloth covering the coffee table, his eyes widened with surprise. He stared at the glittering gems as if hypnotized, and said without looking at me, "You found them? Already?"

"I need your formal identification, Mr. Castleton," I said, "that these are the missing jewels."

"Yes," he said, picking them up and putting them down one by one, "yes, yes, yes, these are they! I'm sorry, I don't know what to say!"

"I beg your pardon?"

"I owe you an apology, Mr. Armes," he said.

I asked him why, and he told me that hiring me had really been the family's way of showing the old lady that no expense or effort was being spared in the matter of her missing jewelry. None of them had thought I might actually locate it, and never in his wildest dreams had he believed I could do so as quickly as I had. He had been sure the stones had already been re-cut, remounted and resold. He leaned forward in his chair.

"Did you find the thief also?" he asked.

I said that I had, and that it had been a member of his family.

"Oh, no," he said. "That can't be true, Mr. Armes."

"I'm afraid it is, Mr. Castleton," I said, and took him into the adjoining room to face the weeping girl. I signaled Steve, and he came out to join me in the other room, leaving the two of them alone. I knew what would be happening in there. There would be questions and tears, and then more questions and more tears, ending in disgust on the one side and despair on the other. There wasn't anything I could do about either. People have to find out about each other, and sometimes it can cut to the bone.

I kept my promise to Joan by recommending in my report, and personally to James Castleton, that no prosecution be instigated. I even stuck my neck out by suggesting there was really no need for the family—especially the girl's parents—to know. The gems were safe, no harm had been done. Castleton shook his head, and I remembered what he had told me about the family the very first time he came to see me.

There never was any prosecution, and what the family did or did not do I have no way of knowing. I have always preferred to believe, in spite of what happened later, that they forgave the girl and did not cast her out; but the ending was just as sad either way. Seven months later that beautiful girl committed suicide by taking a vast overdose of sleeping pills.

21.

I had just finished an insurance investigation when Mike Constantine telephoned me from London. The investigation—which involved my diving to find a sunken ship that had left Yokohama, Japan, loaded with ornamental work insured for $1.5 million—nearly killed me. In tracing the ship, I went further down than was safe, and came up too fast—getting a bad attack of the bends. Too rapid decompression causes nitrogen bubbles to infiltrate the blood, causing agonizing body pains, which, if very severe, can be fatal. I was lucky to be diving from a vessel with a compression chamber, and came out of it healthy enough to prove that the storm-sunk ship had sailed out from Yokohama with only half the cargo aboard. The other half was still in the loading sheds on the quay, and the insurance company that had retained me saved three quarters of a million dollars on the deal. But that's another story.

Mike Constantine is one of the biggest and most famous of all the show-biz agents in England. He divides his time among three homes, one in England, another in Los Angeles and the third in Monte Carlo. A party at any one of them is like the Pantages Theater on Oscar night. Mike's wife is one of the most delightful French actresses ever to appear in an American musical, and that's all the clues you're going to get.

"I've got a caper for you, Jay," he said. "Are you free?"

"Well . . ." I said. I was up to my eyes in work, as usual, but I told him that I'd make an exception for an old friend, and asked what the trouble was. He told me that a friend of his wife's, an Oriental lady who had married, amid enormous publicity, one of the most famous rock singers of his generation, needed my help in the worst way. Her first husband had taken the little boy who was the only child of that marriage on a day trip to the zoo. Now they had discovered that he had abducted the boy, and nobody could find them. Meanwhile, the mother—let's call her Miko Kisama—was slowly going, as Mike put it in his inimitably British manner, "stark raving bonkers"—meaning out of her mind.

"You want me to find them?" I said.

"That's the general idea, Jay," he said. "Can you get right on it?"

I said I would start immediately, and asked him to send me photos and any other relevant details, before hanging up and dialing the number he had given me for Miko Kisama, or Mrs. Hartman as she now was. I talked with her for a long time, ascertaining all the relevant details: what the child had been wearing, who had seen him last, a routine I described earlier which consists of eleven basic who/what/when/where questions upon which I then elaborate. The information provides me with enough of a basis to evaluate a course of action. I then asked further questions about the husband, who was not Oriental. His name was Richard Carson, and to my surprise, Mrs. Hartman told me that his parents were alive, and living in Phoenix, Arizona, not more than six hundred miles from my office door.

I put Paul Napier to work on a neighborhood survey near the apartment—or flat, as the British call it— where Carson had been living, and the London team ran some checks, which quickly came up with the information that Carson had left the apartment closed, telling his landlady he would be away indefinitely, and flown with the child from Heathrow to Kennedy Airport, New York.

Immigration in New York gave us the information in their records, but the address was a hotel in midtown Manhattan, and there was no Richard Carson staying there, or anyone answering his description. The missing boy and his father might by now be on their way to any country in the world. Which left us only one bell to ring. Accordingly, I got a team together and headed for Phoenix, where Janet and Timothy Carson had a house up in Paradise Valley, near Squaw Peak City Park.

We set up round-the-clock surveillance on the house. It's difficult to do on a suburban street, because a strange automobile parked for a long time tends to attract attention, and nervous parents, rightly fearing for the safety of their children, ask the police to check it out. We operated what we call an FVSR— five-vehicle switch routine. Different agents, all using different cars with local plates, take turns moving in and out of the surveillance area, coordinating their movements so that one vehicle will be leaving position just as the next one draws up. That way, people just see different cars coming and going, the most natural thing in the world.

Now I had to find a way to listen in on the Carsons' telephone, and to do that we had to drop a bug near it. Just to get the facts straight: it is illegal to *wiretap* (connect a listening device to a phone); there are federal laws against eavesdropping and divulging the information gained by doing so. However, *bugging* (placing a listening device in a room) is another matter entirely, and is not illegal. So up the road comes a panel truck marked ACE EXTERMINATORS or ACME INFESTATION SERVICE or some such legend, and we knock on the door of the house we want to get into. We tell them we're making random checks for infestation after finding a plague of German cockroaches or Japanese mites nearby, and we'd be happy to check the house and spray against the pests—entirely free, of course. We call back in a couple of days to make sure everything is in order, and there is no charge, no commitment, except that we hope that if the service works, they will recommend us to their neighbors.

People usually go out of their way to help you, making sure you go into every room, spray every corner. You're using ordinary tap water in the sprays, but they don't know that, of course. In the process, you plant your microtransmitters.

A listening post is then set up nearby in the back of another truck, and we monitor every call that is made on that telephone. Surveillance of the subject family and monitoring of the telephones usually give us the names or locations of the people with whom they are talking. Once that is established, we drop a bug at the other end, and that way, we have the whole conversation without ever having been anywhere near a wire belonging to the telephone company. Without obstructing justice or breaking federal law, we can splice the conversations together on our recorders and use the information during interrogation. This system is also used in industrial espionage cases such as the Sierra Foods caper.

Three long, hot, boring, wearisome days later, we got our break. The telephone rang, and it was Carson. He was calling so that the little boy, who they called Kim, could say hello to his grandparents. Now we could only hear one side of the conversation, of course, and that in itself would have been no help in locating Carson, had it not been for two things said by Mrs. Carson during her conversation. One was to the effect that she was willing to accept a collect call from a Richard Carson. Later in the conversation with her son she asked him what on earth he was doing in Montreal.

Even that information would have been a limited break had Carson dialed direct. However, the collect call involved an operator, and operators keep records.

The fact that I was handling a kidnapping case got me priority service from the telephone computer center in Denver, but nobody has yet learned how to make the computer itself understand the word priority. It was another thirty-six hours before the tapes had been vetted, and we had the Montreal telephone number from which the call had been placed.

I placed the apartment under surveillance, having obtained the address and the name of the subscriber through the cooperation of the RCMP—Canada's famed "Mounties," one of the world's best police forces. With an agent in place, I put in a call to Mike Constantine and told him the news. He said Mrs. Hartman had already left for New York, and gave me the address and phone number of her attorneys there. I reached her in New York and she said she was leaving for Montreal right away. She contacted my agent, and went to the apartment with the RCMP backing her up. Her ex-husband surrendered the boy without any trouble, and was requested to leave the country as an undesirable alien, his visa for Canada and the United States irrevocably canceled. All he could do was return to Britain, where criminal charges awaited him.

I have to confess that the Hartman caper was one of the few occasions when I wasn't "in on the kill." I usually make it a point of honor to be there, but in this case I couldn't do anything for my clients that the Mounties couldn't do, and second, I was deeply embroiled in another celebrity caper—one of the biggest I ever tackled. So I reluctantly let Chris Vaughan, my chief agent in Canada, close out the Hartman caper, while I pursued the almost invisible trail of the shyest millionaire in the world.

It had all started long before the kidnapping of the Hartman boy. I'd had a call from a New York–based television-publishing conglomerate that wanted to retain me.

"We understand you claim to be able to find anyone, living or dead," they said. "Is that right?"

"If a missing person is alive, he can be found," I said. "If the person is dead, there is a record of it, somewhere. Could you be a little more specific? What exactly is it that you want?"

They told me they wanted a man found. He had not been seen in public for fifteen years—fifteen or twenty —although there was no doubt that he was alive. Everyone associated with him in the multinational corporations and conglomerates he owned in California, Nevada and the East swore to the fact that he was alive, but no one outside his own close circle ever saw him.

"He travels incognito," they said. "He could be anywhere in the world because nobody knows what he looks like. He's worth so many millions he can buy the tightest security, and enough silence to stay buried anywhere he wants to hide. He's been subpoenaed and refused to appear. Writs and summonses bounce off him like raindrops off a duck's back. You probably know who we're talking about—Jonathan Crandall."

Jonathan Crandall! The man was a legend in his own lifetime. Books—mostly inaccurate—and magazine stories proliferated around his name like midges in a swamp. Boy wonder of Hollywood, a multimillionaire before he was thirty, racing yacht designer and engineer, aviator and—finally—recluse. Crandall was known to be the world's most elusive man. If I was going to find a man the best researchers of the biggest news magazines and newspapers in the world couldn't, I had my work cut out for me. Just the same, I was confident that I could do it, and I said so. If a man exists, he can be found. I asked the New York people what they wanted Crandall for.

"We want an interview with him," they said. "An exclusive interview."

I said I was not an interviewer—not the kind they had in mind, anyway—and that interviewing was a skilled technique, as I know from all the bad ones I've been subjected to. I told them the best I could do would be to locate Crandall and put their proposition to him. I also said, in fairness, that I didn't think there was one chance in a million that he would accept, and that the cost of getting his refusal would be very high.

"How high?" they said.

"Six figures for openers," I told them. "Expenses as encountered."

They took a very long deep breath and said they wanted to go ahead, and we agreed on terms, leaving the attorneys to go over the fine print. I got to work on what was to prove the most challenging assignment I'd had in a long time. Here was a man who had spent the last fifteen years shaking pursuit off his backtrail, covering his tracks with constant success and, like an old timber wolf, getting cannier as the years went by. Crandall didn't use commercial airlines, as far as anyone knew. He had his own private jets—his own private airline, in fact. He owned hotels all over the world—the Caribbean, the Pacific, North and South America and Europe. He rarely stayed in any of them, or so the reports said. I decided—on the basis of how accurate most of the stories written about me are—that the news stories on Crandall wouldn't provide me with any clues worth having.

I sat in my office as the darkness closed in, psyching out the man, evaluating the prospects ahead. It came to me then that I was going at it entirely the wrong way. Why was Crandall always hiding out? Because the press was always baying at his heels. But who else was looking for him? Was there a contract out on him? No, of course not. Any writs or subpoenas that mattered two cents, apart from nuisance cases, people trying to sue the man to see if they could rip him off? No, again. Was there anyone out there sleuthing, really trying to find him? No, a third time. It was the press that was making all this outlandish stuff up.

Encouraged, I placed a call to an old friend of mine, a script writer whom I'd known for years. I asked him if he had the telephone number of an actress to whom he had introduced me at a party the preceding year, Mary Jean Jorgensen. Cliff gave me the number, and I called Mary Jean, said I was coming out to Beverly Hills, and wondered if she'd like to have lunch with me and Cliff.

It was that easy, and within a few hours I was on my way once again to Baghdad-on-the-Beach. The contacts you make daily are a map, a route to success in the investigative field. I had met Mary Jean through Cliff, and had done a little job for her that involved her sister. I never even sent her a bill, because any friend of Cliff's is a friend of mine, and there was no question of her paying for such a small favor. Until now, that is—for Mary Jean Jorgensen had once been married to Jonathan Crandall.

Over lunch in the Polo Lounge, I talked at length with Mary Jean. I told her I wanted to locate Jonathan, and I told her why. She said she hadn't seen him in quite a while, but that she'd had a letter from him a few weeks earlier, in which he'd told her that he was using the name Patrick Constable. She told me that Jonathan was doing most of his traveling by train these days, and I had to admire the man's sagacity. He knew —as do most investigators—that railroad travelers are among the world's most incurious and unobservant animals. The average railroad passenger is busy worrying about his baggage and his tickets and his wife and his kids and his mother-in-law and the dog getting on. He usually buries himself in a newspaper or a book as soon as the train gets going, or stares out the window at the scenery—something he never gets to enjoy on his business flights—so he has hardly any time to observe his fellow passengers. Take a drawing room on the long-distance train, have your meals sent in, and you can be as isolated as the man in the moon.

Mary Jean told me where the letter had come from, and enough about Crandall's security arrangements for me to be able to trace him within three days of that luncheon in the Beverly Hills Hotel. He was staying in the South Ocean Beach Hotel at Lyford Cay in the Bahamas. I telephoned him but it took me nearly thirty-six hours to convince him to see me. I finally did it by intriguing him: I said if he granted me an interview, I'd tell him how I'd tracked him down. It worked: he said it would be worth it just to make sure he wouldn't make the same mistakes again.

I didn't tell him about Mary Jean, of course. I'd made up a good story about my clients having provided me with the information that had enabled me to tie it to the man in the penthouse suite occupying the top floor of the South Ocean Beach Hotel, and if I say so myself, it sounded convincing enough. Crandall was courtly and intelligent, and nodded as I spoke. He listened courteously to the proposition that I put to him on behalf of the New York people, not commenting on it one way or another. Whether such a deal was ever consummated, I don't know—but I seriously doubt it. Crandall just wasn't the type to reveal the facts about himself to anyone—least of all a television-publishing conglomerate. As he said to me on a later occasion, if he had really wanted to tell his story, he'd have bought a publishing house and published it himself.

We shook hands then, and said goodbye, and I noticed that never once in our conservation did he ask me not to reveal his whereabouts or to discuss the subject of our long conference. I concluded that Jonathan Crandall was a man of honor, and expects everyone else to be. I imagine he gets some disappointments, but I know I wasn't one of them. I called my clients and told them that Crandall would be calling them with his answer. They couldn't believe that I'd found the unfindable man so fast, but twenty-four hours later, they called me in El Paso and confirmed that Crandall had telephoned them.

I don't know what deal they made—if any. What I do know is that three days after I left Nassau, the headlines exploded with the news that Crandall was there. There were TV shots of masses of jostling news-papermen, film crews, newsreels, all the baying hounds of the media on the spoor of the reluctant millionaire. However, they were all wasting their time—Crandall was long gone, and the story died of malnutrition.

It must have been three or four months later that I got a call from a man who told me his name was Richard Bickford of the Crandall Aviation Corpora-tion. He said that Jonathan Crandall would like to speak with me. A moment later, I heard Crandall's well-remembered, slightly reedy voice on the line.

"Armes," he said, "can you be at El Paso Inter-national in fifteen minutes? I'm passing through and I'd like to talk to you."

"No problem," I said, but I was wrong.

When I got up to the airport, the place was crawling with security men. You can always spot them. They are big and wide-shouldered, and they don't have their jackets buttoned: so they can get to their holsters fast. They don't seem to be looking at anything in particu-lar, but in fact they don't miss a thing that moves, and that includes you, brother. In addition to the football players, there were too many EPPD boys standing around looking as if they were doing something unim-portant, like meeting Miss Texas off the plane. I could see an unmarked twin-engined Lear 25, the ten-seat expanded version of the old Model 24 executive jet. The Model 25 will do over five hundred mph at its long-range cruising speed, and has a range of nearly two thousand miles with a full complement of passen-gers. Crandall could use half a mile of the El Paso run-way now, and inside four hours be anywhere in the country. No wonder he was hard to find.

I started to go through the VIP arrival lounge to the tarmac where the plane was standing, but a big man blocked my way. From the bulges in his gray suit I could see he was carrying enough iron to give himself kidney sores.

"Where you goin', buddy?" he growled.

"Out to the plane to see the Man," I said.

"What man?" he said.

Oh, I thought, one of that kind. I told him I had an appointment to see Crandall, and predictably, he asked me who Crandall was. I repeated that I had an appointment, and he told me that it had just been canceled. He wasn't unfriendly or anything. Just obtuse and a little bored.

"I want to hear it from the Man himself," I told him.

He looked at me and I looked at him, and things might have warmed up considerably around then, but at that moment a tall man wearing a pilot's suit came hurrying toward us.

"Mr. Armes," he said, "I'm Richard Bickford. Would you follow me, please?"

I blew Gray Suit a kiss as I went by, but his expression didn't alter. He looked like he was auditioning for a spot on Mount Rushmore. We hurried up the ramp into the plane, where Jonathan Crandall was sitting at a small table in an area clearly used as an office. He was wearing a brown suede jacket, Levi boot pants and moccasins. His face was tanned and healthy, his moustache neatly trimmed. He was extremely light in weight. You'd have passed him in the street and would never have given him a second glance.

He told me he wanted to retain me to do some work for him in Canada. He was very meticulous and precise, and I could sense that he was holding back, stopping himself from telling me how I should go about it. He told me he had checked me out with some people we both knew, and asked me a lot of questions about how I work.

"Okay, Mr. Armes," he said. "You're on the payroll."

We shook hands and I left the plane. The ramp was up before I got back into the glass-fronted lounge, and I stood and watched as the neat white plane soared like a bird into the brassy blue of the sky over Franklin

Mountain. When I went out into the concourse, I had
to fight my way through a knot of reporters who'd
been hanging around, trying to find out who the mystery man was, and what I was doing talking to him.
They asked me who had been in the plane, and I said
that I had no idea, I'd been talking to the pilot, a man
named Bickford. Since that isn't now and wasn't then
his real name, it made no difference what I told them.

I shook them off and got into the car. I spent most
of the next couple of days fending off telephone calls
and cables from UPI and AP and Reuter and all the
rest of them. They all wanted to know the same thing
—was the mystery man Jonathan Crandall, and what
had he wanted and where was he now? I made don't-
know noises until they got fed up, and then I got on
with the work Jonathan Crandall had retained me to
do.

The investigation concerned some lumber holdings
in Mexico, and was connected with some mining interests Crandall had in Montana. When I concluded
the investigation, I sent my report to New York—a
firm of highly respected and enormously expensive
attorneys—by registered mail. There would be no ac-
knowledgment, no thank-you note, nothing—that's the
way the Man works. You do your job and you get
paid and that's that. Or so I thought.

It must have been a month later that I got a call
from Railway Express saying they had a big package
for me, a small wooden crate that seemed to weigh a
ton. The point of origin was Las Vegas, Nevada, but
there was no sender's name or address on it. They
brought it over and I opened it up. When I stripped
the excelsior away, I couldn't believe my eyes. Inside
was a pair of solid gold hooks. My size, too.

22.

In June 1972, not along after I wrapped up the Brando
caper, I received a person-to-person call from President
Alfredo Boyacá of Carazuela. You don't have to be a
student of geography to know that no such republic
exists, nor of politics to conclude that there has never
been a president of any South American republic
named Alfredo Boyacá. Nevertheless, there was such a
call from such a country, and it was that country's
president for whom the secretary at the Palacio Na-
cional asked me to hold. I hung on for perhaps five
minutes, listening to the strange, unearthly music of
the relays and rectifiers and repeating coils between
El Paso and Carazuela City, and turning out the file
in my mind on that country. It was a pretty slim one:
I knew that Carazuelan presidents were vested with
executive power but only allowed to serve one term,
that cocoa, coffee, rubber, tropical fruits and oil were
its main exports, and that its population was around
the four million mark and Spanish-speaking. The econ-
omy was pastoral rather than industrial, cattle raising
in the central plains of the country being a major industry. Religion Catholic, currency the peso, history
turbulent. In other words, I knew about as much about
Carazuela as the average encyclopedia owner.

President Boyacá came on the line. He said he had
read about me in the newspapers, and had grave need
of my services. His nephew, Raul, had married an
American girl, and there had been five children from
the marriage. Raul, in the classic South American

manner, had gotten himself a mistress, but his wife Valerie had found out about it and reacted in a most unclassical manner. Valerie Boyacá was the daughter of a president, too—Henry O'Sullivan, president of the Houston International Oil Corporation. She called her dad and told him her story. O'Sullivan immediately sent his private plane down to Carazuela City and spirited Valerie and the five children out of the country.

President Boyacá said that neither he, his brother nor his nephew had any idea where Valerie and the children might be. Houston International had offices all over the world, and O'Sullivan could have arranged for them to be taken anywhere. Boyacá said that he was not only distressed by the family quarrel, but also by the fact that the children had been—effectively— kidnapped from their native country by a foreigner. He felt that Henry O'Sullivan might have been forgiven for interfering in the affairs of Raul and Valerie Boyacá, although that was a matter, surely, for the two people most involved. But he could not forgive such high-handed disregard for the sovereign republic of Carazuela, and he wanted to retain me to locate the Boyacá children and bring them back to Carazuela.

I told him I would need a Power of Attorney from the father giving me a free hand to take any action I deemed proper in locating and returning the children. He said he would have it flown up to El Paso by courier, together with a dossier about the children and Valerie O'Sullivan Boyacá and a cashier's check for my retainer. He begged me to use extreme caution, and to take no action that would put his nephew's children at risk. I read between the lines of his request, realizing that he was hiring me because he didn't want to protest officially, through diplomatic channels, and create an incident that would air the family squabble publicly.

I put down the phone, put up my feet and started planning. It looked to me as if the first thing I would need would be a dossier on Henry O'Sullivan, since he would be the pivot around which everything else we might do would revolve. I called someone I know in the oil capital, and he told me that sixty-seven-year-old Henry O'Sullivan was one of the city's leading lights. Born in Oklahoma, O'Sullivan was the son of a commodity dealer who'd moved into oil in the days when Pennsylvania was the center of the oil industry. Even if he hadn't done as well as another commodity dealer called John D. Rockefeller who did the same thing, O'Sullivan had obviously done all right. He bequeathed his son the nucleus of what was now a multimillion-dollar oil empire, and Henry O'Sullivan was drawing over a quarter of a million a year in salary, plus a further $600,000 in bonuses. He lived in an enormous house, set on its own eight-acre grounds, in an exclusive part of Houston, patrolled night and day by armed guards. He and his wife Veronica—I later learned that all the women in the O'Sullivan family had names beginning with the letter V—were patrons of the Houston Symphony, the ballet and the grand opera at the Jesse H. Jones Hall. O'Sullivan was widely known for his charitable donations, and was on the committee of many Houston institutions, among them the Texas Medical Center and the Museum of Fine Arts. He sounded as if he wasn't going to be an easy nut to crack, but that was what I had to do, so I grabbed my Val-Pak and headed for Space City.

Houston is the biggest city in Texas, with a population of one and three-quarter million people. It has beautiful tree-lined avenues, fountains, skyscrapers and waterways. It is the most Texan of cities in striving to be the richest, the most air-conditioned, the most chic, the biggest training and command post for NASA—and everything else. It's almost exactly the same distance away from San Francisco as it is from New York, sitting on a bayou fifty miles from the Gulf of Mexico. It never gets much below sixty degrees at any time of the year in Houston. There are fine restaurants, beautiful parks and terrific facilities, as befitting the sixth largest city in the United States. But it's a hard place to love.

The O'Sullivan place was up beyond Delta Downs, and I set up surveillance on it. There was no chance of our using the standard procedure for dropping bugs, which meant we had to get in some other way. Surveillance revealed that the O'Sullivans went to some function or dinner most evenings. The times varied, but it would usually be around seven-thirty that they left the house in the chauffeured Jaguar XJ12—O'Sullivan's pride and joy, the very first one off the production line, and the only one in the United States. There were three servants in the house, maid, valet and cook, plus the security guards at each gateway.

Waiting for the O'Sullivans to leave, I positioned my two agents—both dressed in neat but unidentifiable blue uniforms with "Inspector" shoulder flashes—and found myself a good place to park our station wagon with its tinted windows. They are, in fact, opaque from the outside. From the inside of the vehicle, one can see through them as clearly as ordinary glass—ideal for surveillance. About ten minutes after the O'Sullivans left (it was already nearly dark), I let down the tailgate of the station wagon. Lying prone in the rear, using the infrared Sniperscope, I zeroed in from about three hundred yards on the guard at the gate nearest to us, the special tranquilizer rifle trained on his right shoulder. In the breech was the special load, carrying enough of the drug to disable an animal of up to 180 pounds. I squeezed the trigger, and the guard turned, frowning, as the missile struck him on the shoulder. His turn changed into a wilting pirouette, and he slid into a sitting position by the gatepost. My two agents were already on the move, and they dragged him into the bushes behind the gate, disarming him in the process. Meanwhile I headed across the grounds, this time carrying the smaller tranquilizer pistol. The other guard was catching a smoke, and I put him to sleep without his even seeing me. They would wake up later with headaches, wonder what had happened, check the house and discover that two "fire inspectors" had arrived at the door saying that one of the guards had reported smelling smoke. They had gone into every room in the house, found nothing and left. It was my conviction that even if they reported it to O'Sullivan and he reported it to the police, none of them would guess that the reason for the visit of the mythical fire inspectors had been to drop bugs near every phone in the house.

With our listening devices in place, we supplemented the station wagon with a panel truck with a sign reading SPACE INSTRUMENTS INC. There may even be such a firm, for all I know, but a name like that is as common in Houston as the name Smith is in telephone directories. We caught a fish in less than forty-eight hours. Veronica O'Sullivan was talking to someone called Vanessa and asked her whether she'd heard from Valerie. Vanessa must have told her that the price of a call was expensive, because Mrs. O'Sullivan told her that if Valerie called her, she should tell her to call her parents collect, they quite understood how expensive European calls were.

They chattered on about other things, but I already had an agent on the move. His job was to drop a bug at the home of Vanessa, the O'Sullivan's elder daughter. She was married to Samuel McConville, an engineer working at NASA, and from our dossier on O'Sullivan, we knew she lived in the Clear Lake area. Bugging the McConville house was effected, and all we had to do now was wait. Two days later, I was on my way to Zürich, Switzerland.

My contact in Switzerland is a former CIA man who once worked with Allen Dulles, when that worthy was running his espionage shop from a house on the Herrenstrasse in Berne. Walter Hagen retired from the company and stayed on in Switzerland, and his range of contacts there is astonishing. Mind you, the Swiss, as is well known, are a methodical people, and all records pertaining to the citizenry are impeccably kept. In Switzerland, believe it or not, it is possible to buy a book listing the name and address to go with every license plate owned by anyone in the country. When you register an automobile in Switzerland, you are given a license number that's yours for life as long as you keep paying the tax. Hence, the book. Unfortunately, they don't have one for telephone numbers, but Hagen knew where they did, and in short order I learned that Valerie O'Sullivan Boyacá was living in a Zürich suburb called Herrliberg, in the vacant apartment of Hans Roth, manager of the Houston International office in Zürich. Roth was in the Middle East with his wife on an extended business trip, and O'Sullivan had craftily closeted his daughter and her brood there, together with a nurse-housemaid.

I left Houston Intercontinental early the following morning, and twenty-four hours later Walter Hagen was picking me up at the arrivals building in Kloten airport. We drove out of the city, and along a short stretch of motorway that Walter said would get us to Herrliberg quicker than going through the city. On the way, he told me that he had the apartment under surveillance, and that Valerie Boyacá and the children were there. He said our best time to move would be around 10 A.M., when the mother normally went out for a while. Her usual destination was Meilen, a place further along the lake, where there was a shopping center. Sometimes she took the kids along, but mostly they stayed home with the nursemaid.

We worked out our timetable, which had to be split-second. Before picking me up, Walter had checked out optimum travel arrangements to get us to Carazuela from Zürich. There was only one way—from Zürich we would fly direct to New York, taking Swissair's daily Flight 100, leaving at midday. From New York, we could pick up a flight direct to Carazuela City.

Herrliberg is a tightly-packed little place situated on a south-facing hill that slopes sharply downward from an eight-hundred-meter ridge called the Pfannenstiel to Lake Zürich. The apartment was on a street called the Schulstrasse, which ran parallel to the lake. Hagen's man was already there, watching the place in a locally registered Volkswagen. To our surprise and delight, Mrs. Boyacá timed her departure to the second, coming out of the door almost as Walter slid his big Mercedes to a stop behind the Volks. She opened up her garage, and a few minutes later puttered off in a little blue Opel, with Hagen's man Hardmeier in close pursuit. Should Valerie Boyacá change her plans and return without warning, he would let us know by radiophone.

As soon as the coast was clear, we went to the door and told the maid who we were and why we had come. She said she could not permit us to take the children without telephoning the police. We told her that it made no difference whom she telephoned, the Power of Attorney signed by the children's father gave us carte blanche to do whatever we felt necessary for their safety and welfare. The first of those things was to take them away from here and back to the country of their birth. Knowing that the mother would be out of her mind with worry when she returned to find her children gone, Walter Hagen told the maid that he would stay and tell Mrs. Boyacá what had happened. She was mollified by this, and Walter told me to take the Mercedes and get to the airport fast. He told me the simple route: along the lakeside road into the city, and then just follow the signs. Meanwhile, he would telephone one of his people to meet me at Kloten and take over the car while I got the kids through passport control and onto the plane. He said he would also telephone Swissair to make sure that everything was done to expedite our departure. He did, and it was. The Power of Attorney was sufficient grounds for the Swiss authorities to waive passport requirements, and promptly at midday the New York flight departed Zürich, made a big circle over the city and headed west.

The five kids—two girls and three boys, the oldest girl eight, the youngest boy three—were spoiled utterly by the Swissair hostesses, who played games with them and gave them soft drinks, showed them the flight deck, brought them picture books to read and taught them a few words in the unpronounceable Swiss dialect. I leaned back, relaxed and contented, sure that the rest of the caper was just flight time, but I was wrong.

Swissair and TAP, the Portuguese airline that would take us to Carazuela, arrive and depart in the same building at Kennedy, and we were hurrying through the transit lounge when I was intercepted by a New York City Police detective and an agent of the FBI. They marched me away from the ramp with my hands on my head, like a common criminal. Valerie Boyacá had returned to the Zürich apartment, found the children gone and telephoned her father to say that an investigator named Armes was taking them to Carazuela. Knowing our flight, Henry O'Sullivan had phoned the FBI and told them I was a kidnapper, so they were there to arrest me!

They backed off some when they saw the Power of Attorney signed by Raul Boyacá, and my personal credentials. Even so, they insisted that I accompany them to the Administration Building to "get it all straightened out." I told them it was straightened out just fine right now. I told them that I had established that no court order of any kind existed to prevent Raul Boyacá from giving me power of attorney to retrieve his children, and that it was the mother who was, in fact, technically guilty of abduction. Guilt or innocence was not, however, my concern. My concern was to take the children back to their father, and I was going to do it on the waiting TAP jet, and nobody had either the right or power to stop me. The NYPD detective looked a bit uneasy, but the FBI agent said peremptorily that he would have to take the document and make a photostat copy of it.

"You've seen it," I said flatly. "That's all you're entitled to. I'm taking that plane, and you know and I know you know, that there's not a damned thing you can do to stop me."

He knew I was right. I was a duly sworn law-enforcement officer acting within the letter of the law and entitled to his cooperation rather than harassment. I got back on the plane, with everyone staring at me as if I were Frank Sinatra. And that, really, was that.

President Boyacá later became a close personal friend, and we have met many times since then, either in the United States or in the National Palace in Carazuela City. The kids all call me "Uncle Jay" and they're as happy as the day is long. As I understand it, Valerie Boyacá divorced her Carazuelan husband and remarried, whereupon President Boyacá closed the doors of his country to her forever. A harsh measure, perhaps, but as he put it himself, Texas millionaires are not the only ones who can take unilateral action.

23.

The pièce de résistance *in the glass-fronted gun case on
the wall of Jay Armes' library is a .38 Smith & Wesson
with ivory butt plates, on which is carved the head of
a longhorn steer, its eyes made of two real rubies. According to legend, the gun was used to administer the
coup-de-grâce to one of the dying victims in the garage
at 2122 North Clark Street, Chicago, the day Machine
Gun Jack McGurn, John Scalise and Albert Anselmi,
dressed as policemen, burned down seven of Bugs
Moran's gang back in 1919.*

*The St. Valentine's Day Massacre gun belonged to
an Atlanta, Georgia, doctor named Matthew Tomlinson, for whom Armes once worked on a missing jewelry case that developed into a theft-ring caper with
international ramifications. Years later, when he was
in failing health, Dr. Tomlinson committed suicide
with the gun, doing so just as his wife came into his
study. He fired the gun twice, killing himself with the
second shot and never knowing that the first had
grazed his wife. She called the police, only to find herself the center of suspicion. They were convinced that
she had killed her husband and wounded herself to
"make it look good." The distressed woman called in
Jay Armes, whose investigation conclusively established
the fact that Dr. Tomlinson's death had been suicide,
and that his wife's wound could not have been self-
inflicted. She asked him to take the gun as a token of
her thanks. Above it sits a German Luger 9 mm model
08, the most famous of all the pistols designed by the
famous Georg Luger. Armes correctly refers to it as
the 9 mm Parabellum, rattling off the other statistics—
eight-round box magazine, right-hand twist rifling,
four-inch barrel, muzzle velocity 1150 fps, weight un-*

loaded 1 pound 15 ounces. It is an unusual weapon to see on the wall of an El Paso home—even the home of Jay J. Armes.

That was the gun used in the Beach case—the Lonely Widow Caper. It nearly cost me my life, and yet it started out very innocuously. A Mrs. Martha Beach telephoned me from her home up on Cumberland Circle, which is just south of the military reservation, above Trowbridge. She told me she would like to retain my services, and when I asked why, she told me that her husband was trying to kill her.

Her husband, Arthur, was a certified public accountant. His business headquarters were in El Paso, but he had a chain of affiliate offices throughout Texas and New Mexico, and was, if not wealthy, at least comfortably fixed. Mrs. Beach told me that her husband had been acting erratically for several months, so much so that she had at one time thought he might be having mental problems. About two months ago, he had said he was leaving her, and that was when her problems began. There had been telephone calls which, when answered, turned out to be an empty silence or the sound of breathing. She had heard someone moving around the outside of the house in the middle of the night. She had informed the police, and they had sent a prowl car up there, but after a few nights of seeing nothing but an empty street, the car had gone on to other duties, other problems, other lonely women who imagined things. She asked me if I would come up to see her. I drove up there late that evening.

The Beach house was a nice-looking three-story place set back among trees. The fresh green smell of money was everywhere. Martha Beach turned out to be a very attractive woman of perhaps forty, with auburn hair and green eyes. She was wearing a dark housecoat, and there were the dark smudges of sleepless nights beneath her expressive eyes. She invited me into the house, saying that she'd seen me on TV in the *Hawaii Five-O* segment where I had played an explosives expert called Hookman who tries to assassinate Jack "Steve McGarrett" Lord—my only caper on the wrong side of the law. She said that somehow she had expected me to look much older, and I told her I didn't worry as much as some people.

She told me once more about her husband's behavior, and how he had moved away from the house. Living alone had not bothered her much at first. Then she started hearing strange noises, unexpected sounds in back of the house. Her nervousness had increased to the point where she really was convinced that her life was in danger, and she told me that she had not had any sleep worth talking about for nearly a week. I asked her why she didn't take a sleeping pill, and she said she was afraid to drug herself, lest her fears be all too real.

I suggested that perhaps the answer was to close up the house and move to an apartment with a doorman and plenty of security until her situation vis-à-vis her husband was clarified, but she wanted none of that. It was her house, in her name, and she wasn't going to be scared out of it so that Arthur could take possession and sell it over her head, leaving her with nothing. She repeated that she believed he was trying to kill her, and I asked her what, specifically, he had done to make her think so.

"Well, for instance, he called me the other night at eleven-thirty, and asked me to meet him in the backyard at midnight," she said. "He told me he wanted to talk things over."

"In the backyard?" I echoed. "At midnight?"

"Yes," she said. "I told him if he wanted to talk to me, he could come to the house in the daytime like a normal civilized human being. He called me a dirty name and hung up."

"Does he have a key to the gate in back?"

"That was what worried me, afterward," she said. "He was supposed to have handed all his keys over to me when he left. But if he had, then how did he expect to get in?"

"You think he may have keys to the house?"

"I don't know. He might."

I asked her what had happened then, and she told me that at midnight a cab had pulled up outside the house, and the driver told her he had come to collect a party. She had not called for a cab. He said he was supposed to take a fare to a place downtown, Tony's. She said she had never even heard of the place. The cab driver left, and she went back to bed. About fifteen minutes later, her husband called and wanted to know why she hadn't come downtown to meet him, after he went to the trouble of sending a cab for her. He sounded drunk.

"The taxi driver didn't tell me any of that," she told him. "Even if he had, I wouldn't have gone."

"Oh, then, the hell with it and the hell with you as well," Arthur Beach said. "That was your last chance." That was the last contact she had had with her husband, but she had spent the time since then in a constant state of tension, jumping every time the doorbell rang or the telephone jangled. She was afraid he was going to come to the house and harass her— Arthur Beach had a violent temper, it transpired, and he had assaulted her physically before.

I told her that I could arrange for a female investigator to come and stay with her, but she said that she didn't want that, she wanted me to do it. I told her it would be exactly the same. All my people are trained operatives, and well able to take care of themselves. Some of the girls can pull tricks that would make *Police Woman* Pepper Anderson's hair stand on end.

"Mr. Armes," she said, "I want someone here I can rely on. I can't eat and I can't sleep. I'm falling apart. Couldn't you stay and look after me?"

I told her that it just wasn't possible, and that she ought to be able to see why it wasn't possible. The more I said it, the more highly-strung and hysterical she became, until in the end she was weeping, begging me to not leave her alone.

In the end, I capitulated. What harm could it do? I

thought. Mrs. Beach really was in bad shape, and one night's loss of sleep wasn't going to hurt me. I had a lot of paperwork to catch up on in my briefcase, and I could spend the empty hours of the night doing just that. So I called my office and gave them my ten-twenty, and told them the number where they could contact me. I felt sorry for Mrs. Beach, who looked as if she would jump out of her skin if anyone so much as clapped their hands. I told her to go on up to bed, and I would get a chair and sit outside her room in the hall.

She went ahead of me upstairs, and I got a chair and a small folding card table, and started to get ready to do some work. I hadn't read more than the first couple of reports when Mrs. Beach opened the door of the bedroom and poked her head around it.

"The balcony!" she hissed.

I looked at her blankly. "The balcony?" I said.

"There's a balcony outside my room," she said. "It runs all around the house. Anyone could climb up and get into my room!"

I told her nobody was going to do that, and even if they did, I would hear them instantly. She said there was no way I could be certain of that, how could I possibly know? Her voice rose a note on each word. I asked her if she would prefer me to sit out on the balcony, and she shook her head. Then I wouldn't be able to watch the door, she said.

"Mrs. Beach," I said patiently. "I can't spend the night in your bedroom, if that's what you mean."

"Oh, for goodness' sake," she snapped, "this is the twentieth century, not the eighteenth! You're supposed to be acting as my bodyguard, and if you're going to do it properly, I don't see how you can do it sitting in the hallway!"

I could see I had a straight choice—a two-in-the-morning argument with an hysterical woman, or a compromise. The compromise was that I'd set the card table up inside the room and leave the door ajar, so I could watch both the hallway and the balcony. I rigged up a table lamp so that I could see to work without the light shining on Martha Beach, and told her to please settle down and go to sleep. At three o'clock she called me, and asked if I was awake. I told her that I was reading reports, wide awake, and the time was just after three.

"Go back to sleep," I said. "Everything's fine."

I was never more wrong. The words were hardly out of my mouth when the door was kicked back against my table, and I went over backward in a cascade of paper, chair, table and lamp. Framed in the doorway stood a big man with a face like six miles of bad road. There was a German Luger in his hand.

"So you're the little rat she's shacking up with!" he shouted. It was Arthur Beach, and he was mad enough to chew railroad ties. I got to my feet warily, and Mrs. Beach sat up in bed, her eyes wide with fright, clutching the bedclothes about her.

"Arthur!" she said, her voice shrill with fright. "Arthur, he—"

"He nothing!" Beach said, swinging the gun back toward me. I didn't let him finish the movement or even complete whatever thought was in his mind. I was already off the floor, and my flying kick sent him back against the wall with a crash that shook the house. The Luger was jarred from his hand and skittered on the parquet floor. Before I could go after it, he came off the wall with a roar of rage, hands clutching for my throat. I didn't want to do what I did, but I knew I had to, so I hit him very low and very hard. He stopped in his tracks with his eyes bugging out, staring at me as if I had done something completely unmentionable. I had no more conscience than a cow in a stampede. This looked like a simple variation on the old badger game to me, and if I was being set up, the first thing to go would be the Fourth Marquess of Queensberry's rules on pugilism. However, Beach was a big man, tough and sinewy, and he had far too much adrenaline in his pump to be stopped by one punch. So I hit him again, and then again, and he sank to his knees, his face a bright mask of blood. From that position, he launched himself at my knees, but that was a sucker play. Whether you are black belt of the Tenth Dan or a barroom brawler, the first rule of survival in a fight is to stay clear of elbows and knees. The former, driven backward, or the latter, brought upward, are, literally, killing weapons. They will smash bone like a hammer striking china. My training has made the movement in self-defense instinctive and when Beach went for my legs he ran head-on into my sharply-lifted knee. I felt bone crack in his face and he went backward, up and over in a sort of inverted U.

To my astonishment, Martha Beach was out of her bed, hair flying, nightdress agape, calling me names that would have grown hair on a Mexican dog, and trying to get her long fingernails into my eyes. I managed to fend her off, and she pushed past me and ran to the phone, frantically calling the police. I shrugged: that was what I'd been going to do, anyway.

I knelt down to check Arthur Beach. He was breathing badly, and I discovered that his jaw was broken. Martha Beach slammed down the telephone and told me in a voice like a turpentined cat that if I didn't get away from her husband, she was going to do things to me that would give the doctors a lot of problems. I backed away, hands in the *Kamerad* position, and got to the phone.

I called my attorney, who at that time was Mickey Esper, and told him exactly what had happened, and that I expected there would be some problems. I was right. Mrs. Beach told the EPPD that I had assaulted her husband without provocation. They whisked him away in an ambulance, while a policewoman comforted the hysterical woman. Then I had to sit still for a one-hour interrogation, with Mrs. Beach yelling away in the background that I'd tried to kill her husband, and why didn't they put me in jail? Finally, I managed to tell the detectives my side of the story, right up to the time they had received the call. They nodded, and then asked me where the gun was.

"It's on the floor someplace," I said. "A Luger. Nickel-plated."

"We're from Missouri," the cop said. "Show us."

I searched every corner of the room, beneath the bed, chairs, tables, even out on the balcony and in the hall. No Luger: it had disappeared as completely as if I'd dreamed it. The boys from downtown pressed home their advantage, and asked me if I had been having an affair with Martha Beach. It was such a dumb question that I grinned.

"If she's in love with me, she certainly isn't acting that way," I said.

"Answer the question."

"I did," I said. "Now go ask her."

They did, and she told them she would no more have had an affair with me than she would with a leper. She told them she thought I was the most brutal, awful, terrible—well, fill in the rest for yourself. She told them that if she had known I would do what I had done to her husband, she would never have hired me in the first place. The moment she said that, of course, I was off the hook, and Arthur Beach was very firmly on it. The detectives encouraged Mrs. Beach to think she was making trouble for me, and she told them everything—except for one startling omission. She still didn't mention the gun. While they were checking one or two points of the story with me, the telephone rang. It was Arthur Beach. He wanted to tell his wife that he had called his attorney, who would handle everything, and that she should not make any statement to the police. I don't imagine it improved his day to learn that she had been singing like a canary.

It was obvious what his game had been. He had wanted to frighten his wife into hiring protection. Then he could burst into the house and accuse whomever he found there of having an affair with her, sue for divorce and get everything in settlement. It didn't matter who it was: I just happened to be the patsy. So he'd gotten into the house up the stairs at the back, come along the balcony, in through a back bedroom, and jumped me before I even knew he was there. The DA's office asked me whether I wished to prefer countercharges against Beach.

"You produce that gun, Jay," they said, "and you could nail him for attempted murder!"

It was a tempting thought, but there was no point in vindictiveness. I reflected that Arthur Beach already had enough troubles, not to mention a broken jaw and some rather more private bruises. I thought I knew where the gun was, however, and decided to test my theory by driving up to Cumberland Circle to see Mrs. Beach. If she was thrilled to see me, she didn't show it, but she readily admitted to having hidden the gun once I told her that I had no intention of filing suit or charges against her husband.

"I still love him, Mr. Armes," she said, and there was a quiet dignity in the way she said it that touched me. "I thought that if the police came and found that he'd had a gun with him, he would be in terrible trouble, so I hid it."

It seemed superfluous to comment. She took me to the wall safe in the spacious living room and gave me the gun. It was fully loaded and ready to fire. I took it down to the DA's office, and handed it over to the boys. They took it up to Beach, who denied ever having seen it before in his life. They took it back up to Mrs. Beach, but all they could get her to admit was that she'd found it on the floor after the fight, and put it in the safe.

So they called me, and told me they couldn't get anyone to admit owning the Luger. They couldn't even get anyone to admit there had been a crime. They said everyone was just so goddamned angelic around El Paso, it was a wonder there was any work for honest cops. They told me to come downtown sometime and pick up the gun, which was, as of now, technically lost property that nobody was ever going to pick up—and therefore I could have it. A present, they said, from the EPPD. It's just about the only one they ever gave me.

24.

Rape was an emotional subject long before Susan Brownmiller wrote a bestseller about it. In the South and Southwest especially, rape—particularly if it involves a black man assaulting a white woman—can and has inspired bloody lynchings and mob violence of the worst kind. I didn't imagine for a second that anything of that kind was likely to happen at Fort Bliss, but all the same I wasn't anxious to get involved in such a case because of the intense feelings engendered by the very subject.

However, when Captain Malcolm Oram of the Army's legal branch called me and asked me to check it all out as a very special favor, I felt obliged to do it: one way or another, I do a lot of business with the United States—especially the IRS!

Fort Bliss is the largest air defense training center in the free world, its payrolls and local purchases contributing a staggering $258 million to the El Paso economy. It is a vast undertaking with its own airport, schools, hospital and even a national cemetery, a city within a city whose size can be estimated from the fact that out of every hundred dollars spent in El Paso county, five of them are U.S. military post exchange and commissary sales.

I went up to the reservation and contacted Captain Oram. He told me the basic details of the case. A fifteen-year-old girl, a dependent of a warrant officer at Bliss, had accused a Negro noncom of rape. Army CID had already completed its own investigation, but the brass had decreed that, so there should be no question of pressure or unfairness to the accused man, an independent inquiry be conducted by some civilian organization to confirm CID's findings.

"Or not, as the case may be?" I said.

"Or not, as the case may be," Oram agreed. "But CID has got it all pretty well buttoned up."

"Tell me."

Oram told me that CID was not only satisfied that the sergeant was guilty as charged, but that they had supporting evidence to the effect that he had been observed on a number of occasions trying to pick up white girls in El Paso prior to this incident. All in all, the general consensus seemed to be that if all the soldier got was twenty years' hard labor, he'd be getting off light.

I read the CID report, and found it at best cursory. A good defense attorney would have been able to drive a stagecoach and team of horses through it had the defendant been white. In this case, it looked pretty bad for Sergeant Lester Prince.

To my surprise, CID hadn't even bothered to check out the girl's background, so that seemed the sensible place to start. She lived with her parents on the reservation, in a nice little house on a starkly tidy tree-lined road near William Beaumont General Hospital. There was no record of her ever having been detained in a home for incorrigibles in any of the cities where her father had served, no file on her in any law-enforcement agency dealing with juveniles. I started interviewing some of her friends—with startling results. Sue-Ann Moffatt was like the girl in *West Side Story:* anybody's. The boys who knew her all told me the same thing: she was "easy," a pushover who'd have sex with anyone who took her out and bought her a drink. This was a surprising contrast to the picture of the demure, innocent rape victim portrayed in the Army CID file, but there was more to come. One boy told me that Sue-Ann was pregnant. Her eighteen-year-old boyfriend had skipped town when he knew she was in trouble, and someone had told Sue-Ann that if she cried "rape"—especially rape by a black—she could ask for a legal abortion and get it with no questions asked. I put a tracer out on the boyfriend, whose name was Jim Marshall. Meanwhile, I persuaded all the youngsters who'd talked to me that Sergeant Prince deserved better than to be sent to prison for something he hadn't done. I got statements from four men who had been intimate with the girl—so much for the violated virgin pose. Other statements confirmed that Sue-Ann got boyfriends to buy liquor for her, and that she was a long way over on the wild side.

Next I interviewed the accused sergeant. He was tall and erect, a good-looking man who hailed from Atlanta, Georgia. Married, with two kids, Lester Prince lived on the base and had a good service record. His file didn't show any reprimands or demotions. He'd never even been CB—confined to barracks. I asked him to tell me what had happened in his own words.

"I didn't do it, Mr. Armes," he said. "I want to tell you, I've done a few things in my life I ain't too proud of, and a couple I never got caught for, but this—this is just crazy. I never touched that little girl!"

He told me that Sue-Ann babysat regularly at his house, which was only a dozen blocks or so from where she lived. On the night of the alleged assault, she had stayed with the two Prince children while Lester and May Prince went to a party thrown by a fellow noncom who was being transferred overseas. They got home sometime after one in the morning, by which hour, according to Prince, his wife was drunk.

"She'd really taken on a skinful, man," he said. "I had to carry her upstairs and put her to bed."

After he'd done that, he came downstairs and put Sue-Ann in the car to take her home. He had hardly turned the ignition key before she pretend-pouted that it wasn't fair that Mrs. Prince had had all those drinks and she hadn't even had one. He knew Sue-Ann drank

—she often took something out of the liquor cabinet at the house—and there was a bottle in the dash. He told her to help herself—no skin off his nose if she stank of booze when she got home. He figured her daddy ought to take a strap to the girl, but noncommissioned officers don't give advice to warrant officers in any army in the world, and he kept his counsel. The girl took a swig out of the bottle—like a wino on a park bench, Prince said. Then he dropped her off at her house, said good night, turned around and went home.

His story sounded genuine enough, but I was up against the sworn deposition of Sue-Ann Moffatt's father, who had stated that his daughter came running into the house sobbing, her clothes torn and her body scratched, saying she had run all the way from the bottom of the road, after jumping out of Prince's car, in which he had raped her. The military police were called in, and Prince had been placed under close arrest.

He had asked for a polygraph test, and failed, which was marked heavily against him. Sue-Ann Moffatt was taken to the hospital, where a test for semen in the vagina proved positive. I had seen that test report, and remarked on the fact that apart from very minor scratches, Sue-Ann had not been bruised, nor were there any lacerations of the kind usually associated with rape. If he was a rapist, Sergeant Prince was an unusually gentle one. The Army CID investigators' attitude was that Prince had to be responsible, so they weren't looking for anyone else. Mine was different: if he hadn't had intercourse with the girl, who had?

It took a lot of effort and a lot of time and a lot of shoe leather, but I found that someone. An intensive neighborhood survey turned up a witness who had seen a man going into the Prince home after the sergeant and his wife had left for the party. Although the woman didn't know the man's name, she knew him by sight, and roughly where he lived. She came with us in an observation car—a panel truck fitted with one-way windows at the sides and back through which a suspect may be observed without seeing the observer, and photographed or even filmed without his knowledge. She picked him out for us and I went to his house. Under questioning, he admitted having gone to the Prince house with a bottle of bourbon, and he and Sue-Ann had watched TV and gotten mildly drunk. About eleven-thirty they had sexual intercourse on the sofa. This was not the first time he had been intimate with the girl.

I let him in on the nasty little conspiracy of which he was a part, and he couldn't make a statement fast enough.

"Listen," he said, "I didn't know what she had in mind, you gotta believe me."

"Sure," I said. The story about Sergeant Prince's arrest and the crime of which he had been accused had been in all the newspapers, and was common knowledge on the base. "That's why you came forward of your own free will."

"Hell, Armes," the man said. "That's a low blow."

"So is twenty years in the hole for something you didn't do," I said.

The sergeant's trial was a mere formality. We had lined up such a formidable array of witnesses that when the defense attorney read out the list, which included Sue-Ann's boyfriend, the man who'd been with her on the night of the alleged rape, and all the others who'd told us about her slack morals and her drinking, the girl made a strangled sound, somewhere between a sob and a scream, and ran from the courtroom. Her father just sat there looking as if he had been shot in the belly.

I didn't feel any sense of triumph. Rather like that lawyer in the novel *The Caine Mutiny,* I had saved my client only by destroying someone else. I took no pleasure in holding that little girl's life up for everyone to see. Sue-Ann Moffatt had kept a card tacked above her bed carrying this unattributed quotation:

"Although I am not yet known as an outlaw, I am without law whenever I feel so inclined." She just hadn't realized what the price was.

I suppose in a way you could say the same about Bernie Jordan's kids. Bernie was a nice man who loved his wife and spoiled his two daughters all their lives. He was a loving father, but those kids got no real discipline at all. They never ran wild like Sue-Ann Moffatt, but they had that same streak of rebel—the inclination to be without law if they felt like it. People—particularly young people—*will* do things they're not supposed to, once in a while, law or no law. That's why the Noble Experiment failed back in the twenties, and that's why we have so many drug addicts today.

Bernie ran a wholesale vegetable business, with branches all over the Southwest. I had known him since forever, and had last seen him when his daughter Jean had married the boy next door about a year before. Yes, they were that kind of family. One day Bernie called and said he'd like to come in and see me. He came with his son-in-law, Bill MacDonald. They both looked tanned and healthy, as if they'd been on vacation. Bernie said gloomily that they had, and that was the problem. He had taken his wife, Jean and Bill, and Jean's thirteen-year-old sister Kathy, for a vacation to Spain. They had flown to Barcelona and rented a Volkswagen camper, planning to drive all the way down the Mediterranean coast, stopping off at resorts on the Costa del Sol as and when the mood took them.

They had been staying at Marbella when Jean and Kathy decided they would like to drive up to Ronda. Everyone else wanted to stay on the beach, so the girls went off alone. They had been involved in an auto accident in which Kathy and the driver of the other vehicle had been killed, and Jean, who had been driving, was hospitalized. Although she was still unconscious, the Spanish police had charged her with negligent homicide due to dangerous driving.

For a tourist, one of the worst things that can happen on vacation is an auto accident. The worst place to have it happen is in Spain, and if there is a fatality involved, it can be an experience not far short of harrowing. The police are extremely severe—especially if the fatality is a Spaniard and the guilty party a non-Spanish tourist. The Jordan family was required to post bonds so that Bernie and his son-in-law could leave the country. They also took Kathy's coffin back to the United States. Mrs. Jordan stayed in Spain to be with Jean. The American consul had done what he could, but the police had remained adamant about Jean. If and when she regained consciousness, she would have to stand trial for causing the death of the Spanish driver. They regretted that amnesia would probably preclude her testifying in her own defense, but all the physical evidence seemed to point to the accident having been caused by her. It was this attitude that decided Bernie Jordan to fly to El Paso and ask me to go out there and investigate the case.

I asked him to give me as much detail as he could.

"We were staying at the Hotel Don Pepe," Jordan said. "Great big place a little to the south of the main part of town, right on the sea. The girls said they wanted to go up to Ronda, see the old town."

"We said we'd rather stay on the beach," Bill MacDonald said. "So the girls said they'd go on their own. They took the camper and the next we knew was the police were at the hotel, telling us they'd been in an accident at the main crossroads just out of town."

The basic facts of the crash seemed to be that the Spanish driver, a twenty-four-year-old boy working as a representative for an engineering firm in Barcelona, had been driving his Seat 500—the Spanish version of the little Fiat "bug" that they call the Topolino, or Mickey Mouse—down the main highway, when the Volkswagen came through a red light. It hit the little car broadside so hard that it flipped over four times, killing the boy, Eduardo Spinelli, instantly. Kathy died in the ambulance on the way to the hospital.

I asked Bernie and Bill whether Jean was usually a careful driver.

"Always," Bill said. "Especially lately. She's five months pregnant."

They told me that they had retained a lawyer recommended to them by the American consul, and gave me his name and address in Malaga. I said I would fly to Spain right away, and Bernie Jordan shook my hand like a man who's been promised a miracle. I hoped I could give him one.

Before I left the United States, I contacted my agent in Madrid, Pedro Amaya. We rendezvoused at Barajas, and while we were waiting for our connection, an Iberia flight to Malaga, Pedro told me that he'd lined up a local man to help us in Marbella. He also told me that the tourists had taken over Madrid, and the city was going to hell in a handbasket. You couldn't get a reservation at Botin's anymore, the good bars were all full of high-class whores and the price of everything had gone through the ceiling. I told him he ought to come to the States, where we don't have any of those problems, and he grinned and shrugged. Pedro looks a little bit like Iron Eyes Cody, and may even be older, but he's one of the smartest investigators on the Iberian peninsula. He's a professional grumbler—it's his avocation—and he kept in practice all the way across to Malaga. Pedro Amaya telling you what is wrong with airline food, and what ought to be done to the men who design airports, and why Spain is in the shape it's in for several hours on end is about as much of Pedro Amaya as I can take at any one time. I was glad to get off that Caravelle and head down the coast road in our rented Mercedes.

The Mediterranean coast between Malaga and Marbella is one vast strip of overdeveloped concrete. From the sea, it looks like nothing so much as one huge set of very bad teeth, and as an aesthetic experience, it is catastrophic. It gave Pedro a chance to vent his spleen on another favorite topic, and he vented it with a vengeance. I tuned him out—I'm used to Pedro—and concentrated upon what needed to be done in Marbella.

Although we were in a foreign country and there were certain diplomatic niceties to be observed with the local law-enforcement agencies, my procedure would be much the same as if the accident had happened right on my own doorstep in El Paso. I had no fear about getting police cooperation: my International Police Congress credentials would ensure it. I planned to explore three main areas. The first would be to interview anyone and everyone who had been at the scene of the accident: police, doctors, passersby, newspaper reporters, anyone. The second would be to conduct a vehicular survey. The third was happening already—in El Paso. I had agents working on an intensive and top-priority neighborhood survey around the Jordan home on Hillcrest Drive in Mission Hills.

A vehicular survey is as useful a tool as the neighborhood one. People do things out of habit, or by rote. They go to lunch at the same time every day, to and from work at roughly the same time. They will stop and buy a newspaper or a cup of coffee at the same spot. Men even shave the same way every day: always starting at the same place on their face. Most trades call them "regulars." In the private investigating business, these people are known as "routines," and their existence is one of our greatest assets.

We have the time and location of the accident. What we do is to stand at the scene of the accident and note the license numbers of every car that goes by for ten minutes on either side of the vital time. Then we check out the owners. If it's in America, we use DMV —the Department of Motor Vehicles, which maintains a comprehensive file of ownerships. In Spain, as in most European countries, it's even easier because automobiles are registered locally, at the large town nearest to where the owner lives. In our case, it was Malaga, which provided the bulk of our collection. Once the owners have been identified in the records, we go and visit them and ask them what, if anything, they saw as they went past the scene of the accident. It never fails to surprise me how many people tell me that they "don't want to get involved" in anything to do with a fatality—as if we can avoid being involved in the death of another human being!

The vehicular survey, and the neighborhood survey back home in El Paso, came up with some extremely pertinent information, and we had one enormous piece of luck. A local TV station had sent a team down to Marbella on an assignment. They had heard about the crash and had filmed the scene of the accident for the late evening news. I managed to persuade them to lend me the film, and I ran and reran it until the sprocket holes started to wear out.

From my viewings of the film and the testimony of witnesses on the scene minutes after the crash, I had a pretty clear picture of it all. The cars were a long way away from their original point of impact. The Volkswagen camper was lying on its side across the middle line of the highway. The little Seat was maybe 250 yards away, upside down on the center dividing strip. They'd had to use cutting gear to get the dead boy out. The car looked like a mashed beer can.

Thirteen-year-old Kathy Jordan's body was lying face down near the open door on the driver's side of the camper. Her sister Jean lay face up near the front wheel on the opposite side. The camper itself was in gear, although the odometer showed zero—but that's fairly common and not conclusive proof of anything. I drew and redrew accurate scale diagrams, and experimented with toy cars on a model of the junction that we made.

When I had got it all togther, I took my findings to the police. My El Paso neighborhood survey had turned up reports around the Mission Hills area that lots of people had seen Kathy driving the family car, although why Bernie Jordan let her when she didn't have an operator's license nobody knew. One woman stated that her husband had almost been knocked down by a car with Kathy at the wheel and Jean in the passenger seat. Altogether, we had ten people in El Paso who could testify to having seen Kathy driving on more than one occasion.

Our vehicular survey revealed that the Volkswagen had kangaroo-jumped into the crash, and had not been moving smoothly as it would have been if properly driven. Kangaroo-jumping happens when an inexperienced driver uses a clutch and gear shift, or—as was my guess—when someone used to driving only automatics uses one, lets in the clutch too quickly and buck-jumps forward out of control. One witness said that the driver had been wearing a bright red blouse. Jean was pregnant: she was wearing a pale blue smock. Then there was the position of the bodies after the crash—further supporting my theory that it had been Kathy who had been behind the wheel, not Jean.

I think it was the statement of the witness who told us about the bright red blouse that clinched it with the Spanish police, who had been absolutely splendid throughout, giving us as much, if not more, cooperation than we had any right to hope for. They accepted that there was more than a reasonable probability that Kathy Jordan had been the driver, and not her sister Jean. Charges against Jean were dropped, and when she was well enough to return to the States she was allowed to leave without trouble.

A couple of months later, I was invited to a party up in Mission Hills to meet Bernie Jordan's new grandson, Bill Jr. The new father looked as conceited as the barbershop cat, and Jean looked radiant. I heard recently that she has regained most of her memory—although not completely.

25.

*The Jay Armes story keeps developing faster than any-
one can write it down and there are already enough
cases in Jay's files to fill six books. So this book is
really only part of the story of a most extraordinary
man. The most important part, though, isn't really the
capers but the fact that it's Armes who pulls them, a
man whose hands were blown off when he was a pre-
teen and who fought to win his own special place in
the sun.*

*Friend of paupers and Presidents, nonentities and
the world-famous, Armes has become a Celebrity, to
be stopped in hotel lobbies for Instamatic snapshots by
people who have seen him on TV or read about him
in magazines. The kid from the Lower Valley is now,
officially, the World's Greatest Investigator.*

*To this CinemaScope projection of the real man the
supplicants come in endless procession, as to kings of
old, seeking a boon. They want him to open a supermarket, endorse a product, write a syndicated column,
star in a TV show, have his picture taken with them,
finance a search for uranium, plan a safari park, find
the body of Jimmy Hoffa, give a speech, run for office,
dig out the truth about the Kennedy assassination. Reporters come in from all over the world, sure of a good
story. Armes never disappoints them. The London*
Sunday Times, *the Toronto* Star, *the Melbourne* Age,
the Boston Globe, *the Chicago* Tribune, *the St. Louis*
Globe-Democrat, *Bolivians, Italians, Spaniards, Ger-
mans. He entertains them all in his imperturbable way,*

always good value for the money. He shows them his animals and his cars and his helicopter and his house, his guns and his gymnasium and his shooting range and his electronic surveillance equipment, mild of voice and gentle of eye and endlessly polite. The jaws chomp rhythmically on the Care-Free Sugarless gum as he drives around El Paso in his black limousine, with Anne Murray singing country on the stereo, telling and retelling the stories and hinting at others he still can't tell.

He's rich and famous and successful and happy. He's the world's best-known private investigator, and yet you get the feeling always that he could stop doing it tomorrow and start on something else. Behind the facade the reporters see, Jay Armes is still a very private and thoughtful man, with a lot of unfulfilled ambitions and plenty more mountains to climb. The present is bright, but the future's even brighter.

"Me, I think of the ideas and then I put them into operation," he says, "so they won't bother me anymore. When I get an idea, I get it done. It's like a thirst: you're thirsty, you drink water. All the things I do, I do now. That's my philosophy."

One last story. It's about the lady who accused me of being gay. Now over the years I've made a few enemies, some of whom have called me names that would have taken the frost out of a zero morning, but until I was retained by Susan Evans, nobody ever called me gay.

Susan Evans was the wife of a big-name movie star —his fourth. He was forty-five, she twenty-three, and she came to me because, as she put it, her husband was evading his marital responsibilities. I found it hard to imagine why. Susan Evans was a really beautiful woman, built, as they say, like the proverbial brick shipyard, with a long mane of chestnut hair, wide expressive eyes and a mobile mouth that could break into a stunning smile. She'd played some decent parts on

television, the kind that encourage your agent to take
a quarter-page ad in the back of the *Hollywood Reporter* on the morning before the show airs, and was
beginning to make a name for herself when she met
Jacob Evans. He was well on his way to being legendary already, his life a tumultuous procession of films
and brawls and benders and talk-show appearances—
and women. Susan Peterson, as she then was, couldn't
believe her luck in marrying a man she had adored for
years, he of the fabulous ice-blue eyes, the boyish, lop-
sided smile that melted female hearts, and the crinkly,
slightly graying hair that they all wanted to run their
fingers through. Susan fell for Jacob like the proverbial ton of bricks, and they had a whirlwind romance,
a Tijuana wedding and an Acapulco honeymoon—all
faithfully reported by Radie and Hank and *People* and
Modern Screen and *Time.* It was sheerest bliss for
Susan, the Kansas City girl with stars in her eyes, and
she simply reveled in her new life—for a while. At first,
she thought Jacob's neglect was simply due to his
work, but then he started neglecting her even when he
wasn't working, leaving the house in the evening and
not coming back until 1 or 2 A.M., then falling into bed
and going to sleep without explanation. Jacob was *muy
macho,* though, and she thought maybe he had problems he didn't want to talk about. So she let it slide,
and then there would be another mad whirl of activity, a new movie, a vacation—hyperactivity into which
Jacob plunged as if possessed, dragging her along. Not
that she minded, she told me.

Going on location was great when you were part of
the entourage of a Big Name. They played in the
plushest of plush hotels, and every night there would
be people in for drinks, dinner, theater parties. One
service that Jacob insisted upon no matter where he
was filming, whether it was Griffith Park or the far
side of outer Mongolia, was that the producers supply
him, daily, with a crate of Taittinger Blanc de Blanc
champagne. He drank the stuff the way kids drink
Coke in midsummer.

Even when there was no movie, no location excitement, there was still the chalet in Gstaad, and seeing Dick and Liz and ex-Queen Soraya and all the in-crowd on the slopes and in the chi-chi *après-ski* places. There was the Park Avenue apartment in New York, the November vacation at the exclusive club in Fuengirola, the suite at the Fontainbleu in Miami Beach and the house in Benedict Canyon. Susan had clothes, clothes, clothes, furs, jewelry, everything. Anything she so much as expressed a wish for was delivered to her, with roses. Everything, except for one thing she wanted most—the man she loved.

She confided that she was sure Jacob was playing around, and asked me to put him under surveillance and report to her.

"If he's with another woman," she said, "I want you to call me—wherever it is, I want you to call me so I can come there and see it with my own eyes. I want to see what she's like, what she has that I don't have."

Susan Evans gave off sex appeal the way television screens give off static, and I found it hard to imagine anyone being able to find a lady who had anything Susan didn't have—in spades—already.

I promised her that I would check her husband out and report back to her. I added that if I called her to join me in surveillance, the condition was that she come *sans* guns, knives, poisons or blunt instruments. No mayhem. That was out, all the way out.

"Don't you trust me, Mr. Armes?" she said.

I told her of course, I trusted her. I trusted dynamite, too, and look where that got me. You would be surprised how many instances there have been of women—and men—being confronted with the visual proof of their suspicions, and going berserk. Normal, everyday, reasonable human beings just like you and me. They turn a motel room into something looking like a butcher's backyard, and afterward say, in complete honesty, that "something snapped." In Texas, even today, it's difficult to get a jury to convict anyone who kills a spouse caught in the act of infidelity, and if the lover also happens to get killed in the process, that's the next thing to accidental homicide. I resolved that if the opportunity arose for Susan Evans to see her husband *in flagrante delicto,* it would be through very long long-distance binoculars.

Not that I really hoped to be able to arrange it. Surveillance on the average man or woman is one thing, but putting a tail on a major movie star is something else altogether. If he is in a movie, the production company protects him as if he is made of brittle eggshells. There are millions tied up in his whims and perversities, and somehow, they all have to be coped with, catered for. I know one big female star who suddenly fell in love with her hairdresser and demanded that he be given co-director status immediately. When the producer tried to reason with her, she said either the boy-friend was made co-director or she was walking off the picture. The answer was no, so she walked. And $6 million went straight down the chute.

There are male stars who expect—not hope for, expect—that an assortment of nubile and ever-ready lovelies will be provided to soothe their oversized egos, others whose first question on set is "Where's the car?" One really big-name actor demands a "gift" of a luxury car on the first day of every movie he makes —and not just your everyday Cadillac or Rolls. This guy wants Lamborghinis and handmade Maseratis and Ferraris—and gets them. Others want enormous dinner parties at Sardi's or "21," and there are others with demands far more bizarre. This is why there are very few movie producers who do not have gray hair and worry wrinkles six inches deep. In the context, Jacob Evans' insistence on a daily shipment of Brut champagne was almost sweet reasonableness itself.

Stars are cosseted, and come to expect it. They are protected, and come to dislike it. They walk through a world from which all the horribles and nasties have been removed. They stay only in the finest places, eat only the most delicate goodies and drink only at the most exclusive watering holes. They step from hotel to limousine, limousine to restaurant, restaurant to limousine, limousine to hotel, hotel to studio, to roped-off area, to private box, to top-security suite, first nighters only, taking everything and paying for nothing, as thousands cheer. When they're working.

When they are "resting," they become ordinary people again, and sometimes the change of gear unsettles them. An actor uses the word "resting" when he is unemployed. It's a period of uncertainty, and sometimes even fear, particularly if his last movie bombed. In Hollywood circles, you are still only as good as your last movie, but these days it doesn't matter if you acted well, if the critics loved you, if the performance you gave will win an Oscar—none of these things matter. What matters is how the movie stood up at the box office, and you live or die on that. Actors—especially actors like Jacob Evans, whose style is the man, nervous, tense, wary of commitment, impetuous—live on their emotions. "Resting" wears them out. There's nothing to do but go to parties at homes exactly like one's own, and talk shop, shop, shop. There is no other subject in the movie business.

When Susan Evans came to see me, Jacob was "resting." She said he would pace up and down like a caged animal, then toss aside some script he had been reading with an impatient epithet, curse all the damn fool producers who sent him carbon copies of the script of his last movie and slam out of the house. He didn't talk about where he'd been, but he was always late coming home. He was moody and drinking a lot, and snapped her head off if she tried to be sympathetic.

I decided to play the Jacob Evans caper alone. He was too big a name to bring other people into it, even people one trusts. It's a very small town, Los Angeles, and it's very difficult to keep quiet the fact that your subject is one of its most famous names. Better, I figured, not to take any chance of a leak. I flew out to California the next day, rented a tan Chevrolet wagon

—for some reason, tan automobiles seem instantly for-gettable—and set up my surveillance on the house, late in the afternoon. Susan Evans had already confirmed by phone that Jacob was in the house. All I had to do was wait until he came out.

The sleek red Mach 1 Mustang slid out of the gate just before 7:45, with Jacob Evans at the wheel, alone. He was as easy to follow as a spider on a whitewashed wall, and I followed him down the canyon to Santa Monica, to Beverly Hills and into LeDoux road, which holds on to the fringe of that exclusive suburb like an urchin hanging on to a rich man's coattails. I hung back as Jacob Evans' Mustang turned into the already-open garage of a shabby-looking bungalow on the right side of the street. Wearing dark glasses and a raincoat, Evans came out of the garage, closed the door, and went into the house with a key.

It looked like what an old-time newspaper would have called a "love nest." I scouted the block, check-ing out possible observation points. LeDoux is one side of a rectangle formed by Wilshire Boulevard, La Cienega and Clifton Way. La Cienega at Wilshire isn't what you'd call overbuilt. A coffee shop, a filling sta-tion and a couple of restaurants. One of them, a steak and lobster place, had a rear parking lot that backed directly onto the walled backyards of the LeDoux roadhouses, but there was nowhere I could get any height without making myself conspicuous. A little further north, I found there was a vacant lot, which, while not perfect, was at least better. The angle per-mitted sight of the living-room windows of the houses down LeDoux, and if I could get a little more eleva-tion, I'd be able to get a clear shot of the one I was interested in. Since by now it was pretty dark, I climbed onto the hood of the station wagon and screwed the Sniperscope to a tripod with rubber suc-tion-cup feet. Clamping these to the roof of the car, I zeroed in on the house. There were no lights show-ing, but that made no difference to me. I could see detail through the scope as clearly as if it were day, and what I saw nearly made my eyebrows climb past my hairline. The great screen idol was playing a love scene, as I had expected. What I hadn't expected was that it would be with another man!

It looked to me as if Evans and his inamorata—or, in this case, is it inamorato?—were likely to be staying put for at least an hour, maybe longer, so I climbed down and unscrewed the scope before I attracted the attention of any passerby, and headed for a telephone. I called an old pal of mine at the LAPD and asked him for a favor.

"No sweat, Jay," he said. "This another of your capers?"

I told him it was, and he made a few calls before phoning me back at the restaurant where I was waiting. The name of the tenant of the LeDoux Road house was Geoffrey Wheatcroft, actor. As far as my friend in the police department knew, Wheatcroft was "clean" but he hadn't run the name through NCIC.

At around ten, Wheatcroft and Evans came out of the house, and drove up to the Beverly Hilton, where they had dinner together in Trader Vic's. They drank a lot of wine during the meal, and returned to the house afterward. I didn't bother to go in back and watch through the scope. I didn't need a diagram to know what would be going on, and playing Peeping Tom doesn't appeal to me one little bit.

One of the lousiest parts of surveillance is the dull, endless hours of waiting. The subject you are watching is living his life, doing things, going places. You are his shadow, and you have about the same amount of fun as a real shadow does. You spend nights huddled in a fogged-up car wondering why anyone would want to do a job like the one you do. You spend evenings in Muzaked, half-empty restaurants, beginning to believe the United States is exclusively populated by plain girls with long dark hair and gold-rimmed glasses who are studying speech therapy. It's the other side of the coin

—not glamorous, not exciting, not really very interesting. But it's part of what you do, so you do it.

Around one, Evans got into his Mustang and headed back up Benedict Canyon. I followed him until it was obvious he was heading for the barn, then turned off and headed back for my bungalow at the Beverly Hills.

Susan Evans awoke me early the following morning with a call. She was eager to know what I'd discovered, and I told her I had some news, but I wanted confirmation, and that confirmation took a little time. The Wheatcroft thing didn't look like a one-night stand, but I wanted it tied with a ribbon. There are far too many people in my business who jump to the nearest conclusion. Sometimes it's the only exercise their minds get.

I kept Jacob Evans under surveillance for a week. He went to the LeDoux Road address four of those nights. The other engagements were legitimate.

I did a couple of other things, too. I rented a big camper, and parked it on the vacant lot so people could get used to seeing it there. Its "upstairs" window was high enough so that I could set up the Sniperscope for perfect observation into the LeDoux Road bungalow.

I also checked out Geoffrey Wheatcroft. He was one of that all-too-numerous brigade who gravitate to the movie business like wasps to honey. A former male model, he was from Chicago—a town not noted for its tolerance towards male models—and had worked in Los Angeles as a window dresser, a hairdresser and a quondam actor. He was a known frequenter of gay and singles bars on Hollywood Boulevard, and one or two even less attractive areas. He'd met Evans, it appeared, at a party thrown by a New York publisher during a convention held in Los Angeles a couple of years earlier, which Wheatcroft had crashed.

Now I had to gussy up to the big question—did I tell Susan Evans to come down and see for herself, or simply tell her and keep her away? I wondered whether she could take such a low blow. That Jacob Evans was gay—or bisexual, as seemed likelier—was going to come as a considerable shock to the beautiful bride of less than eighteen months, as was the news that Evans had known and been seeing Wheatcroft before the marriage. I called her and told her, and listened to the empty silence on the other end of the line for perhaps five minutes. Then she told me to stay right where I was, she was coming down.

Half an hour later, her car slid to a stop behind mine and she got out. I was sitting in the camper with a cup of coffee and offered her one. Her face was a white mask of anger, and she shook her head, the chestnut hair swinging like a fan.

"No," she said. "I just want to see this. I want to see it for myself. I want to see what that bastard is doing!"

"All right," I said. Without giving her a chance to argue, I took her purse off her and checked it. No gun. She was wearing a turtle-neck sweater and wine-colored pants that looked as if they had been put on with a spray gun. She went in and came out in all the right places, and there was no way she could have been concealing a weapon.

"You still don't trust me!" she said, surprised.

"The telescope is up there," I said, pointing with my chin. She got up and squinted through the viewfinder. That scope magnifies the objective three hundred times, and what you see is crystal clear. I heard her suck in her breath and then let it out in one long, angry exhalation.

"That your husband, Mrs. Evans?" I asked.

"You know damned well it is!" she hissed. "Who is this other—man? What's his name?"

I told her Wheatcroft's name and what I knew about him. There were tears welling in Susan Evans' eyes as I spoke, but she bravely held them back. We went out of the camper and got into the station wagon. She cried then, shaking her head as if there was something inside it she wanted to get out. After a while, she stopped.

"Why?" she asked me. "What's wrong with me? Am I ugly, or something?"

I said I didn't know why. Nobody ever does.

"Don't I have a good figure?" she said. "Good legs, a good body?"

She wasn't really asking me. She was asking Someone, Everyone.

More to console her than anything else, I told her that she was a beautiful woman, and she had nothing to worry about in that department.

"Well," she said suddenly, "take a good look."

She reached down without warning, and with that curious cross-armed movement only women can do, pulled off the turtleneck sweater in one smooth movement, and confirmed my earlier conclusion that she wasn't wearing a bra.

"Well?" she said. Her eyes met mine challengingly. If he can do it, she was saying, so can I. She looked very sweet and very vulnerable and terribly young, and I felt angry that such a nice kid was going to be turned sour by a man who patently didn't give a damn for anyone, as long as he got his kicks. I told Susan Evans, as gently as I could, that what she had in mind was not part of the service I provided for my clients. She looked nonplussed for a moment, but she was committed to a course of action by what she had already said and done. She thought I was playing hard to get. She bit her lower lip gently, and then smiled, and before I could say anything, slid out of her wine-colored slacks.

"Be nice to me, Jay," she said, sliding nearer. "Please?"

"Mrs. Evans," I said very formally. "There's no point to this. Get your clothes on or I'll open the door and dump you on the street the way you are."

"You're joking," she said.

"Try me."

There was a long silence. It lasted maybe a minute. Then she let out a long impatient sigh, the way a schoolteacher will sigh when one of her intelligent pupils plays difficult. It meant that she thought I still needed persuasion. Which left me no alternative. I switched on the ignition.

"What—what are you doing?" she faltered.

"I told you," I said. "I'm going to take you to the corner of La Cienega and Wilshire and drop you there."

"You wouldn't dare!" she said, eyes flashing with affront. For an answer, I rolled the car forward a couple of yards, and she gave a squawk of panic and told me to stop, dammit! Then she did some wriggling and scrambling and under-the-breath cursing as she got her slacks and sweater back on. Breathing heavily, her hair all mussed and her eyes glowing like an angry puma, she looked at me with infinite contempt.

"You're the same as him!" she hissed. "You're gay, aren't you!"

Hell hath no fury, I thought. I knew she was trying to salvage a little of her wounded pride, and I understood why. She had just offered me the great gift of her fair white body, a gift not capable of being refused. She had been brought up to believe this, as have a lot of American women who think that using their femininity is a substitute for using their heads.

"Susan," I said, softly. "I'm not gay. It just so happens that I'm into a very heavy love affair right now. I can't see anyone else. You understand, don't you?"

She looked at me for another of those long moments, and as she did, her eyes flooded with warmth. She reached over and touched my face with her hand, and then gave me a quick, sisterly kiss.

"I understand," she said. "You're a lucky man, Jay Armes."

Then she got out of my car and walked back to her own, head held high, so the tears wouldn't fall. I was glad that I had at least given her back a small piece of her pride to walk away from this mess with. I watched her drive away, and then put the station wagon in gear.

I had things to do. Arrange for the camper to be

collected. See if there was a flight to Dallas that would get me back to El Paso before midnight. I felt the old familiar urge to move that comes as soon as a caper is ended—I've got to get back, read all the messages, answer all the phone calls, plunge ahead into the next caper, the next encounter with the unexpected. The world is full of adventures I haven't yet had, people I haven't yet met. My only enemy is Time. There was also another reason I wanted to get back to El Paso— that very heavy love affair that I had told Susan Evans about. I hadn't made it up.

The lady's name is Linda.